Palgrave Studies of Marketing in Emerging Economies

Series Editors
Robert E Hinson
Dept of Marketing and Entrepreneurship
University of Ghana Business School
Accra, Ghana

Ogechi Adeola
Pan-Atlantic University
Lagos Business School
Lagos, Nigeria

This book series focuses on contemporary themes in marketing and marketing management research in emerging markets and developing economies. Books in the series cover the BRICS (Brazil, Russia, India, China and South Africa), MINT (Mexico, Indonesia, Nigeria and Turkey), CIVETS (Colombia, Indonesia, Vietnam, Egypt, Turkey, and South Africa); EAGLE economies (those which are expected to lead growth in the next ten years, such as Brazil, China, India, Indonesia, South Korea, Mexico, Russia, Taiwan, and Turkey) and all other African countries (classified under developing countries), taking into consideration the demographic, socio-cultural and macro-economic factors influencing consumer choices in these markets. The series synthesizes key subject areas in marketing, discuss marketing issues, processes, procedures and strategies across communities, regions and continents, and also the way digital innovation is changing the business landscape in emerging economies.

Palgrave Studies of Marketing in Emerging Economies presents a unique opportunity to examine and discuss marketing strategy and its implications in emerging economies, thereby filling a gap in current marketing literature.

All chapter submissions to the series will undergo a double blind peer review and all book proposals will undergo a single blind peer review.

Frederica Brooksworth
Emmanuel Mogaji • Genevieve Bosah
Editors

Fashion Marketing in Emerging Economies Volume II

South American, Asian and African Perspectives

palgrave
macmillan

Editors
Frederica Brooksworth
Fashion Education Group
London, UK

Emmanuel Mogaji
Greenwich Business School
University of Greenwich
London, UK

Genevieve Bosah
University of Hertfordshire
Hatfield, UK

ISSN 2730-5554 ISSN 2730-5562 (electronic)
Palgrave Studies of Marketing in Emerging Economies

https://doi.org/10.1007/978-3-031-07078-5

This Palgrave Macmillan imprint is published by the registered company Springer Nature Switzerland AG.
The registered company address is: Gewerbestrasse 11, 6330 Cham, Switzerland

Contents

Notes on Contributors

Mamun Ala is Lecturer in Strategic Management and International Business at the Australian Institute of Business. He holds a PhD in Applied Economics from the University of South Australia (UniSA) and a GradCert in L&T from Swinburne University. He has long experience in teaching in higher education institutions, including UniSA and Flinders University. His research interests include teaching and learning, entrepreneurship, international competitiveness, political economy and industrial policy.

Aurore Bardey is Associate Professor of Marketing at the Burgundy School of Business. Having designed the BSc (Hons) Psychology of Fashion, her expertise sits in applying psychology in fashion. Her research interests fall into three topics: (1) applying cognitive and experimental psychology concepts to enhance green consumer behaviour in fashion; (2) applying social psychology concepts to assess the impact of inclusive fashion on consumers; and (3) evaluating the impact of fashion on well-being and cognitive performance.

Genevieve Bosah is a Senior Lecturer at the University of Hertfordshire where she teaches and researches in Public Relations, Corporate Communications, Media and Branding. She is the Programme Leader for the MA Journalism and Media Communications and the newly developed MA Public Relations and Digital Communications. She is the Convenor/Founder of African PhD Scholars Network. She is a chartered practitioner of the Chartered Institute of Public Relations (CIPR) UK and board member of Public Relations and Communications Association (PRCA) UK qualifications board.

Frederica Brooksworth is a British-Ghanaian academic, researcher, strategist, editor and author. She is the executive director of the Fashion Education Group which comprises initiatives such as the Council for International African Fashion Education (CIAFE), Professional Development and the Fashion Knowledge Challenge. Brooksworth is also regional editor (Africa) of Bloomsbury Publishing for Fashion Business Cases.

Brooksworth has taught at numerous universities and is a lecturer at the London College of Fashion, British School of Fashion, Hult International Business School and Conde Nast College of Fashion and Design. She is a board member at BlueCrest University College.

Coy Griffin is a TEDx speaker, fashion analyst and fashion-tech enthusiast. Griffin is a guest lecturer specialising in fashion analytics, technology and operations with experience in teaching at Virginia State University and the London College of Fashion. She has also worked with Nike and Black Girls Code. Griffin works with fashion organisations to integrate the latest technological innovations with the creative world. She has been featured in media outlets such as Blavity and New York Fashion Week and often participates in educational and interactive events in Accra, Ghana.

Damilola Joseph holds a PhD in Strategy, Enterprise and Innovations from Portsmouth Business School. She is a lecturer at Teesside University Business School and teaches across a range of modules like research methods, enterprise and practice, and the relationship between buying and selling. She also supervises undergraduate, postgraduate and doctoral students.

Pandora Kay has a life-long passion for fashion and creative industries and, as a marketing academic, is excited by recent research on intersections between them. She has first-hand experience in the arts, cultural and creative industries as a practitioner, as an administrator and recently as a collector, patron, philanthropist and fundraiser.

Utkarsha Mehdiratta is a first-class honours graduate from London College of Fashion, where she studied BSc (Hons) Psychology of Fashion. She was born and brought up in India and is now pursuing her post-graduate studies and research at Goldsmiths, University of London. She was a recipient of the BPS Undergraduate Research Assistantship Scheme Award in 2019. Her area of research includes understanding consumers' attitudes and behaviour towards sustainability and inclusive fashion; the psychological principles of effect and persuasion involved in consumer decision-making; and the evolving relationship between technology, data, and consumer behaviour.

Emmanuel Mogaji is Senior Lecturer in Advertising and Marketing Communications at the University of Greenwich. His primary area of interest is ABCDE of marketing communications—advertising, branding, communications, digital and ethics. He has authored and edited over ten books on branding, fashion marketing and higher education.

Sumesh Nair works at the Australian Institute of Business as a senior lecturer, and he previously worked with Monash and Murdoch Universities for 11 years. His research appeared in the *Journal of Macromarketing*, *Journal of International Consumer Marketing*, *Business Strategy* and *the Environment and Ergonomics*, to name a few.

Yasmina Nessim is the founder and CEO of pstyled—the world's first-ever styling service that uses fashion psychology to optimise mood and productivity. Her initial academic background is in business management from King's College London and an MSc in Strategic Marketing from Imperial College in London. She holds a second MSc degree in Applied Psychology of Fashion from the London College of Fashion. She conducts her scientific research proving the significant correlation between outfit curation and the human psyche, focusing on emotive fluctuations, productivity levels and self-expression. Consequently, pstyled was born. She is running the business from Cairo, Egypt, but continues to collaborate and cater to both men and women across the globe.

Ken Kweku Nimo is pursuing an MA in fashion design at the University of Johannesburg. His research focuses on luxury in Africa, with a specific interest in South Africa's emerging luxury fashion industry. He believes in the fashion industry's potential as a vehicle for job and wealth creation. He seeks to contribute to the development of local luxury fashion brands through research and practice. He is keen on charting the history of luxury across diverse cultures in Africa and developing and managing local and international luxury brands on the continent.

Tareq Rasul is a senior lecturer at the Australian Institute of Business, Australia. He holds a doctorate in marketing from the University of South Australia, Australia, and an MBA from East London, UK. His research has been published in many international journals such as *Australasian Journal of Information Systems, Tourism Recreation Research, Journal of Strategic Marketing, International Journal of Web-Based Communities, Journal of Knowledge Management* and *Journal of Open Innovation: Technology Market, and Complexity*. He is also a Certified Practising Marketer (CPM) and a member of Australian Marketing Institute (AMI) and Action Learning Action Research Association (ALARA).

Fábio Shimabukuro Sandes is Assistant Professor of Marketing at Universidade Lusófona. Marketing professional with 15+ years of work in the Fashion Industry, working in multinational companies like Vicunha Textil and LYCRA® Brand. Sandes holds an MSc and PhD degrees in Marketing at EAESP Fundação Getulio Vargas, São Paulo, Brazil.

Rose Turner is a cognitive scientist and Lecturer in Psychology at UAL: London College of Fashion. She studies relationships between engagement with stories and artistic practices, empathy and sustainability. Having previously worked as a theatre artist taking creative arts interventions into education, criminal justice and social care contexts, she is interested in the real-world impact of arts engagement and research methods, emphasising quantitative approaches and statistics.

Caroline Young is a creative diplomat; her innate understanding of cultural and creative sensibilities encompass decades of collaborating with exceptional creative visionaries, including Vogue, Hermes, Balenciaga, Shiseido, Peter Saville, Brian Eno, Peter Lindbergh, Joyce Ma and Li Edelkoort. She studied art history and then lived in London, Paris, Milan, Tokyo, and India since 2005.

List of Tables

Part I

An Introduction

1

Fashion Marketing in Emerging Economies Volume II: South American, Asian and African Perspectives

Frederica Brooksworth, Emmanuel Mogaji, and Genevieve Bosah

Introduction

Emerging economies have often been under-researched, and models of comparison to global markets are ill-suited to conceptualize the contextual factors that are specific to the market. There is a growing interest and research in this area which poses challenges for existing models and the need for adaptation or creation of hybrid models for market integration, segmentation and consumption. The new models also contribute to

F. Brooksworth (✉)
Fashion Education Group, London, UK
e-mail: frederica@internationalfashioneducation.org

E. Mogaji
Greenwich Business School, University of Greenwich, London, UK
e-mail: e.o.mogaji@greenwich.ac.uk

G. Bosah
University of Hertfordshire, Hertfordshire, UK
e-mail: g.bosah@herts.ac.uk

F. Brooksworth et al. (eds.), *Fashion Marketing in Emerging Economies Volume II*, Palgrave Studies of Marketing in Emerging Economies,
https://doi.org/10.1007/978-3-031-07078-5_1

economic growth, employment and productivity because of the integrated ecosystems of operation. These emerging markets have become co-creation hubs for the societies in which they operate. This book highlights the different perspectives in such markets by presenting empirical evidence on strategies and tools employed by the contributors in this volume to unpack the evolving phenomenon in the Fashion Markets in markets considered emerging.

The term "emerging markets" is defined as developing countries with high growth expectations and increasing influence, which have proven to become more attractive to investors because of their high return potential (Wilson 20,026). These countries considered as emerging markets are characterized by the level of economic development, economic growth and market governance by Czinkota and Ronkainen (1997). Emerging Economies are home to approximately 80% of the world's population (Alon and Welsh, 2001), and constitute the primary destinations not only for exports but also for direct investment, as more and more equity investors are seeking opportunities in these economies. According to Cavusgil, Ghauri and Agarwal (2002), emerging markets will be responsible for a high share of the world's growth in the next two decades as they are rapidly transforming their economies. Cities within emerging markets also provide the most dynamic opportunities and varying market potentials for companies mostly in developed countries to extend their markets.

According to the Financial Times and Stock Exchange (FTSE), the countries identified as emerging markets propelling consistent economic growth and active across all sectors of the economy are Brazil, the Czech Republic, Hungary, Mexico, Malaysia, Poland, South Africa, Turkey and Taiwan. The secondary emerging countries are Chile, China, Columbia, Egypt, India, Indonesia, Malaysia, Morocco, Pakistan, Peru, the Philippines, Russia, Thailand and the UAE (FTSE, 2012), with Brazil, Russia, India, China and South Africa (BRICS) being the most popular, and their capacity to provide investors with higher profits and boost the world economy cannot be underestimated (Goldman Sachs, 2003). Mexico, Indonesia, South Korea and Turkey (MIST), which followed years later as the second tier of nations. According to Goldman Sachs' projections, within the next 20 years, BRICS will add to their populations some 225 million "middle class" consumers who earn at least US$ 15,000 a year. The economy of BRICS will overtake the U.S., Japan, Germany, France, the UK, Italy and Canada by 2040 (BusinessWeek, 2006). According to Hanlon Investment Management, the market capitalization of emerging markets are as follows: China 38%, India 10.9%, South Korea 8.7%, Taiwan 6.3%, Brazil 5.0%, Russia 3.2%, South Africa 2.8%., Thailand 2.8%, Saudi Arabia 2.5%, Indonesia 2.5%, Malaysia 2.3%, Mexico 1.9%, and all other emerging markets represent 13.0%.

Emerging markets offer several advantages to equity investors. They include, but are not limited to, an expanding middle class necessary for e-commerce and retail to excel, relatively unsaturated markets, urbanized and highly populated cities, for the most part, a growing youth market, free trade zones, relatively friendly business laws, liberalized markets and transitioning economies, and a huge pent-up demand for Western-style goods and services.

Fashion in Emerging Markets

How is fashion looking like in emerging markets? It is estimated that by 2035, the gross domestic product of emerging markets will permanently surpass that of all advanced markets (Wilson and Purushothaman 2003). Emerging markets have enormous raw material advantages ranging from human capital (China, India), industrial raw materials (Brazil, Central America), energy (Russia, Nigeria) and other natural resources (Peru, Africa). Many of these markets also have strong agricultural (Brazil) and cattle-based natural resources (India). With developing markets becoming saturated, equity investors have turned to emerging markets for future growth.

The fashion multinational industries in emerging markets have been widely acknowledged as important global players and have initiated unique strategies that aid the development of these industries. Since the term "BRICS" was coined (O'Neill, 2001), much has been learned over the past decades on mature and developed markets; yet our knowledge is incomplete on several major issues happening in emerging markets that offer a variety of opportunities, whether it is sourcing, producing, selling, disposal or engaging in other relevant activities and conversations along the fashion value chain and some of the world's most important issues (Cavusgil, Ghauri & Agarwal, 2002). The paucity of historical Literature on Emerging Economies is part of the reason why researchers interested in the field have come together with the ultimate goal of shaping the agenda for research work on Fashion Marketing in Emerging Economies through identifying Fashion Multinational Corporations, interesting research topics, collaborating, exploring and sharing insights and findings from the field on fashion marketing strategies in emerging economies (Agarwal & Malhotra, 2019; Malhotra, Schaller, & Patil, 2017; Malhotra & Uslay, 2018, Mogaji et al., 2022).

Fashion is one of the most important and competitive industries in the world, and emerging markets are employing the right tools and strategies to keep up with the competition. It is one of the most progressing industries in the world and worth billions (Australian Bureau of Statistics, 2009). The fashion multinational apparel industries in emerging markets have undergone profound transformation due to various changes in the business environment; efforts have been made to improve technology, design, business management and service delivery (Mogaji, 2021), which have results in an intensified global competition in the emerging market's fashion businesses. The industrial sectors in emerging markets have seen a rapid growth and are playing a vital role in the global economy by contributing to shaping international standards (Allwood, Laursen, De-Rodriguez and Bocken, 2006, Mukonza et al., 2021).

With the rise of fashion consumption and industrial upgrading, fashion in emerging economies has emerged as a lucrative business model as they have been successful in attracting global equity investors and offer arguably the widest array of market opportunities (Gereffi, 2005). The fusion of digital technologies, where technologies mean "knowledge, methods, tools, devices" mediates communication, including internet-enabled technologies (Varadarajan et al., 2010, Abdulquadri et al., 2021). The fusion of digital technologies, such as computer-aided design (CAD), computer-aided manufacturing (CAM) and enterprise resource planning (ERP) into clothing production and manufacturing, has pushed these economies into becoming leading fashion manufacturing and production hubs and the cornerstone for global fashion exports. These have seen a significant internal change in the labour process: impressive employment growth and expanding and fuelling consumption, raising wages and income, accumulating wealth and reducing poverty (Cavusgil, Ghauri and Agarwal, 2002).

The global fashion apparel procurement industry has been dominated by strong players in emerging markets. With a considerable amount of expertise in the industry, along with decades of experience, modern infrastructure, efficient supply chain management, and high productivity, apparel manufacturers and retailers, primarily from the developed markets have developed interests in doing business in emerging markets as they present plentiful business opportunities for them (Cavusgil, Ghauri & Agarwal, 2002). The Chinese textile and apparel industry has seen a rapid development within the global apparel and textile supply chain as it has become the largest producer and supplier of fibres, yarns, fabrics and apparel (Gereffi & Memedocic 2003). In 2007, the industry accounted for 20% of China's manufacturing employment, 7% of China's GGDP, 14% of its manufacturing value added and 15% of its total exports (China Textile Industry Development Report 2006/2007, 2008).

There is an emergence of a unique and local apparel chain in Brazil (Pinto, 2011; Pinto & Souza, 2013; Pontual, 2010). Brazil ranks among the world's top producers of textiles and the second major supplier of indigo (Vilasboas 2012). The textile and clothing production chain is present in all 27 Brazilian States, with more than 32,000 companies, located mainly in the South and Southeast regions of Brazil, especially in the State of São Paulo, which concentrates 27% of production units (Brasil, 2014). There are approximately 1.585.6 million direct jobs, representing 17% of the total of workers engaged in the manufacturing industry, distributed in all segments of the production chain, from the natural and synthetic fibre production, spinning, weaving, knitting, finishing and sewing (ABIT, 2015). The industry is worth US$ 797 billion in global value according to the World Trade Organization (WTO, 2015).

The Indian clothing industry is labour-intensive, and it provides employment to those with simple skills, including women. Some of the countries, such as Bangladesh, Sri Lanka, Vietnam, and Mauritius, have experienced high output growth in this sector (Chakrabarty, 2014). Bangladesh is a growing country in the emerging market (Khan and

Ullah, 2017), and its most vital export industry is the Fashion Industry. According to Barua and Ansary (2007), there are more than four million employees in Bangladesh's Fashion Industry. It has been identified as being the second biggest exporter of fashion products after China (Khan and Ullah, 2017). The country has joint ventures with different companies in developed countries and export clothes all over the world. The apparel industry in India is one of the leading apparel industries globally by adopting new production and technological techniques (Cavusgil, Ghauri & Agarwal, 2002).

The growing markets of Asia, especially in Korea, Japan, India and China (Morton, 2002; Bryck, 2003), have proven to become an important sourcing and control centre for the global garment industry, and a lot of equity investors have dedicated their attention even more than before to the market potential beckoning in these markets, with production plants mainly in China, Indonesia, Thailand and India (Hong Kong Government Industry Department, 1995). Global value chains in the fashion industry have been motivated by the emergence of these new markets (Markusen, Wassall, DeNatale, & Cohen, 2008; Nika, 2010; Pontual, 2011; Prideaux, 2009). Any discussion on this substantial growth would not be complete without understanding the positive and favourable fashion marketing strategies and factors attributing to this global competitiveness in emerging markets.

The dominant patterns in the fashion industry that the industry gets called out for are polluting the environment, producing enormous amounts of waste, and exploiting people but changes are slowly happening highlighting the many enormous hurdles to overcome in the fashion networks (Lacy and Hayward, 2011). There is an increasing pressure for Fashion Multinational Corporations to take a greater role in addressing global societal issues such as eradicating poverty and environmental protection. Emerging economies are beginning to contribute to environmentally sustainable challenges. There are several allocations and relocations of resources for production activities to cities within emerging economies, thereby putting pressure on the world's resources (Barba-Navaretti and Falzoni, 2004; Pennings and Sleuwaegen, 2000). Fashion sustainability has gained considerable attention and has become one of the crucial conversations in the fashion industry (Niinimaki, 2011,

Nguyen & Mogaji, 2021a). An important element identified in emerging markets is the growing expectations and preferences of customers to shift towards a more transparent, sustainable, less negative but positive social impact brands, because they believe fashion brands have the responsibility of addressing environmental and social issues (Marchand and Walker, 2008).

Objective of the Book

There is little academic and contemporary research about Fashion Markets in Emerging Economies. The fashion industry is growing rapidly in emerging markets; in addition to this, marketing strategies, tools and technologies have also evolved. There is a growing demand for additional research, information, recommendations and insight from practitioners, entrepreneurs, students and academics. The book aims to provide and shed light on insights, challenges and opportunities to support the development and economic growth of the fashion industries within emerging markets.

Target Audience

This book will aim to satisfy the needs of our audience by providing timely information on growing areas such as sustainability, luxury, digital, trends and psychology.

The book could be implemented as a manual to help with organizational activities and will be relevant to policy makers interested in growth and development of economies.

The book will also satisfy the needs of scholars by filling in a research gap for research papers, case studies and journal articles and by pursuing their own personal projects.

For undergraduate and postgraduate students this will also be very useful to support them with research for their thesis and assignments. Additionally, it will give them insight into various job roles within the industry and educate them on opportunities within the emerging market.

The Book Outline

This volume contains ten chapters, which include introductory and concluding chapters. In the series, there are 17 contributing authors from different emerging markets across the globe including Brazil, Nigeria, South Africa and India. Authors who have presented their contributions to theories, knowledge and discussion around Fashion Marketing in Emerging Economies. Drawing from the contributions, these chapters provide an understanding of effective marketing strategies employed by Fashion Multinational Corporations within Emerging Markets.

The authors made important contributions to their host literatures, and they encompass and should however be noted that the portfolio of these chapters is a focused selection from a far wider corpus of research output, conducted over a period of 12 months. Presentations, collaborations and other published outputs, while excluded from the core portfolio, provide relevant evidence along the research journey, and are referenced accordingly. The individual portfolio papers are distinguished throughout by writing style. This academic research bridges the gap to not only the relatively neglected area of marketing activities happening in emerging markets but also the growth of emerging economies entirely.

This volume compliments the first volume which had a focus on brand, consumer and sustainability perspectives (Brooksworth et al., 2022a, 2022b). This volume examined fashion marketing from various contexts and across other emerging economies such as Sect. "Fashion in Emerging Markets"—South America and Asian perspectives with case studies from India, Brazil and markets in Southeast Asia and Sect. "Objective of the Book", which considers the emerging economies of the fashion market from the African and Middle East perspective with contributions from Nigeria, Egypt, South Africa and the Middle East.

While Chap. 1 offers an introduction to the book, Bardey et al. (2022) in Chap. 2 provided insights into Generation Z Indian consumers' attitudes towards Western and Indian Fashion. This chapter reports on the current state of the Indian fashion industry and describes Indian fashion consumers. It focused on an under-researched demographic: young Indian fashion consumers. Specifically, the authors assessed their attitudes and brand equity towards Western and Indian fashion as well as their environmental attitudes and behaviours. The study provides insight into how Western and Indian fashion brands can be successful in their marketing towards Indian Gen Z fashion consumers.

Chapter 3 by Sandes (2022) discusses the characteristics of fashion's menswear market in one of the biggest emerging countries in the world: Brazil. In-depth interviews were conducted with experts to build a point of view of the dynamics present in this market. Fashion designers, product managers, journalists and brand managers' perspectives offer the reader a qualitative perception of relevant characteristics of the men's buying behaviour in fashion in Brazil, an emerging country that still faces gender discrimination in fashion consumption and usage.

Chapter 4 focused on the Southeast Asia markets. Ala et al. (2022) presented theoretical insight into the power of neuromarketing and highlighed the huge possibilities of taking luxury fashion marketing to a whole new level. This chapter highlights some of the ways neuromarketing can be applied in social media to better understand and influence the psychological motivation and decision-making of consumers, and it provides a summary of scholarly insights into effective strategies for using neuromarketing in e-commerce and social commerce. This chapter presents a comprehensive analysis of the application of neuromarketing to support market research, product development and marketing communication associated with luxury fashion marketing in SE Asia markets.

In Chap. 5, Kay and Young (2022) recognized the impact of the COVID-19 pandemic on fashion brands and further presented evidence of how artisanal fashion in India is building the brand through storytelling, even in challenging times. This is the first chapter under the fashion brand positioning theme. Like other markets in the world, the Coronavirus pandemic has created massive challenges and opportunities (Ding et al. 2020) for fashion industries within emerging markets. There is the need to also discuss the impact of the Novel Coronavirus on Fashion Businesses and Corporate Social Responsibility activities in Emerging Economies. This chapter highlights the resilience of some fashion brands that emerged during the pandemic environment in India.

Section "Objective of the Book" with a focus on the African perspective starts with Chap. 6, where Joseph (2022) presented a study on how

Nigerian fashion brands influence customer purchasing behaviour. With a case study approach on a select number of well-established Nigerian Brands such as Lisa Folawiyo, Lanre Da Silva and Orange Culture, the study revealed that Nigerian fashion brands influence purchase behaviour through the use of psychological factors like Cultural and ethnic identity, Influencer marketing. An important implication is that since consumers' consumption of fashion has moved beyond materialism, and towards culture and self-identity, fashion brands need to communicate brand messages that deeply resonate with the values and ideology of their customers.

In the same manner, in Chap. 7, Appiah-Nimo (2022) presented a snapshot of contemporary retail in South Africa. This chapter presents a condensed overview of contemporary fashion retail in South Africa. Its core objective is to offer valuable insight and a critical point of entry for brands and retailers prospecting the South African market. This chapter briefly explores the country's fashion retail history, examining the contemporary retail environment, while providing a glimpse into its fashion retail future. Furthermore, the trajectory of growth in the fashion retail market, contextualized by the recent COVID-19 global pandemic and the emergence of frontier technology, is discussed. The study adopted a qualitative approach, through a combination of document analysis and case studies to analyse the phenomenon.

Chapter 8 by Pstyled and Bardey (2022) recognizes the rise of female empowerment in Egypt and the fashion Psychology Behind Their Attire and Armour. The study assessed the use of clothing practices as a means of communicating and expressing the woman's newfound confidence in the MENA region, with a particular focus on Egypt. The evolution in local fashion designers and consumer demands paint a clear and beautiful picture of how women across the region are using fashion to express their growth, their power and their love——for themselves and for their cultures. The findings revealed ways in which neighbouring and international brands and fashion houses can appreciate and empathize with the women of the MENA region: communicate, market and support their growth and energy.

Chapter 9 authored by Griffin (2022) presented Strategies and Tools for Fashion Analytics in Africa and Middle East. This chapter analyses the effectiveness of advanced data-driven marketing practices and fashion consumer analytics in emerging markets in the Middle East and African regions (MEA). It inspects the analytical tools facilitating decisions within the arising landscapes and examines data-driven marketing case studies, literature reviews, and reference frameworks to obtain a current view of fashion marketing in emerging markets. Additionally, this chapter investigates digital disadvantages in MEA markets, and the analytical tools facilitating decisions within the arising landscape. Brooksworth et al. (2022c) present the conclusion in Chap. 10. Research agenda for Fashion Marketing in Emerging Economies were also presented.

Conclusion

The main intention of Fashion Marketing in Emerging Economies is to focus attention on how the fashion apparel industries in emerging markets have significantly expanded their boundaries (Djelic and Ainamo 1999). The book develops a classification of the major impacts of emerging markets around the globe. Fashion Marketing in Emerging Economies is a timely contribution to highlighting the most significant economic growth and rapid transformation happening in emerging markets (Thompson and Reynolds 2018), which are not only undervalued but also under-researched, yet embody and offer enormous opportunity for investors and entrepreneurs (Mckinsey, 2014; Kaur et al., 2022).

The book describes the Influence and Power of Emerging Markets and some effective Fashion Marketing Growth Strategies adopted by Fashion Multinational Corporations in these markets, while highlighting things that have noticeably improved, concurrently, and why it is compelling to investors and worth investing in (Atsmon, Kertesz & Vittal, 2011). The book provides a detailed analysis of numerous indisputable strengths and attractive attributes of Fashion Multinational Corporations within emerging markets and some interesting challenges.

Highlighting the differences and unique characteristics between the various emerging markets, the authors strongly suggest the need for investors to use different approaches to marketing in emerging markets (Atsmon, Kertesz & Vittal, 2011, Gökerik et al., 2018). By highlighting the developments of Fashion Multinational Corporations in Emerging

Markets, these chapters in the book respond to the call that emerging markets are a distinct cluster rather than a set of discrete regional stories and must be treated as such (Austin et al., 2017). These chapters further identify, profile and evaluate the performance of some emerging markets in Africa with compelling growth stories that not a lot of investors are aware of, thereby tilting their resources towards what's familiar resulting in them missing out on a world of potential opportunities (Mwenda 2000). The contributions will serve as a roadmap to encourage corporations and investors looking for investment opportunities in emerging markets to be strategic and establish localized and more tailor-made approaches and suitable actions/solutions (Bespoke) and not a generic or standardized go-to-market models for each market (Aaker and Shansby 1982).

With the sluggish growth in developed markets, equity investors, fashion marketers and retailers are increasingly becoming aware of the benefits in these markets and are forced to seek their future growth potential in emerging economies. Although billions of dollars of apparel business are conducted in emerging markets, relatively little knowledge about the management of supply chains is reported in published research. In view of this data limitation, all the authors use multiple methods and theories to uncover, analyse, demonstrate and present the facts in their chapters and provide integrated guideposts for future research. This book posited the strong characteristics of emerging markets. The authors further provide integrated guideposts for future research.

References

Abdulquadri, A., Mogaji, E., Kieu, T. A., & Nguyen, N. P. (2021). Digital transformation in financial services provision: A Nigerian perspective to the adoption of chatbot. *Journal of Enterprising Communities: People and Places in the Global Economy, 15*(2), 258–281.

Ala, M., Rasul, T., & Nair, S. (2022). The power of neuromarketing: Taking luxury fashion marketing in Southeast Asia markets to a whole new level. In F. Brooksworth, E. Mogaji, & G. Bosah (Eds.), *Fashion Marketing in Emerging Economies (volume 2)—South American, Asian and African perspectives*. Springer.

Appiah-Nimo, K. (2022). South Africa: A snapshot of contemporary retail. In F. Brooksworth, E. Mogaji, & G. Bosah (Eds.), *Fashion Marketing in Emerging Economies (volume 2)—South American, Asian and African perspectives*. Springer.

Bardey, A., Turner, R., & Mehdiratta, U. (2022). Fashioning the future generation: Generation Z Indian consumers' attitudes towards Western and Indian fashion. In F. Brooksworth, E. Mogaji, & G. Bosah (Eds.), *Fashion Marketing in Emerging Economies (volume 2)—South American, Asian and African perspectives*. Springer.

Brooksworth, F., Mogaji, E., & Bosah, G. (2022a). Fashion Marketing in Emerging Economies: An introduction. In F. Brooksworth, E. Mogaji, & G. Bosah (Eds.), *Fashion Marketing in Emerging Economies (volume 1)—Brand, consumer and sustainability perspectives*. Springer.

Brooksworth, F., Mogaji, E., & Bosah, G. (2022b). Fashion Marketing in Emerging Economies: Conclusion and research agenda. In F. Brooksworth, E. Mogaji, & G. Bosah (Eds.), *Fashion Marketing in Emerging Economies (volume 1)—Brand, consumer and sustainability perspectives*. Springer.

Brooksworth, F., Mogaji, E., & Bosah, G. (2022c). Fashion Marketing in Emerging Economies: Conclusion and research agenda. In F. Brooksworth, E. Mogaji, & G. Bosah (Eds.), *Fashion Marketing in Emerging Economies (volume 2)—South American, Asian and African perspectives*. Springer.

Gökerik, M., Gürbüz, A., Erkan, I., & Sap, S. (2018). Surprise me with your ads! The impacts of guerrilla marketing in social media on brand image. *Asia Pacific Journal of Marketing and Logistics, 30*(5), 1222–1238. https://doi.org/10.1108/APJML-10-2017-0257

Griffin, C. (2022). Fashion Analytics in Africa & Middle East: Strategies, Tools and, Insights for Fashion Brands. In F. Brooksworth, E. Mogaji, & G. Bosah (Eds.), Fashion Marketing in Emerging Economies (volume 2)—South American, Asian and African perspectives. : Springer.

Joseph, D. (2022). Towards understanding how Nigerian fashion brands influences customer purchasing behaviour. A case study of Nigerian fashion brands. In F. Brooksworth, E. Mogaji, & G. Bosah (Eds.), *Fashion Marketing in Emerging Economies (volume 2)—South American, Asian and African perspectives*. Springer.

Kaur, J., Mogaji, E., Wadera, D., & Gupta, S. (2022). "Sustainable consumption practices in Indian households: A saga of environment management linked to Indian ethos and generational differences", Society and Business Review, Vol. ahead-of-print No. ahead-of-print. https://doi.org/10.1108/SBR-08-2021-0132.

Kay, P., & Young, C. (2022). Afloat in a changing COVID-19 world: The rise of artisanal fashion in India for brand story relevance in challenging times. In F. Brooksworth, E. Mogaji, & G. Bosah (Eds.), *Fashion Marketing in Emerging Economies (volume 2)—South American, Asian and African perspectives*. Springer.

Mogaji, E. (2021). *Brand Management*. Palgrave Macmillan.

Mogaji, E., Hinson, R. E., Nwoba, A. C., & Nguyen, N. P. (2021). Corporate social responsibility for women's empowerment: A study on Nigerian banks. *International Journal of Bank Marketing, 39*(4), 516–540. https://doi.org/10.1108/IJBM-04-2020-0195

Mogaji, E., Adeola, O., Adisa, I., Hinson, R. E., Mukonza, C., & Kirgiz, A. C. (2022). Green Marketing in Emerging Economies: Communication and brand perspective: An introduction. In E. Mogaji, O. Adeola, I. Adisa, R. E. Hinson, C. Mukonza, & A. C. Kirgiz (Eds.), *Green Marketing in Emerging Economies. Palgrave studies of Marketing in Emerging Economies* (pp. 1–16). Palgrave Macmillan. https://doi.org/10.1007/978-3-030-82572-0_1

Mukonza, C., Hinson, R. E., Adeola, O., Adisa, I., Mogaji, E., & Kirgiz, A. C. (2021). Green marketing: An introduction. In C. Mukonza, R. E. Hinson, O. Adeola, I. Adisa, E. Mogaji, & A. C. Kirgiz (Eds.), *Green Marketing in Emerging Markets. Palgrave studies of Marketing in Emerging Economies* (pp. 3–14). Palgrave Macmillan. https://doi.org/10.1007/978-3-030-74065-8_1

Nguyen, P. N., & Mogaji, E. (2021a). Brand development through sustainability certifications in emerging markets: Adoption of B corporation certification in Vietnam. In O. Adeola, R. Hinson, & A. Sakkthivel (Eds.), *Marketing communications and brand development in emerging markets* (pp. 255–274). Palgrave.

Pinto, M. M. B., & Souza, Y. S. D. (2013). From garment to fashion production: An analysis of the evolution of the apparel industry in Brazil. *BAR-Brazilian Administration Review, 10*(3), 304–322.

Pstyled, Y. N., & Bardey, A. (2022). The rise of female empowerment in Egypt: The fashion psychology behind their attire and Armour. In F. Brooksworth, E. Mogaji, & G. Bosah (Eds.), *Fashion Marketing in Emerging Economies (volume 2)—South American, Asian and African perspectives*. Springer.

Sandes, F. S. (2022). A closer look at the menswear market in Brazil. In F. Brooksworth, E. Mogaji, & G. Bosah (Eds.), *Fashion Marketing in Emerging Economies (volume 2)—South American, Asian and African perspectives*. Springer.

Part II

Fashion Marketing in Emerging Economies: South American and Asian Perspectives

2

Fashioning the Future Generation: Generation Z Indian Consumers' Attitudes Towards Western and Indian Fashion

Aurore Bardey, Utkarsha Mehdiratta, and Rose Turner

Introduction

India's high-end fashion industry emerged in the 1980s. Since the early 2000s, Indian fashion has become a functioning and well-established industry, earning revenues of approximately 2 billion Indian rupees (KPMG India report, 2020; almost £21 million). According to McKinsey's Fashion Scope (2019), India's fashion market will be worth £45.5 billion in 2022 (compared to the United Kingdom's £49.8 billion), making India the fifth largest apparel market in the world and one of the emerging markets with the highest growth rates. In addition to this unprecedented growth,

A. Bardey (✉)
Burgundy School of Business, Dijon, France
e-mail: aurore.bardey@bsb-education.com

U. Mehdiratta • R. Turner
London College of Fashion, London, UK

F. Brooksworth et al. (eds.), *Fashion Marketing in Emerging Economies Volume II*,
Palgrave Studies of Marketing in Emerging Economies,
https://doi.org/10.1007/978-3-031-07078-5_2

the Indian apparel industry has evolved greatly over the past three decades. Western fashion brands' presence in India (Nagrath, 2003), the rise of e-commerce (Chanana & Goele, 2012), consumers' rejuvenation (Sinha, 2003) and their desire to shop sustainably (Kaur et al., 2018; Mukonza et al., 2021) have transformed Indian consumerism. Even though the Indian fashion industry is one of the largest and fastest-growing apparel industries to date, there is still a lack of studies focused on Indian consumers (Ganguly & Ayres, 2006; Kaur et al., 2022). This chapter aims to address this gap by reporting on the current state of the Indian fashion industry and describing Indian fashion consumers. We will focus on an under-researched demographic: young Indian fashion consumers. Specifically, we will assess their attitudes and brand equity towards Western and Indian fashion as well as their environmental attitudes and behaviours. We aim to provide insight into how Western and Indian fashion brands can be successful in their marketing to Indian Gen Z fashion consumers.

Literature Review

Theoretical Background

In the past four decades, the world has seen significant and unprecedented growth of emerging markets (Nguyen & Mogaji, 2022b), and particularly the Indian economy (Kaur et al., 2022). While Indian GDP steadily increased from 37.03 billion USD in 1960 to 468.39 billion USD in 2000, it increased remarkably to 2.65 trillion USD in 2017 (World Bank Data, 2020), making India the 12th largest consumer market (McKinsey & Company, 2007). This growth led economists to identify India as a future major global economic power (Indian Week, 2005). Indeed, if the country's growth continues at the same rate, India will become the fifth largest worldwide consumer market by 2022 (Beinhocker et al., 2007; McKinsey & Company, 2007; McKinsey's Fashion Scope, 2019). This impressive economic growth is paired with increased consumer demand, which will expand three to four times faster than the global economy (Nguyen & Mogaji, 2021; Zainulbhai, 2005).

Indian retail appears to be one of the sectors that has benefited most from worldwide economic growth, with a Compound Annual Growth Rate (CAGR) of 13% in 2013 (KPMG report, 2014). On the one hand, the rapid growth of internet penetration in India made the Indian retail sector the earliest to adapt to retail mobile applications (Bhattacharya & Anand, 2019; Ming 2017). On the other hand, the fact that India is one of the main raw material suppliers, and provides cost competitiveness for several international retail chains, places Indian retail as the most attractive retail sector worldwide. Although organized retailing is currently only 3% in India, the Indian retail industry is expected to keep expanding in the next decade, thanks to Indian demographics, increasing urbanization, increased number of malls, growing preference for branded products and change in consumer habit towards foreign brands (Kang, 2015).

Apparel retailing is one of the sectors expected to obtain the highest growth (KPMG report, 2014). With 40–50% of Indian women's salaries spent on clothing and footwear (Hasan, 2016), the Indian apparel market accounts for $3.5 billion and for almost 39% of the organized retail sector (being the second-largest organized retail sector after food and groceries; Fernandes et al., 2000; Pani & Sharma, 2012). According to Pani and Sharma (2012), the Indian apparel market growth has been instigated by several factors: (1) increase in average household income, (2) rise in special occasion trends, (3) women empowerment, (4) access to fashion by middle-class women, (5) use of fashion as a tool for self-expression, (6) increased urbanization, (7) growth of organized retail and shopping malls, (8) circulation of fashion innovators due to the rise of internet use and (9) presence of Western brands in India.

This last factor is particularly interesting as Western products were restrained in India before the 1980s, and they were mainly available to the higher social classes only (Batra et al., 2000). In the late 1980s, the Indian government chose to ease these restrictions allowing foreign competitors to bring their branded goods to the local markets (Field, 2005). With an annual growth of 25%, a rise in consumer demand for fashion and increasing middle-class salaries, the Indian apparel industry today offers significant opportunities for multinational fashion retailers (Bellman, 2005; Moreau & Mazumdar, 2007; Nicholls et al., 1996). Many international apparel brands have launched in India (see Table 2.1),

Table 2.1 Foreign brands launched (by entry year) in India from the late 1980s to 2007 (from Son, 2011)

Brand	Entry year	Country	Brand	Entry year	Country
Adidas	1989	Germany	Bossini	2005	Hong Kong
Pierre Cardin	1994	France	Christian Dior	2006	France
Levi's	1994	USA	Promod	2006	France
Nike	1995	USA	Giordano	2006	Hong Kong
Lee	1995	USA	Mango	2006	Spain
Reebok	1995	USA	Zara	2006	Spain
Benetton	1998	Italy	Nautica	2006	USA
Ermenegildo Zegna	1999	Italy	Guess	2006	USA
Van Heusen	2000	USA	DKNY	2006	USA
Marks & spencer	2001	UK	Seven jeans	2006	USA
Ralph Lauren	2001	USA	Versace	2006	Italy
Wrangler	2001	USA	Fendi	2007	Italy
Allen Solly	2001	UK	Dolce and Gabanna	2007	Italy
Louis Vuitton	2002	France	Armani	2007	Italy
Hugo boss	2003	Germany	Gucci	2007	Italy
Daks Simpson	2004	UK	Diesel	2007	Italy
Bvulgari	2004	Italy	Sisley	2007	Italy
Mexx	2004	Netherlands	Banana republic	2007	USA
Calvin Klein	2004	USA	Gap	2007	USA
Tommy Hilfiger	2004	USA	Kipling	2007	Belgium
La Senza	2004	Canada	FCUK	2007	UK
Channel	2005	France	Jimmy Choo	2007	UK
Esprit	2005	Hong Kong	Canali	2007	Italy

offering new shopping formats to Indian consumers, that is, shopping malls and department stores similar to the Western type. Table 2.1 illustrates the wide offer from Western Fashion, from mass-market and fast fashion brands to mid-market brands as well as luxury brands. Foreign branded products are now in competition with traditional and mostly unbranded Indian apparel (Bandyopadhyay 2001; Kinra, 2006). The branded apparel sector is a growing market (Nguyen & Mogaji, 2022a) and is considered to be the second-largest retail sales in India (Vaid, 2007). These multinational apparel brands that entered India have transformed Indian consumerism over the past decade (Gopal & Srinivasan, 2006).

The impact of multinational, and also Western, brands on Indian consumerism can be better understood through the lens of cross-cultural research. Traditionally, cross-cultural studies have depicted Indian society as an Eastern culture with Eastern cultural preferences such as collectivist orientation, respect for status and power, primacy of personalized relationships, desire to be embedded in an in-group and familism (Hofstede, 1991; Panda & Gupta, 2004; Sharma 2015). Foreign brands have 'created a powerful image among the upper-middle-class that foreign goods were exotic, showy and better than Indian-made products' (Bullis 1997, p. 64). Western brands have heightened the need for uniqueness in young Indians (Handa & Khare, 2010) and increased brand consciousness among Indian consumers (Shashidhar, 2004). Western brands have also increased the choice of products with emotional benefits such as the communication of status, wealth and prestige (Batra et al., 2000; Sinha, 2003) as well as utilitarian benefits such as quality and low price (Batra et al., 2000). Table 2.2 summarizes cross-cultural studies that have assessed Indian consumer decision-making characteristics since the 1980s. Overall, research depicts Indian consumers as brand loyal, brand and price-value conscious, new fashion and recreational-shopping conscious, perfectionist, time-energy conserving but also confused by over-choice and impulse (see Table 2.2).

Research has underlined that Indian consumers, particularly young generations such as Generation Z (18–24-year-old), have a more positive attitude and higher consumer preferences towards foreign brands as compared to local brands (Jin, Chansarkar & Kondap 2006; Kumar et al., 2009). Indian consumers are more inclined to prefer and purchase Western rather than Indian fashion brands because of the perception that Western goods are of higher quality, depict high social class and provide modernity and nonconformity to traditional values, uniqueness and emotional values (Batra et al., 2000; Jin, Chansarkar & Kondap 2006; Kinra, 2006; Kumar et al., 2009).

Despite the Indian growth rate, Indian fashion consumption has been the subject of relatively little research. Furthermore, 500 million Indians were under the age of 25 in 2011 (KPMG report, 2014) representing

Table 2.2 The decision-making characteristics of Indian consumers (adapted from Mishra, 2010)

Decision-making characteristics	Articles							
	Sproles & Kendall (1986)	Hafstrom et al. (1992)	Lyonski et al. (1996)	Fan & Xiao (1998)	Mitchell & Bates (1998)	Hiu et al. (2001)	Mokhlis (2009)	Mishra (2010)
Brand conscious	x	x	x	x	x	x		x
Confused by over choice	x	x	x		x	x	x	x
Dissatisfied shopping consciousness								x
Fashion-conscious								x
Habitual, brand loyal	x	x	x		x	x	x	x
Information-utilization				x				
Impulsiveness	x	x	x		x		x	x
Novelty-fashion conscious	x		x		x	x	x	
Perfectionist	x	x	x		x	x	x	x
Price-value conscious	x	x		x	x	x		x
Quality conscious				x				x
Recreational-shopping conscious	x	x	x		x	x	x	x
Store loyal					x			x
Time-energy conserving		x		x	x		x	
Variety-seeking							x	

20% of the world's population under the age of 24 (Sinha, 2003), and young female Indian consumers are more involved in fashion than mature Indian women (Khare et al., 2012). Interestingly, young consumers, including young Indian consumers, choose to engage with sustainability (Dabija et al., 2019; Goswami, 2008; Kaur et al., 2018; Singh et al., 2011). In order to cope with unethical image of fast fashion as well as to attract young consumers, Western fast fashion brands tend to focus their image and strategy on sustainability (McNeill & Moore, 2015). Considering Gen Z Indian consumers' prevalence and ease of access to fashion, and understanding the attitudes of these consumers towards Western fast fashion, Indian traditional fashion and sustainability will enable brands to enhance their targeted marketing strategies.

Research Objectives and Rationale

This research is aimed at evaluating the fashion consumer behaviour of Gen Z Indian consumers. Our specific research objectives were (1) to assess the opinion of these consumers towards Western and Indian fashion, (2) to measure Indian Gen Z's brand equity towards Western and Indian fashion and (3) to measure Indian Gen Z's behaviours and attitudes towards sustainability. Two studies were conducted in order to address these objectives.

Study 1 aimed to evaluate Gen Z's attitudes and opinions towards Western and Indian fashion. Given the lack of academic research into Indian fashion consumers, Interpretative Phenomenological Analysis (IPA; Smith et al., 2009) was used to explore the qualitative features, depth and richness of individuals' experiences of, and perspectives on, Western and Indian fashion.

Study 2 aimed to quantify the brand equity (brand awareness, perceived quality, brand associations and brand loyalty) of young Indian consumers towards Western and Indian fashion, as well as to measure their environmental behaviours and attitudes (fast fashion purchasing, disposal, value-oriented hoarding and recycling, and environmental attitudes). Specifically, Study 2 addressed the following hypotheses:

H1. There will be a difference in brand equity (brand awareness, perceived quality, brand associations and brand loyalty) between Western and Indian fashion.
H2. There will be associations between fast fashion purchasing, environmental behaviours (disposal, value-oriented hoarding and recycling) and environmental attitudes.
H3. Brand equity will predict environmental behaviours and attitudes.

Study 1

Participants

Participants were recruited using convenience[1] and snowball sampling[2] methods. As explained in the literature section, only Gen Z consumers were invited to participate in this study. As women are more involved in fashion than men (O'Cass, 2000), only women were recruited for this study in order to obtain a homogeneous sample. The sample included five Indian Gen Z (1997–2013) females aged between 18 and 24 years. Participants were recruited from across the country: Hyderabad (P1, participant 1), New Delhi (P2, participant 2), Chandigarh (P3, participant 3), Lucknow (P4, participant 4), Noida (P5, participant 5). All participants declared having an interest in fashion and volunteered to participate in this study.

Methods

Participants were invited for a one-on-one interview.[3] Prior to the interview, an information sheet and consent form were signed by all participants. The interviews were set up on a video call, and the participants were

---

[1] Nonprobability sampling technique where participants are recruited because they are 'convenient' source of data for researchers, that is, easy to contact or to reach.

[2] Nonprobability sampling technique where participants are recruited from existing participants' referral.

[3] This study has been carried out during the COVID-19 lockdown. As a result, all the 1:1 interviews were carried out online.

informed that their interview would be audio-recorded. Participants were then asked five to six open-ended questions about their experiences and opinions on Indian and Western fashion. Topics explored during the interview were their opinions towards both Indian and Western fast fashion brands, their consumption habits over the last few years as well as their opinions about sustainability. To explore these topics in-depth and encourage elaboration, questions were adapted in response to each participant's answers during the interview. At the end of the interview, participants were debriefed and thanked for their valuable time and input.

Data Analysis

All interviews were transcribed, and IPA (Smith et al., 2009) was used to explore the qualitative features, depth and richness of individuals' experiences of, and perspectives on, Western and Indian fashion. The first stage of analysis consisted of reading each transcript several times, highlighting descriptive words and phrases. The second stage was a more systematic and critical reading of the transcript in order to identify developing themes in the text. The third stage was grouping together these themes into clusters. The fourth stage consisted of summarizing each participant's themes, keywords, and quotations. The fifth and final step was consolidating superordinate themes across all transcripts to identify shared themes about their experience and attitude towards Western and Indian fashion (Smith et al., 2009).

The second author carried out all the interviews and transcribed all the interviews. The first author carried out the data analysis with the help of the second author. Considering that the second author is Indian, and the first author is French, this dual data analysis provided an *insider* and *outsider's* point of view in the analysis.

Results

The data analysis highlighted two superordinate themes: (1) fashion as a communication tool and (2) opinion about fashion in India. As Table 2.3 shows, the analysis featured several subordinate themes.

Table 2.3 Superordinate and subordinate themes highlighted by Study 1 IPA analysis. Note that P1 stands for Participant 1, P2 for Participant 2 and so on

Superordinate themes	Subordinate themes	P1	P2	P3	P4	P5
Fashion as a communication tool	The social self	x	x			
	The authentic self			x	x	x
	The cultural self	x		x		
Opinions about fashion in India	Positive opinion Western brands	x			x	x
	Negative opinion Western brands		x	x		
	Positive opinion about traditional Indian fashion	x	x	x		
	'They don't get it'.	x	x			x

Fashion as a Communication Tool

While all participants perceived fashion as a communication tool used to express themselves, the analysis highlighted two trends of thought. Indeed, P1 and P2 communicated the notion of social perception in their use of fashion while P3, P4 and P5 focused on their authentic selves.

P1 mentioned using fashion to *'convey a message'* with the way she dresses; to show people who she is. P2 went beyond this communication tool idea by stating that fashion is *'a general statement about a person'*, which reflects the personal and social characteristics of a person, that is, fashion *'reflects how you think, how your life is, and that generally reflects your socio-economic factor, your social status, where you come from'*. In addition to being herself, P3 mentioned using fashion to feel comfortable, being in her *'own comfort zone'*. P4 and P5 echoed this statement by describing the use of fashion as a means to *'be authentic and be comfortable'* (P4) and to *'feel comfortable and attractive'*.

Indian culture seemed to impact two of the participants in their fashion choice. P1 explained that her Indian culture, which she defines as *'strong and rigid'*, affects the way she dresses. Even though she described using fashion to express her true self, this expression seems constrained within a social and cultural context. Among all the different models she has access to, P3 focuses her dress style on her Indian peers, that is, her mother and her law school peers.

> *'I dress according to the place I'm going, and not the way I want to dress. I dress according to what people would perceive of me and how I should maintain myself in that place - but it's not like I can dress in whatever because somewhere a thought would come, about what people will think of me if I wear something like this?'* (P1)

> *'Since I am in my fourth year of law school and I belong to such a place where people around me are wearing mostly Indian ethnic wear suits, and I feel that, over the past 3-4 years, I have changed my consumption patterns from the mainstream patters of jeans and shirts to mostly wearing ethnic suits in college; and I have also seen all my friends do that.'* (P3)

Before going further into the consumers' opinion about Western and Indian fashion, it is interesting to notice the importance of fashion to the consumer's self, identity and culture.

Western Versus Indian Fashion

All of the participants defined Indian fashion in two different categories. On the one hand, they described traditional Indian fashion, defining this concept as unbranded fashion, sold on local markets or homemade and tailored. On the other hand, participants talked about branded Indian fashion, defining this concept as branded fashion using Indian style, which could be bought online or in stores.

The data analysis did not reveal opinions about branded Indian fashion, however it did highlight an apparent dichotomy between participants' perceptions of Western fast fashion and traditional Indian fashion. P1, P4 and P5 mentioned being attracted to Western fast fashion brands due to the wide range of products, their style and their affordable price-points. While P1 underlined the lack of sustainability of Western fast fashion brands, she described being amazed by the wide product range that these brands offer. She also highlighted the innovative visual merchandising of these products and it appeared that the vast offer of products was more attractive to her than the lack of sustainability. P4 also mentioned being attracted to Western fast fashion brands as these brands offer affordable products with better style. She confirmed that the presence of Western fast fashion had changed the way Indian consumers dress. In line with P1 and P4, P5 underlined the success of her favourite brand H&M, pointing out that the wide range of products they offer can suit any consumer.

> *'The kind of products Western brands have and the way they market it or the way they show how people are wearing them. I think that convinces me to go and get it.'* (P1)

> *'H&M is my favourite brand. Anytime I need to buy something I just need to open the website, and I KNOW I will find something for sure.'* (P5)

On the contrary, P3 was put off by the wide range of Western fast fashion products. She mentioned not being particularly brand conscious and described Western fast fashion as *'versatile'*. Although she said that she sometimes purchased Western fast fashion brands such as H&M, Zara and Forever 21, P2 had been trying to move away from these brands due to their lack of sustainability; how these brands treat their workers and the lack of sustainable materials. She also perceived Western fast fashion brands as too pricey for the products they offer. She explained the success of Western fast fashion brands as due to their affordability, but also underlined the possibility of finding affordable Indian fashion, either fashion brands (she referred to *W* or *Biba*) or traditional fashion clothing that can be homemade or found in a market.

With this idea of being more sustainable while being stylish, P2 talked about wearing ethnic clothes, bought from local markets or having it made by local artisans. Having an increased fashion or style awareness, coupled with a desire to be environmentally friendly, made P2 naturally turn towards local ethnic fashion. As mentioned earlier, P3 also described herself as having turned towards ethnic clothing, which she explained in terms of the influence of her social groups.

> I live in Delhi, which is I think, quite a very convenient thing for college students to just go to Sarojini (local market), which is just like a thrift store but Indian version. Like you can get a lot of clothes there for very cheap prices. (P2)

P1 also discussed the influence of social groups on her traditional Indian fashion choices, which are influenced by Indian culture. It is thus not surprising that she, like her friends, still wears traditional Indian clothes. She described traditional Indian fashion as *'expensive'* and thus *'aspiring'*.

> *'Indian factories have started having their own brands and people have started encouraging them and I naturally turned to them.'* (P1)

> *'So many girls think that "this (traditional Indian fashion) is what I'm gonna wear at some point in my life".'* (P1)

Interestingly, while P3 underlined the success of Western fast fashion brands in India, she also highlighted that many Indian consumers still buy and wear Indian fashion. While the rise of social media has helped the entrance of Western brands into the Indian apparel market, P3 suggested that the rise of social media would also help Indian Fashion to reach global consumers.

> *'What I feel is, people from India locally, they are sticking to Indian fashion; but on the other hand, the people from outside India (from US, UK, whatever countries), they are also slowly and steadily coming and recognizing Indian fashion brands, and they are using it.'* (P3)

P1 emphasized that, even though traditional Indian fashion has been successful for a long time, there has been a lack of progression. While Western fast fashion is a fast-paced and changing industry, she viewed traditional Indian fashion as stagnant with a need for progress. P2 echoed this statement by commenting that the Indian fashion industry needs to understand the consumers' demands better and increase the affordability of sustainable fashion. P5 described being put off by the price and the lack of style of traditional Indian fashion. Young Indian consumers seem to wear Indian fashion but feel that it needs to progress in terms of the range of style and quality of products that it offers.

> *'They (traditional Indian fashion people) just still don't get it.'* (P1)

> *'I mean that's what I think India needs at this point; sustainability, but at an affordable price.'* (P2)

'Indian traditional fashion brands are either too gaudy or too simple. I feel these brands have not managed to find that common ground.' (P5)

While there is no distinct definition of Indian fashion in the literature, our participants have provided us with a definition of Indian fashion as compared to Western fashion.

Study 2

Participants

Convenience [1] and snowball [2] sampling were used for participants' recruitment. As with Study 1, only women aged between 18 and 24-year-old were invited for Study 2, and 44 female participants aged between 18 and 24-year-old completed the online survey.

Materials and Procedure

Having read an information sheet, all participants were required to sign a consent form before proceeding to the online questionnaire. Participants were required to anonymously complete two questionnaires—the brand equity questionnaire (CBBE) and the consumers' post-purchase behaviour questionnaire.

The brand equity questionnaire (CBBE) was based on the four brand equity dimensions defined by Aaker and Equity (1991) and Christodoulides, Cadogan & Veloutsou (2015): (1) brand awareness, (2) brand association, (3) brand quality and (4) brand loyalty. Each dimension was measured using three items scored on a seven-point Likert scale from 1 (strongly disagree) to 7 (strongly agree).

Brand awareness was measured via the following items: (1) I have heard of this brand, (2) I am quite familiar with this brand and (3) I can recognize this brand among other brands.

Brand association was tested using the following items: (1) This brand has strong associations, (2) This brand has favourable associations and (3) It is clear what this brand stands for.

Brand perceived quality was measured with the following items: (1) This brand is good quality, (2) This brand has excellent features and (3) Compared to other brands in its category, this brand is of very high quality.

Brand Loyalty was tested using the following items: (1) I feel loyal to this brand, (2) This brand is my first choice and (3) I am committed to this brand.

Participants were required to complete a CBBE questionnaire for Indian traditional fashion, Western fast fashion brands and branded Indian fashion. The decision to examine Indian traditional fashion and branded Indian fashion separately was based on the qualitative findings from Study 1. In order to assess traditional Indian fashion brand equity, the terminology 'this brand' was replaced by 'traditional Indian fashion' and the terminology 'other brands' was replaced by 'other type of fashion'.

The consumers' post-purchase behaviour questionnaire, designed by Joung (2014), measures fast fashion purchasing, disposing, hoarding, recycling efforts and environmental attitudes. In order to assess fast fashion purchasing, participants were invited to answer two questions: (1) I purchase apparel products in stores that carry fast fashion brands (e.g., H&M, Forever21, ZARA, Topshop, Gap) using a yes/no answer; and (2) approximately how many items of apparel products do you purchase in a year, using a ten-point scale with five-apparel item intervals (1= fewer than 5 items, 2= 5–9 items, ..., 10 = 45 or more items). Participants were then invited to answer the question, 'how many items of apparel products do you dispose of in a year?' in order to measure the apparel disposing. Value-oriented hoarding, participation in recycling and environmental attitudes were measured using five-point Likert scales from 1 (strongly disagree) to 5 (strongly agree). In line with Joung (2014), seven items reflecting time for organizing apparel, investment value, usability and fit were used to assess value-oriented hoarding; seven items probing donation, reuse, pass-on, resale, swap and throw-away were used to measure participation in recycling, and five items assessing concerns and attitudes towards environment were used to quantify environmental attitudes.

Data Analysis

The data were analysed using SPSS v.25. Average scores for each dimension were computed to enable interpretation of scores in relation to scale labels (e.g., 'somewhat agree'). Kolmogorov-Smirnov analysis showed that the CBBE dimensions (brand awareness, perceived quality, brand associations and brand loyalty) and consumers' post-purchase behaviour dimensions (disposing, hoarding, recycling efforts and environmental attitudes) followed a normal curve ($p > 0.05$) and so parametric tests were conducted.

Repeated measured analyses of variance (ANOVAs) were used to assess the effects of fashion type (traditional Indian fashion, branded Indian fashion and Western fast fashion) on each of the CBBE dimensions (hypothesis 1), and post-hoc Bonferroni pairwise comparisons were used to examine significant effects. A Pearson bivariate correlation analysis was conducted to examine relationships between the sustainability dimensions and apparel purchasing (hypothesis 2). Linear regression analyses were used to examine how far the CBBE dimensions for each brand type predicted attitudes and behaviours related to sustainability (hypothesis 3). For all tests, statistical significance was accepted at $p < 0.05$.

Results

H1. There will be a difference in brand equity (brand awareness, perceived quality, brand associations and brand loyalty) between Western and Indian fashion.

Average brand awareness, perceived quality, brand association and brand loyalty scores are presented in Table 2.4. Repeated measures ANOVAs identified significant effects of the type of fashion on brand awareness ($F(2, 84) = 11.35$, $p < 0.001$), perceived quality ($F(2, 84) = 7.93$, $p = 0.001$), brand association ($F(2, 84) = 32.66$, $p < 0.001$) and brand loyalty ($F(2, 84) = 6.97$, $p < 0.001$). Bonferroni pairwise comparisons revealed that brand awareness and brand loyalty were significantly lower for branded Indian fashion compared to both traditional Indian and Western fast fashion (all ps < 0.01). Traditional Indian fashion was

Table 2.4 Means (and standard deviations) for awareness, quality, association, and loyalty across the three fashion categories (Western fast fashion, traditional Indian fashion) and branded Indian fashion

CBBE	Western fast fashion	Traditional Indian fashion	Branded Indian fashion
Brand awareness	5.88 (0.93)	5.91 (0.88)	5.08 (1.22)
Perceived quality	4.26 (1.25)	5.14 (0.97)	4.46 (1.09)
Brand association	4.72 (1.22)	5.12 (0.90)	4.38 (0.90)
Brand loyalty	4.05 (1.37)	4.35 (1.62)	3.28 (1.48)

Note. Ratings from 1 (strongly disagree) to 7 (strongly agree) were averaged across three items within each category

Table 2.5 Means (with standard deviations) and correlations between sustainability dimensions

Sustainability dimension	Mean (SD)	1	2	3	4
1. Apparel purchase	3.68 (2.13)	–			
2. Apparel disposal	8.30 (6.12)	0.47**	–		
3. Value-oriented hoarding	3.89 (0.78)	0.55**	0.30	–	
4. Participation in recycling	3.36 (0.77)	-0.01	0.04	0.02	–
5. Environmental attitudes	3.25 (0.44)	0.32*	0.004	0.22	0.32*

Note. Mean scores were averaged across 5-point Likert scales. *$p < 0.05$; ** $p < 0.005$

perceived as higher quality compared to branded Indian and Western fast fashion (both *p*s < 0.05), and had more positive associations compared to Western fast fashion ($p < 0.001$).

H2. There will be associations between fast fashion purchasing, disposal, environmental behaviours and attitudes.

Means, standard deviations and correlations between sustainability dimensions are presented in Table 2.5. On average, respondents purchased three to four apparel products each year (M = 3.68, SD = 2.13), but they disposed of around eight per year (M = 8.30, SD = 6.12). Average scores were 3.89 (SD = 0.78) for value-oriented hoarding, 3.36 (SD = 0.77) for participation in recycling, and 3.25 (SD = 0.44) for environmental attitudes, where higher scores indicated more sustainable attitudes on five-point Likert scales. A Pearson correlation analysis revealed that apparel purchasing was positively associated with disposal ($r = 0.47$, $p = 0.001$), value-oriented hoarding ($r = 0.55$, $p < 0.001$) and environmental attitudes ($r = 0.32$, $p = 0.03$), and that participation in recycling was positively associated with environmental attitudes ($r = 0.32$, $p = 0.05$). Disposal was not associated with recycling or environmental attitudes (both rs < 0.04, both ps > 0.05), and the relationship with hoarding approached, but did not reach, significance ($r = 0.30$, $p = 0.058$).

H3. Brand equity will predict environmental behaviours and attitudes.

Regression analyses were conducted to predict sustainability attitudes (value hoarding, participation recycling and environmental attitudes) using each CBBE dimension (brand awareness, perceived quality, brand association and brand loyalty). Separate models were computed for each CBBE dimension with all three brand types included in each model. These relationships are depicted in Table 2.1.

Perceived quality of brands predicted participation in recycling ($F(3, 39) = 6.40$, $p = 0.001$); while perceived quality of traditional Indian fashion was a significant positive predictor ($B = 0.33$, $p = 0.003$), perceived quality of branded Indian fashion was a significant negative predictor ($B = -0.26$, $p = 0.007$). Brand associations also predicted participation in recycling ($F(3, 39) = 6.33$, $p = 0.001$); again, traditional Indian fashion was a positive predictor ($B = 0.41$, $p = 0.005$), whereas branded Indian fashion was a negative predictor ($B = -0.35$, $p = 0.01$). Brand associations positively predicted environmental attitudes ($F(3, 39) = 3.76$, $p = 0.02$), with traditional Indian fashion ($B = 0.26$, $p = 0.003$) as the only positive predictor. Brand loyalty also positively predicted environmental attitudes ($F(3, 39) = 3.01$, $p = 0.041$); again, loyalty to traditional Indian fashion was the only significant predictor ($B = 0.12$ $p = 0.006$). No other predictions were statistically significant (Fig. 2.1).

Discussion

General Discussion

In this chapter, we aimed to assess the fashion consumer behaviour of Gen Z Indian consumers. Our objectives were (1) to assess the opinion of these consumers towards Western and Indian fashion, (2) to measure Indian Gen Z's brand equity towards Western and Indian fashion and (3)

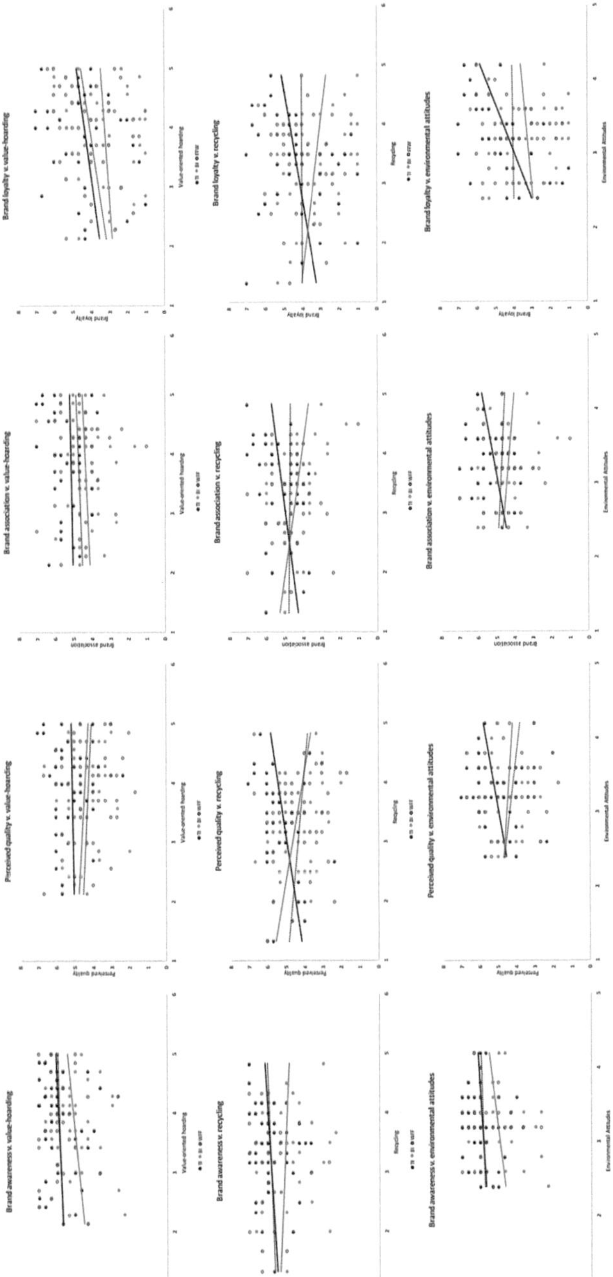

Fig. 2.1 Relationships between brands and sustainability dimensions presented for each CBBE dimension. TI: traditional Indian fashion (black line). BI: branded Indian fashion (grey line). WFF: Western fast fashion (dotted line)

to measure Indian Gen Z's behaviours and attitudes towards sustainability. Two studies were implemented in order to address the research objectives. Using Interpretative Phenomenological Analysis (IPA), Study 1 assessed the attitudes of these consumers towards Western and Indian fashion. Using a quantitative approach, Study 2 measured Indian Gen Z's brand equity towards Western and Indian fashion as well as their environmental behaviours and attitudes (fast fashion purchasing, disposal, hoarding and recycling and environmental attitudes).

Indian Consumers: The Authentic Self and the Cultural Self

It is well established that fashion is used a tool for self-expression (Moody et al., 2010; Entwistle & Wilson 2001). Specifically, Hefferon and colleagues (Hefferon & Boniwell, 2011; Masuch & Hefferon, 2014) have highlighted the use of clothing in negotiating selfhood, allowing self-expression and creating sameness. Our first study outcomes align with this, as the participants described using fashion to find and communicate their sartorial self. This outcome also reflects Pani and Sharma's (2012) evaluation of the Indian apparel growth, which suggested women's empowerment to be one factor of this growth. Specifically, our participants described using clothing practice as a way of expressing their authentic self (i.e., who they really are), their social self (i.e., their authentic self, expressed within a social context such as a family or friendship group) and their cultural self (i.e., their authentic self, expressed within Indian culture and codes). Most of the Study 1 participants referred to the impact of social groups and Indian culture on their sartorial self.

While some research suggests that the presence of Western brands in India has changed the behaviour of Indian consumers (Batra et al., 2000; Bullis, 1997; Handa & Khare, 2010; Shashidhar, 2004; Sinha, 2003), suggesting that they have developed an attraction towards foreign products, our Study 1 results suggest that Gen Z Indian consumers still integrate the traditional cross-cultural dimensions in their sartorial self. Indeed, cross-cultural studies (Hofstede, 1991; Panda & Gupta, 2004; Sharma 2015) have portrayed Indian society as a culture with a collectivist orientation, respect for status and power, desire to be embedded in an in-group and familism. Study 1 indicates that some young Indian consumers are still very much anchored in their traditional culture. As further explained in the next section, this cultural anchor has an impact on Indian consumers' opinion and brand equity towards Western and Indian fashion.

Indian Consumers' Opinion and Brand Equity: Western Fast Fashion Versus Traditional Indian Fashion

Study 1 highlighted two trends in participants' opinions about Western and Indian fashion. Some participants had positive opinions of Western fashion brands, praising their style, affordability and the wide range of products available. Other participants had a positive opinion of traditional Indian fashion, particularly praising the quality, social influence and sustainability of traditional Indian fashion, while underlining the versatility of Western fast fashion brands. Interestingly, the participants who mentioned expressing their social and cultural selves (as described above) showed positive opinions about traditional Indian fashion.

While the outcomes from Study 1 identified Indian fashion as either traditional or branded, the participants did not particularly discuss branded Indian fashion. Overall, participants viewed branded Indian fashion as an unsuccessful mix of Western fast fashion brands and traditional Indian fashion. Participants explained that branded Indian fashion offers a wider range of apparel compared to traditional Indian fashion, but they did not consider this wider range of products as less stylish and lower quality as compared to traditional Indian fashion. Moreover, participants described branded Indian fashion as having a smaller range of products when compared to Western fast fashion brands, while not being as novel as Western brands.

In line with Study 1, Study 2 indicated that there was a lower brand awareness and brand loyalty for branded Indian fashion in comparison to both traditional Indian fashion and Western fast fashion. Interestingly, brand awareness and brand loyalty between Indian and Western fast fashion did not differ significantly, which could reflect the two trends mentioned above; an equal number of participants being more aware and loyal to traditional Indian fashion or to Western fast fashion could attenuate any effect. As suggested by the results of the first study, Study 2 highlighted that branded Indian fashion was perceived as lower quality when compared to traditional Indian fashion. Although there was no significant difference between brand awareness and brand loyalty, results showed that traditional Indian fashion was perceived as higher quality and had more positive associations compared to Western fast fashion. This outcome, along with Aaker's (1991) assertion that the main role of brand associations is to create meanings for consumers, mirrors the findings from Study 1.

While Shashidhar (2004) argued that the presence and growth of Western fashion brands had increased brand consciousness among Indian consumers, the present study failed to show a difference in brand awareness or brand loyalty between Indian and Western fashion. Concerning branded Indian fashion, the presence of Western fast fashion brands and traditional Indian fashion seems to have led to a neutral, if not negative, opinion towards branded Indian fashion.

Contrary to Handa and Khare (2010) who found that Western brands had enhanced the need for uniqueness in young Indian consumers, our research highlighted the importance of novelty, breadth of product choice and affordability for participants inclined to appreciate Western fast fashion brands. This outcome is in line with studies describing Indian consumers as novelty-fashion and price-value conscious (Sproles & Kendall 1986; Hafstrom et al. 1992; Lyonski et al. 1996; Fan & Xiao 1998; Mitchell & Bates 1998; Hiu et al. 2001; Mokhlis 2009; Mishra 2010). While, in line with previous research (Batra et al., 2000; Sinha, 2003), our participants did mention the importance of increased choice and low price, they did not raise the importance of emotional benefits such as the communication of status, wealth and prestige (Batra et al., 2000; Sinha, 2003). Instead, participants described the importance of their authentic self, their traditional cultures and ethnic fashion, and the novelty of Western brands. Moreover, Study 2 results contradict Batra et al. (2000) who found that Western brands increased utilitarian benefits such as quality; our participants rated traditional Indian fashion as higher quality than Western Indian fashion. However, Study 1 results suggest that price is an important utilitarian factor which contributed to a preference for Western fast fashion in young Indian consumers.

Indian Gen Z's Behaviours and Attitudes Towards Sustainability

The Study 1 results suggest that sustainability is an important factor in brand preference. Participants with a positive opinion about traditional Indian fashion described being put off by the versatility of Western fast fashion, referring to the increased sustainability of traditional Indian fashion. Participants with positive opinions about Western fast fashion initially described its brands as sustainable but ended up softening this perspective when asked to elaborate. Thus, it appears that novelty was perceived as more important than sustainability for these participants.

The findings of the second study were interesting, particularly in comparison to those of Joung (2014), who recruited Gen Z American consumers. Our participants reported having purchased 3 to 4 fashion items each year, which is much lower than the 20–24 fashion apparel items bought by Joung's young American participants. Moreover, the participants in Study 2 reported disposing of fewer items per year (around 8 per year) compared to Joung's (2014) participants who disposed of 14 or fewer items per year. While both groups, that is, Americans (Joung, 2014) and Indians (our participants), seem to have similar scores in value-oriented hoarding (3.89 ± 0.78 in our study and 3.18 ± 0.98 in Joung's study) and environmental attitudes (3.25 ± 0.44 in our study and 3.59 ± 0.64 in Joung's study), our participants reported participation in recycling to a greater extent than Joung's participants (3.36 ± 0.77 in our study compared to 2.39 ± 0.78 in Joung's study). Our correlation analysis showed similar results to Joung's; that is, positive correlations between apparel purchase and disposal ($r = 0.47$ and $r = 0.36$ for our study and Joung's, respectively, ps <0.001) and value-oriented hoarding ($r = 0.55$ and $r = 0.18$, for our study and Joung's, respectively, ps < 0.001). However, while Joung (2014) failed to show a correlation between apparel purchasing and environmental attitudes ($p > 0.05$), our results showed a positive correlation between environmental attitudes ($r = 0.32$, $p = 0.03$) and apparel purchasing. Both our study and Joung's showed that disposal was not associated with either participation in recycling or environmental attitudes. Contrary to Joung (2014), our results showed a positive correlation ($r = 0.32$, $p = 0.05$) between participation in recycling and environmental attitudes. Moreover, we found that the perceived quality and positive associations with traditional Indian fashion positively predicted consumers' participation in recycling, and brand loyalty and association for traditional Indian fashion positively predicted consumers' environmental attitudes. In line with Joung, we found that although fast fashion consumers were interested in the environment, they did not participate in recycling. These results are in agreement with previous research showing that recycling behaviours positively relate to environmental attitudes (Joung & Park-Poaps, 2013; Shim, 1995).

The current study indicated that (1) positive brand associations towards traditional Indian fashion positively predict participation in recycling and environmental attitudes; (2) perceived quality of traditional Indian fashion positively predicts participation in recycling and (3) brand loyalty towards traditional Indian fashion positively predicts environmental attitudes. This is in agreement with previous research (Koch & Domina, 1997; Niinimäki & Armstrong, 2013) that suggested that consumers are more likely to recycle than to throw away valued fashion items due to personal attachment and investment. In line with the outcomes of Kumar (2019), the present study indicates cultural differences in environmental behaviours, particularly between Americans and Indians.

Implication of the Research

By understanding the attitudes of these consumers towards Western fashion, Indian fashion and sustainability, the present research aimed to enable brands to enhance their marketing strategies in order to better streamline their brands' marketing. While Western fast fashion brands appear successful and well-liked by some young Indian consumers, our study revealed positive attitude towards traditional Indian fashion due to its anchoring in tradition as well as its sustainability practices.

While Study 1 showed that some young Indian participants hold positive attitudes towards Western fast fashion brands, we also found that traditional Indian fashion is perceived as better quality and with more positive associations than Western fast fashion brands. Furthermore, the results indicated that (1) perceived quality and brand associations for traditional Indian fashion positively predicted Indian consumers' participation in recycling; and (2) brand associations and brand loyalty for traditional Indian fashion positively predicted Indian consumers' environmental attitudes. Since the 1980s the growing presence of Western brands in India has changed the landscape of the Indian apparel industry. However, the present findings suggest that Western brands could benefit from understanding traditional Indian fashion's emphasis on brand quality, brand meanings and associations, brand loyalty and, most importantly, sustainable practices. Instead of targeting young Indian consumers to purchase Western fast fashion brands, it would be wiser and more beneficial to enhance traditional Indian fashion to meet the needs of young Indian consumers.

Study Evaluation and Future Work

Despite the growth of the Indian fashion industry, there has been a lack of studies focused on India (Ganguly & Ayres, 2006). The present study addressed this gap by assessing the current state of the fashion industry and the attitudes and behaviours of young consumers in India. The findings highlight the need for further understanding of consumer behaviour in the growing fashion industry in India. Using the mixed-method approach facilitated in-depth study of the attitudes and behaviours of young fashion consumers in India, as well as a detailed analysis of the Indian fashion industry. However, there were some limitations in regard to the quantitative approach (Study 2). Studying Indian consumer behaviour is complex due to India being a vast country that is multicultural, multilingual and multi-religious (Panda & Gupta, 2004), as reflected by the heterogeneity of Indian consumers. A larger sample size would have supported the generalizability of the results to the broader population; however, despite the relatively small sample size, participants were selected from across the country, which accounts for some cultural differences across India. Future research should aim to focus on young Indian consumers of fashion, while accounting for the complex and diverse cultural make-up of India.

Conclusion

The present study partially contradicted previous research indicating that Indian consumers have a more positive attitude towards foreign brands when compared to local brands (Jin, Chansarkar & Kondap 2006; Kumar, Lee & Kim 2008) due to their perception of Western goods providing modernity and nonconformity to traditional values (Jin, Chansarkar & Kondap 2006; Kinra, 2006; Kumar, Lee & Kim 2008). The present research suggested a need for improvement in traditional Indian fashion, particularly concerning its lack of pace, its perceived stagnancy and the need to broaden its product offerings and specifically from an emerging economy perspective (Brooksworth et al., 2022a, 2022b). Considering the positive attitudes of Indian young consumers towards traditional Indian fashion, which may soon overtake positive attitudes towards Western fast fashion, the latter could collaborate with traditional Indian fashion in order to help this local apparel sector develop.

References

Aaker, D. A., & Equity, M. B. (1991). The Free Press. *New York, 206.*

Bandyopadhyay, S. P., & Kao, J. L. (2001). Competition and Big 6 brand name reputation: Evidence from the Ontario municipal audit market. Contemporary Accounting Research, 18(1), 27–64

Bandyopadhyay, R., & Morais, D. (2005). Representative dissonance: India's self and western image. *Annals of Tourism Research, 32*(4), 1006–1021.

Batra, R., Ramaswamy, V., Alden, D. L., Steenkamp, J. B. E., & Ramachander, S. (2000). Effects of brand local and nonlocal origin on consumer attitudes in developing countries. *Journal of Consumer Psychology, 9*(2), 83–95.

Beinhocker, E. D., Farrell, D., & Zainulbhai, A. S. (2007). Tracking the growth of India's middle class. *McKinsey Quarterly, 3*, 50.

Bellman, E. (2005). India embarks on a retail boom. *The Wall Street Journal, 8*, A5.

Bhattacharya, S., & Anand, V. (2019). What makes the Indian youths to engage with online retail brands: An empirical study. Global Business Review, p. 0972150918822106.

Brooksworth, F., Mogaji, E., & Bosah, G. (2022a). Fashion Marketing in Emerging Economies: An introduction. In F. Brooksworth, E. Mogaji, &

G. Bosah (Eds.), *Fashion Marketing in Emerging Economies (volume 1) – Brand, consumer and sustainability perspectives*. Springer.

Brooksworth, F., Mogaji, E., & Bosah, G. (2022b). Fashion Marketing in Emerging Economies: Conclusion and research agenda. In F. Brooksworth, E. Mogaji, & G. Bosah (Eds.), *Fashion Marketing in Emerging Economies (volume 1) – Brand, consumer and sustainability perspectives*. Springer.

Bullis, D. (1997). *Selling to the consumer market in India*. Quorum Books.

Chanana, N., & Goele, S. (2012). Future of e-commerce in India. *International Journal of Computing & Business Research, 8*, 1.

Dabija, D. C., Bejan, B. M., & Dinu, V. (2019). How sustainability oriented is generation Z in retail? *A Literature Review Transformations in Business & Economics, 18*(2), 1.

Entwistle, J., & Wilson, E. (Eds.). (2001). *Body dressing* (p. 33). Berg.

Fernandes, M., Gadi, C., Khanna, A., Mitra, P., & Narayanswamy, S. (2000). India's retailing comes of age. *The McKinsey Quarterly, 1*, 94.

Field, A. (2005). Passage to India. http://retailtrafficmag.com/2005

Ganguly, S., & Ayres, A. (2006). Introduction: The state of India studies in the United States, 2006. *India Review, 5*(1), 1–13.

Gopal, A., & Srinivasan, R. (2006). The new Indian consumer. *Harvard Business Review, 84*(10), 22–23.

Goswami, P. (2008). Is the urban Indian consumer ready for clothing with eco-labels? *International Journal of Consumer Studies, 32*(5), 438–446.

Handa, M., & Khare, A. (2010). Need for uniqueness and consumption behaviour for luxury brands amongst Indian youth PAPER RETRACTED. *International Journal of Indian Culture and Business Management, 3*(5), 489–502.

Hasan, B. (2016). Perceived irritation in online shopping: The impact of website design characteristics. *Computers in Human Behaviour, 54*, 224–230.

Hefferon, K., & Boniwell, I. (2011). *Positive psychology: Theory, research and applications*. McGraw-Hill Education (UK).

Hofstede, G. (1991). Cultures and organizations: Software of the mind (London and New York, McGraw hill). *House, RJ, Hanges, PJ, Javidan, M., Dorfman, PW, & Gupta, V.(Eds. 2004), Airaksinen*, pp. 1–25.

Industry week 50. (2005). *Indian Economy Races into 2006*. The Economy. Retrieved November 3, 2020, from https://www.industryweek.com/the-economy/article/21953240/indian-economy-races-into-2006.

Joung, H. M., & Park-Poaps, H. (2013). Factors motivating and influencing clothing disposal behaviours. *International Journal of Consumer Studies, 37*(1), 105–111.

Joung, H. M. (2014). Fast-fashion consumers' post-purchase behaviours. *International Journal of Retail & Distribution Management.*

Kang, A. (2015). Brand love–moving beyond loyalty an empirical investigation of perceived brand love of Indian consumer. *Arab Economic and Business Journal, 10*(2), 90–101.

Kaur, J., Duggal, V., & Suri, S. (2018). To study the factors effecting purchase of green products and their relation to the purchase decision of green products for generation Z in India. *Journal of Asia Entrepreneurship and Sustainability, 14*(2), 21–63.

Kaur, J., Mogaji, E., Wadera, D., & Gupta, S. (2022). "Sustainable consumption practices in Indian households: a saga of environment management linked to Indian ethos and generational differences", Society and Business Review, Vol. ahead-of-print No. ahead-of-print. https://doi.org/10.1108/SBR-08-2021-0132.

Khare, A., Mishra, A., & Parveen, C. (2012). Influence of collective self-esteem on fashion clothing involvement among Indian women. *Journal of Fashion Marketing and Management: An International Journal.*

Kinra, N. (2006). The effect of country-of-origin on foreign brand names in the Indian market. *Marketing Intelligence & Planning.*

Koch, K., & Domina, T. (1997). The effects of environmental attitude and fashion opinion leadership on textile recycling in the US. *Journal of Consumer Studies & Home Economics, 21*(1), 1–17.

Kumar, A., Lee, H. J., & Kim, Y. K. (2009). Indian consumers' purchase intention toward a United States versus local brand. *Journal of Business Research, 62*(5), 521–527.

KPMG India report. (2020). The online private label growth paradigm. February 2020.

KPMG report. (2014). KPMG International Annual Review. KPMG cutting through complexity. https://assets.kpmg/content/dam/kpmg/pdf/2014/12/international-annual-review-2014.pdf

Kumar, A. (2019). Exploring young adults' e-waste recycling behaviour using an extended theory of planned behaviour model: A cross-cultural study. *Resources, Conservation and Recycling, 141*, 378–389.

Masuch, C. S., & Hefferon, K. (2014). Understanding the links between positive psychology and fashion: A grounded theory analysis. *International Journal of Fashion Studies, 1*(2), 227–246.

McKinsey's Fashion Scope. (2019). How India's ascent could change the fashion industry. 05 February 2019.

McKinsey & Company. (2007). *The 'bird of gold': The rise of India's consumer market*. McKinsey Global Institute.

McNeill, L., & Moore, R. (2015). Sustainable fashion consumption and the fast fashion conundrum: Fashionable consumers and attitudes to sustainability in clothing choice. *International Journal of Consumer Studies, 39*(3), 212–222.

Moody, W., Kinderman, P., & Sinha, P. (2010). An exploratory study. *Journal of Fashion Marketing and Management: An International Journal, 14*(1), 161–179.

Moreau, R., & Mazumdar, S. (2007). India turns on Singh at his peak. *Newsweek-American Edition, 150*(23), 34.

Mukonza, C., Hinson, R. E., Adeola, O., Adisa, I., & Kirgiz, A. C. (2021). Green marketing: An introduction. In C. Mukonza, R. E. Hinson, O. Adeola, I. Adisa, & A. C. Kirgiz (Eds.), *Green Marketing in Emerging Markets. Palgrave studies of Marketing in Emerging Economies* (pp. 3–14). Palgrave Macmillan. https://doi.org/10.1007/978-3-030-74065-8_1

Nagrath, S. (2003). (En) countering orientalism in high fashion: A review of India fashion week 2002. *Fashion Theory, 7*(3–4), 361–376.

Nguyen, P. N., & Mogaji, E. (2022a). Emerging economies in fashion global value chain: Brand positioning and managerial implications. In F. Brooksworth, E. Mogaji, & G. Bosah (Eds.), *Fashion Marketing in Emerging Economies – Strategies, tools and insights for fashion brands* (pp. 234–345). Springer.

Nguyen, N. P., & Mogaji, E. (2022b). A theoretical framework for the influence of green marketing communication on consumer behaviour in emerging economies. In E. Mogaji, O. Adeola, I. Adisa, R. E. Hinson, C. Mukonza, & A. C. Kirgiz (Eds.), *Green Marketing in Emerging Economies. Palgrave studies of Marketing in Emerging Economies* (pp. 253–274). Palgrave Macmillan. https://doi.org/10.1007/978-3-030-82572-0_11

Nguyen, P., & Mogaji, E. (2021). Brand development through sustainability certifications in emerging markets: Adoption of B corporation certification in Vietnam. In O. Adeola, R. Hinson, & A. Sakkthivel (Eds.), *Marketing communications and brand development in emerging markets* (pp. 34–45). Palgrave.

Nicholls, J. A. F., Roslow, S., Dublish, S., & Comer, L. B. (1996). Relationship between situational variables and purchasing in India and the USA. *International Marketing Review.*

Niinimäki, K., & Armstrong, C. (2013). From pleasure in use to preservation of meaningful memories: A closer look at the sustainability of clothing via longevity and attachment. *International Journal of Fashion Design, Technology and Education, 6*(3), 190–199.

O'Cass, A. (2000). An assessment of consumers product, purchase decision, advertising and consumption involvement in fashion clothing. *Journal of Economic Psychology, 21*(5), 545–576.

Panda, A., & Gupta, R. K. (2004). Mapping cultural diversity within India: A meta-analysis of some recent studies. *Global Business Review, 5*(1), 27–49.

Pani, A., & Sharma, M. (2012). Emerging trends in fashion marketing: A case study of apparel retailing in India. *International Journal of Business and Management Tomorrow, 2*(10), 1–8.

Sharma, P. (2015). Consumer ethnocentrism: Reconceptualization and cross-cultural validation. *Journal of International Business Studies, 46*(3), 381–389.

Shashidhar, A. (2004). Taking its fashion forward. http://www.thehindubusinessline.com/catalyst/2004/01/29/stories/2004012900010030.htm

Shim, S. (1995). Environmentalism and consumers' clothing disposal patterns: An exploratory study. *Clothing and Textiles Research Journal, 13*(1), 38–48.

Singh, S., Park, J. R., & Litten-Brown, J. (2011). *The economic sustainability of cropping systems in Indian Punjab: A farmers' perspective* (No. 726–2016-50056, pp. 1–12).

Sinha, P. K. (2003). Shopping orientation in the evolving Indian market. *Vikalpa, 28*(2), 13–22.

Smith, J.A., Flowers, P., & Larkin, M. (2009). Interpretative phenomenological analysis: Theory, method and research.

World Bank Data. (2020). https://data.worldbank.org/country/india. Accessed 15 October.

Vaid, M. (2007). Shakeout in store in branded clothing space. http://www.moneycontrol.com

Zainulbhai, A. (2005). What executives are asking about India. *McKinsey Quarterly, 1*, 26–33.

3

A Closer Look at the Menswear Market in Brazil

Fábio Shimabukuro Sandes

Introduction

If we look at any industry statistics in fashion, we can see clearly that the womenswear market is larger and more complex than menswear: men"s apparel market is estimated to have been worth $414 billion in 2019, roughly a quarter of the global apparel market (Euromonitor, 2020b), although the division of society per gender is almost 50/50. This can be explained by the fact that a man's wardrobe is composed of fewer kinds of shapes and fits and a more limited colour pallet where tradition overcomes fashion trends (Lorber, 1991; Otnes & Zayer, 2012) as men are expected to perform in a more restricted manner when expressing themselves in the way they dress (Barry & Martin, 2015). As a result of this restricted demand, the menswear market offers consumers fewer fits and shapes to choose from and products with less fashion trend information.

F. S. Sandes (✉)
CICANT Research Centre, Universidade Lusófona, Lisbon, Portugal

F. Brooksworth et al. (eds.), *Fashion Marketing in Emerging Economies Volume II*,
Palgrave Studies of Marketing in Emerging Economies,
https://doi.org/10.1007/978-3-031-07078-5_3

This scenario started to change at the end of the twentieth century when the image of a more fashion-oriented man coming from celebrities like Brad Pitt and footballers like David Beckham inspired a movement called metrosexuals (Kang et al., 2011; Shephard et al., 2016). This movement portrayed men who cared about what they wore and wanted to include the latest fashion trends in dressing and presenting themselves to the world. This movement has expanded the menswear market options and inspired consumers to explore and include fashion-forward references in their routine.

This change was connected to a change of perspectives in gender roles and expected performances of gender in marketplaces (Barry & Martin, 2015; Lorber, 1991; Thompson & Üstüner, 2015; WGSN, 2020), especially when considering consumers from generations Y and Z who use fashion as a way to express their individualism and social activism principles (Euromonitor, 2020a; Gazzola et al., 2020; WGSN, 2020). Most studies that support this change of behaviour in the fashion menswear market, however, come from WEIRD (Western, educated, industrialized, rich, and democratic) populations, a criticized known bias in social sciences (Nielsen et al., 2017; Soetan et al., 2021) that questions generalizations made using the perspective of these consumers, which reinforces the need to include different perspectives of these changes.

Even though the impact of gender on fashion consumption behaviour has been widely studied in the literature (Cova et al., 2011; Kang et al., 2011; Rocha et al., 2005; Schofield & Schmidt, 2005; Workman & Lee, 2012), little attention has been devoted to considering this impact on emerging countries (Brooksworth et al., 2022a, 2022b). This chapter aims to fill this gap by offering a different and supplementary perception of these changes in the menswear market by discussing how men behave as fashion consumers in Brazil—one of the BRICS countries. This group represents the most relevant emerging economies in the world. This discussion aims to present a critical perspective of men"s behaviour in this market by including 12 experts interviewed to discuss the main characteristics and details of Brazil"s menswear market.

Method

To describe contemporary men"s characteristics in fashion buying behaviour in Brazil, interviews with experts in menswear were conducted to gather their perspectives about how contemporary men are behaving in the market and the trends for this behaviour. An expert is someone with relevant experience in the menswear market, and these criteria vary according to the role this professional plays in the market. I considered product designers and sales professionals as experts when they have worked for at least ten years, specifically in the menswear market. For cool hunters, I considered an expert a professional with at least five years of professional work in fashion trends research for all markets, including menswear (it was impossible to find cool hunters who research the menswear market exclusively). And for media, I included a journalist that writes about fashion in a leading national newspaper in Brazil and a blogger who writes about menswear for more than five years. Interviews followed a semi-structured script, with questions generated from findings in the literature about male consumer behaviour in the fashion context, as discussed in the previous section.

Interviewees are identified in Table 3.1, with their corresponding areas of expertise in menswear. In total, 12 professionals were interviewed, including mainstream fashion designers, product managers from brands, and big retailers focused on menswear, journalists, bloggers, specialized in fashion and male consumption, and cool hunters. In addition, we interviewed four cool hunters to treat the characteristics of different regions in Brazil: two from the southern part of Brazil, one from the northern part, and one from the Central region. All interviews were recorded and transcribed. On average, an interview lasted 47 minutes (varying from 34 to 75 minutes), summing up to a total of 567 minutes of recorded interviews. In addition, there were 187 pages of transcribed text analysed and grouped into 13 topics discussed in the following section.

All data collected from the interviews were analysed using framework analysis (Srivastava & Thomson, 2009), and 12 main topics emerged from these interviews. This technique was used because it allows the researcher to find major topics organized to allow the researcher to build

Table 3.1 Experts interviewed information

	Expert in	Professional experience
João Pimenta	Product designer	Fashion designer focused on menswear, SPFW
Pedro Diniz	Media	Journalist specialized in fashion and lifestyle
Claudio Pessanha	Sales and commercial	Brand manager—Brazil, Diesel brand
Paula Novaes Fernandes	Product designer	Product director at Foxton, a fashion brand focused on menswear
Roni Almeida	Product designer	Product director Jeanswear at Lunelli and Hangar 33, menswear brand
Leonardo Soares	Sales and commercial	Team manager at C&A, menswear, and kids
Igor Dadona	Product designer	Fashion designer focused on menswear, Casa de Criadores, SPFW
André do Val	Media	Fashion blogger, journalist specialized in menswear/fashion
Patricia Sant'Anna	Cool Hunter	Partner at Tender, fashion trends consultancy, and professor in several courses in fashion design (undergraduate and graduate)
Lorena Abdalla	Cool Hunter—Central-West region	Professor in fashion design undergraduate at Universidade Federal de Goiás
Alamo Bandeira	Cool Hunter—Northeast region	Fashion stylist and professor in fashion design undergraduate at Universidade Federal de Pernambuco
Marcelo Vianna Batista	Cool Hunter—South region	Professor in several courses in fashion design (undergraduate and graduate)

frames that, when put together, create a logical narrative that helps to describe the results found in the interviews. The following section presents this framework analysis results by briefly describing the market"s context and the 12 topics surged from these interviews.

Characteristics of Brazilian Menswear Market

Brazil is the largest country in South America and Latin America and the fifth-largest country by area and the sixth-most populous country in the world. Brazil"s coastline is famous worldwide, with an extension of 7491 km facing the Atlantic Sea[1]. Culturally, Brazil is a melting pot that compasses a wide range of cultures. Since colonial times, the country has assimilated various cultures, and intermarriage was more acceptable in Brazil than in most other European colonies. Brazil was the most significant African, Italian, and Japanese diasporas and the second largest German diaspora in the world. Brazil is also the home of the largest Arab community outside the Arab world (Seyferth, 2000).

In Brazil, the menswear market is estimated to be worth $ 29.5 billion (about $5.8 billion). On the other hand, the women"s apparel market is estimated to be worth $ 45 billion in 2019 (Euromonitor, 2020b), surpassing the men"s market by 52%. If we take into account that in Brazil's population, there is a balance between men and women distribution (50.9% women/49.1% men), and if we consider the fact that, in Brazil, men earn 30% more than women, and occupy 61% of managerial positions in the market (IBGE, 2018), the difference of figures in these markets should be much smaller, which suggests that, on average, women spend more on apparel than the man.

Men"s consumption in fashion is more conservative than women"s, where there are fewer categories in the market, but in Brazil, this is even more noticeable. Brazilian men concentrate their purchase even more, where the jeans market is responsible for about 40% of all the sales in apparel in the region (Euromonitor, 2020a, 2020b). But designers and specialists think there is space for innovation to foster the creation of new products in the Brazilian men"s market in the following years, as new consumers tend to be less conservative (Euromonitor, 2020b).

[1] Population stat, World statistic data, available at www.populationstat.com

Sexuality and Machismo Influence Behaviour

The relevance of sexuality in defining men"s buying behaviour in fashion is commonplace amongst all experts interviewed. All of them say the influence of choices men make in the way they dress is restricted by their sexuality or how they want to portray their sexuality to others. These restrictions come from a historical-cultural background of "machismo" in Brazil (for an extensive comprehension, please refer to Stevens"s classic work, Stevens, 1973). This machismo restricts the choices and behaviour of men in the fashion arena. Experts say men tend to repel the idea of enjoying shopping for clothes, which is seen as a feminine characteristic. All product designers interviewed mentioned that the last great innovation in Brazilian menswear was the acceptance of elastane in the fabrics of the garments because there was a prejudice against fabrics with stretch as it was considered exclusively part of the female universe, as indicated by the quotes below:

> *Not too long ago, men repelled fabrics with stretch because they felt it was a woman's thing. It took a while for them to accept it.* (Paula)
>
> *Men are very traditional. It took a long time for them to accept elastane in their pants, but they eventually cave in for a slimmer fit, mostly because of comfort.* (Roni)
>
> *For men to accept the slim fit, it took over than ten years to happen in the market. Skinny fit is still for an exclusive group of consumers, like rockers.* (Leonardo)

Many experts, especially the cool hunters, point out that the new generation is breaking this barrier as these "macho" stereotypes influence them less. But they advise this is still a small part of the market:

> *This new generation does not care if it looks feminine or not. They see this gender question much different than the rest, all they want is to dress the way they feel.* (Patricia)
>
> *There is a tendency to change men's behaviour in the market, men are testing more things, it is evolving a lot, but it is still very traditional.* (Leonardo)

The influence of sexuality in men's buying behaviour in fashion is a global phenomenon, and the perception that there is a connection with gender and garment types is normalized in Western culture: Otnes and Zayer (2012) point out that it is common to see skirts and pants as the icons that symbolize gender in the public lavatories. These cultural pressures make contemporary male consumers feel vulnerable when expressing non-traditional gender practices in the market (Tuncay & Otnes, 2008). Diego Rinallo interviewed 16 consumers, gay and straight, to understand their relationship with fashion consumption and found a list of dos and don"ts that draw lines that separate masculine from effeminate behaviour in fashion. He proposes that it tends to be more acceptable when it is a narcissistic gaze than when the gaze is panoptical (for further information, please read his chapter in Cova et al., 2011). In developed and more prosperous countries, however, the influence of sexuality has been changing for some time now, and companies are expecting men to rise as fashion consumers. Therefore, large groups like Coach and Michael Kors are experiencing exponential growth in their sales for men"s clothing (Stock, 2014).

Nevertheless, even though men"s tendency to adopt a more active shopping behaviour in fashion tends to be constrained by gender norms that have defined what is masculine in Western culture (Gupta & Gentry, 2016), even considering the approach of a new man, an image created in recent years where men are starting to appropriate their active participation in the buying behaviour for fashion items (Gupta & Gentry, 2016). This is, indeed, a step forward from that previous perception that to be masculine, a man must adhere to four principles in their behaviour: worry about being competitive, combative, be physically strong and emotionally stoic, avoid all things that appear feminine, and be aggressive and forceful all the time (David & Brannon, 1976).

In an example of how cultural and social aspects shape consumers" behaviour, Manrai et al. (2001) came across a peculiar finding. Their research about fashion consumption in the recent opening to shopping behaviour in Eastern countries found that men were more fashion-conscious than women because they had more freedom to dress to express their individualities. In contrast, women faced more restrictions during the Communist era.

What is interesting to realize is that the influence of expected gender roles in fashion can be seen not only in the clothes a man chooses to buy but also in the way he behaves in the market as men attribute their masculinity to consumption practices that includes buying and wearing clothes (Otnes & Zayer, 2012). Jacob Ostberg analysed men"s behaviour in fashion by analysing the discourse he found in Sweden"s socks market and found that masculinity is present in two opposing pressures: to defend tradition and stability and to connect to what is happening globally. In this chapter, he wrote about masculinity in consumers" fashion behaviour (Otnes & Zayer, 2012). Ostberg criticizes the fact that men who care "too much" about one's appearance or merely try to dress to look beautiful seems to be constructed as something potentially dangerous for one"s masculinity" (Otnes & Zayer, 2012. p. 278), and men tend to look for including rationality in their fashion consumption behaviour, often referencing authorities of style experts. Two topics arise from this expected masculine behaviour in fashion shopping: the lack of involvement and rational choices, and they are discussed in the following paragraphs.

Shopping for Themselves Is a Novelty for Most Consumers

Following the machismo cultural heritage in Latin America (Stevens, 1973), there is a cultural aspect in Brazil"s menswear market because, in most cases, men don"t buy their own clothes. Instead, they expect that someone else would do it for them, often their mothers, wives, and even sisters. This is one reason why the main event for sales in menswear in Brazil is Father"s Day, where the sales for men"s apparel hit the top (Euromonitor, 2020b). This celebration occurs on the second Sunday of August. Some of the experts say this is a crucial characteristic of the market because there is a cultural perception that shopping is a feminine activity that men must not enjoy, as can be seen in the following quotes:

> *In several cases, who buys the clothes for men are women. That is one of the reasons why Richard's (menswear brand) launched a female collection.* (Paula)
>
> *Usually who buys the clothes are the women. Men expect that someone will do it for them.* (Roni)

In recent years, experts say this behaviour is gradually changing, where men are part of the shopping process:

> *Twenty years ago, there was this clear perception in the market that were women who bought men's clothing. Today, men buying for clothes solo is still a small part of what you see in stores, but now they are in the store, always accompanied by someone else: girlfriend, boyfriend or a group of friends.* (Leonardo)

And when this happens, men tend to change their behaviour, accept more choices, express what they like and do not like. They start caring about the fit and fabric and are often willing to experience products outside their comfort zone.

> *I feel that when a man starts to participate in the process of choosing his clothes, he enjoys and starts to ask for information, to showcase things he likes, he wants.* (João)

This is consistent with findings in the literature. For example, Lertwannawit and Mandhachitara (2012) suggest that brands stimulate men"s awareness of fashion products and educate men in fashion issues, such as new product launches, to develop a sense of connection to fashion experts, as this status would then lead them to increase their desire to improve their fashion consciousness. This new approach where men are getting more involved in the buying process makes menswear brands invest in innovating their product lines and the shopping environment. As a result, Euromonitor expects that most fashion market innovations will come from brands focused on the menswear market (Euromonitor, 2020b).

Shopping for Clothes Is a Rational (Rather than Emotional) Behaviour

Among all interviewees, there is a common perception that men either behave rationally (or want to be as rational as possible) when buying clothes. "Men buy only when they need something" was often mentioned in most interviews. Pragmatic, rational, and reasoning are words commonly used to describe men"s buying behaviour. According to interviewees, men behave very pragmatically when shopping for clothes. This is consistent with the findings from Gupta and Gentry (2016) that realized that when facing low conditions in fast fashion stores, men tend to adopt a pragmatic behaviour of buying as fast and as effectively as possible. Men"s approach to buying clothes is mainly driven by an immediate need, as represented by the following quotes:

> *They go shopping when they need to, and they sometimes try to optimize the buying process, waiting to accumulate things, like, if they need to buy new underwear, they sometimes wait for a while until they need to buy other things as well, so they can buy them together.* (Lorena)
>
> *I think that it is possible to say that in most cases, men are just buying to replace things that are wasted, and they can no longer use.* (Roni)

As men want to be rational when buying clothes, men could either buy cheap clothes, aiming to spend as little as possible, or buy better quality products, choosing products that will last longer (and postpone the need to replace items). Between these two choices, interviewees say the latter is more frequent. They say that men ask more about the fabrics and the quality of material than women and are often willing to pay more for a product that they consider of good quality because they know that this would lead them to have clothes that will last longer and will be a better investment of their money, as illustrated by the quotes below:

> *When men are shopping, they look for the quality of the fit, the fabrics, the touch of materials. He wants to know if the investment he is making in the outfit is worth.* (João)

Men always value good quality garments; he pays attention to the quality of the material used in the garment. (Paula)

Loyalty as a Way to Escape the Process of Shopping for Clothes

Loyalty is often mentioned in most of the interviews as a characteristic of male consumers in fashion. They say that this loyalty, however, is not always to a specific brand. Instead, it may be to a specific fit of the garment or to a specific material. Interviewees mentioned that when consumers find something they like in a brand, they tend to be loyal to this brand because it simplifies their buying behaviour. However, if the fit of the garment changes and they notice it, they would likely look for new options, as can be seen in the following quotes:

When a male consumer likes the fit, they tend to repeat the purchase, or even buy several garments of this fit, wanting to maximize their time. (Marcelo)

Some consumers go to our stores and turn them inside part of their pants to show the salesperson the name of the fit they want to buy. Then, they ask for other colors or washing options of that model. Then, they specifically ask for the models they already know. (Claudio)

I believe that men tend to be loyal when they see that it will facilitate their shopping behavior: it is a store where I know the model and the size that fits me, so I want to return there. (André)

Menswear brands try to instigate this loyalty by providing their customers with a customized and excellent service in their stores. Some experts also mentioned that menswear brands invest in developing a customized relationship with customers, calling them to go to the stores to hang out, have a beer, or a coffee. Then these brands offer these consumers an in-store experience that would make them enjoy the buying process:

> *Most menswear brands grew because of the loyalty concept. Brands realize that when men find a fit that is good for them, they tend to adopt it and repeat purchases over and over.* (Paula)
>
> *I can say that during COVID when our stores were closed, the most impactful resource was not the e-commerce, but instead the sales through WhatsApp where our sales team were connecting with their customers, maintaining their relationship, and offering an excellent service. That is what helped our sales during this period.* (Claudio)

This loyalty, however, is not a consensus amongst all experts because they mention there is no empirical study that supports this perception and that this occurs mainly because the womenswear market is considerably more complex and dynamic than menswear, as can be seen in the quotes below:

> *No, this is inaccurate. I have studied that in the past. Men are not more loyal than women. They have much fewer options of brands in the market, and therefore there is this myth that they are more loyal, but when you go and analyze the behavior, you see that it is no different than women's behavior.* (Patricia)
>
> *I haven't seen statistics about men being more loyal in consumption, but I did see men in stores saying that they own four, five different colors of the same pants because they like the way they fit. I think it is because this gives him confidence.* (Leonardo)

Despite the controversy about loyalty in men"s behaviour in fashion, one thing stood out in all the interviews. Men are eager to buy clothes online. Due to convenience, it is a direct result of being loyal to a brand they like. If they feel confident that the fit will be helpful, they tend to opt for easier ways to shop. And this includes online shopping. This behaviour is consistent with the literature: Workman (2010) compared men and women in their Need for Touch (NFT) and found that men present a higher instrumental dimension in this scale, suggesting that men need to touch objects more due practical reasons than for seeking enjoyment and hedonic motives, reinforcing the notion that when men feel confident about the product they need to buy, they tend to feel comfortable in buying them online.

Fond of Technological Appeals and Comfort, Not So Much About Sustainability

Following the argument of rational shopping in buying fashion, male consumers pay more attention to the garments" technological details. All experts mentioned they see a positive perception and interest of men when these appeals are presented to them. When a salesperson uses the technological appeal to make a garment more attractive, men tend to pay attention, which may help them rationalize their buying decision. Experts say that men value when the product they are buying has technological advancements that will make the garment last longer or perform better, as they feel this is a better investment of their money.

> *Yes, they like when they see that there is a technological advantage in the product they are buying because they feel the product is better.* (Pedro)
>
> *I have seen a couple of times, men bragging about what the fabric does, especially in fitness garments. You see, technology can be seen as a masculine feature, so they value it. (Patricia)*
>
> *I think the future for menswear is investing in products with technological advancements, like formalwear garments that do not need to iron.* (André)

All experts also agree that Brazilian men are not preoccupied with sustainability matters. They say that this is not something they look for when they are buying clothes, and also when this information is presented to them, they usually do not appreciate it as much. They see it as a flattering appeal, but they are not willing to use it as a deciding feature in their buying decision.

> *From what I have seen, they do not care much about it. They often say this is nice when I show them that the fabric is from recycled material or organic, but I do not notice that this has any impact on their perception of the garment.* (Igor)
>
> *They may even think as something cool, but they would not pay more because of it.* (Roni)
>
> *This may be different for younger generations, but for most consumers, this appeal is not as attractive as the technological one.* (Leonardo)

Men Are Learning to Enjoy the Activity of Shopping

According to the experts interviewed, men are now starting to enjoy the activity of shopping for clothes. However, they say it is a recent event, and it is still seen as a trend for more upscale brands, where they have invested in creating a more appealing atmosphere for men, including barbershops, snooker pool tables, beer tasting, amongst other things from what is perceived as a masculine universe. This is important because men present lower fashion clothing involvement than women, leading to lower knowledge and confidence in choosing clothes (O'Cass, 2004). Also, women tend to value owning more things than men: Workman and Lee (2012) found that women scores higher in materialistic values than men, specifically in the centrality dimension of the scale, which is related to the importance of owning things.

However, the behavioural change demands time, and brands must be patient to adhere to the slow pace of breaking down barriers of prejudice men have in admitting their enjoyment of the shopping process, according to the interviewees. The following quotes are examples of this change:

> *Now men enjoy going to our stores, they have a full experience there. Now they go by themselves, and spend some time there, enjoying it.* (Claudio)
>
> *Brands have created all the atmosphere to make men more involved in the process. They need to feel embraced by the atmosphere, they need to feel comfortable, at home.* (Paula)
>
> *Men have been away from fashion knowledge for a long time, but since the David Beckham phenomenon, men are learning more and more about fashion.* (André)

Also, even contemporary men that consciously adhere to an active fashion buying behaviour are subjected to convey to normative, cultured-engendered behaviour: Gupta and Gentry (2016) found that even when this contemporary male consumer faces scarcity situations, like the ones used by fast fashion retailers, that generates a false sense of scarcity of products to induce urgent buying behaviour in consumers, these men tend to adhere to their expected gender role of competing and being aggressive, towards making the best purchase in the least time possible.

Formal Wear Is Restricted to Specific Professions and Occasions

In 2019, the menswear market in Brazil sold about 390.5 mi garments, most of them denim pants (117.4 million) followed by T-shirts (99.5 million) and shirts (57 million). In the same period, 6.7 million suits were sold (less than the 7.1 million swimsuits sold), suggesting that the Brazilian menswear market is a more informal one. This informality is also mentioned as a primary characteristic by all excellent hunters interviewed. They say that Brazilian men chose to dress more casually and informally than consumers from developed countries.

> *I think that the beachwear lifestyle is present in all Brazilians' perception of fashion, even in places where there are no beaches. The leisure and the informality of life on a beach influence menswear perception everywhere.* (Patricia)

A suit—or even a tie—is restricted to those professions that demand this formality, such as lawyers, finance professionals, and so on. For most of the other careers, casual wear is present. With a dress shirt, denim pants are considered formal as a company would expect, and for some parts of the country, even wearing shorts and T-shirts can be seen as acceptable in working places. The polo shirt is often mentioned as a critical garment for menswear in Brazil as its collar offer men the feeling of formality that they want and the comfort they desire. Some regions are known for being more formal than the others, as is demonstrated by the quotes below:

> *A guy from the South needs to wear a polo to feel adequate. They need that collar, the same polo shirt everywhere you look here in the South.* (Marcelo)
>
> *Men from Goias, for instance, they feel the need to dress up; they always were denim pants, button shirts or polos, and shoes. On the other hand, men from Brasilia (that is the closest capital) are much more informal. They wear*

> *Bermuda shorts and flip-flops, which is not seen as acceptable here, so when we spot a man wearing the Bermudas in the mall, we know they are from Brasilia.* (Lorena)

The Influence of Pop-Cultural Icons

Soccer players and famous singers are considered trendsetters in menswear fashion. They influence a specific consumer, usually younger ones, and from specific regions. Funk and Sertanejo are two of the most famous music styles in Brazil. Funk is more connected to a hip-hop style, while Sertanejo is more linked to a country style. In between these styles, there are some footballers, like Neymar, who also influence men's style in Brazil.

One interesting thing to notice is that these styles are much more fashionable, including colourful pieces, lots of prints, and extravaganza garments, such as fluffy jackets and crazy prints. According to the cool hunters we interviewed, this high-end fashion is seen as consumers as reserved to the celebrities on stage. They also say that some characteristics of their looks, however, influence consumers: in places where Sertanejo is more present, like in the countryside, skinny jeans and tight shirts are seen as the standard style for young men, while in places where Funk is more present, pants and shirts with a loose fit are more common. For style references, these are some of the celebrities considered as fashion influencers in Brazil: Luan Santana (singer), Neymar (footballer), Emicida (singer), and Gusttavo Lima (singer).

Regional Differences

Regional differences are a relevant matter when analysing a market in a country as big as Brazil. What is considered as a standard in some regions can be seen as an outsider in another region? A good example can be seen in these quotes below, from cool hunters from different regions:

> *Men here only wear loose pants. Tight pants are seen as clothes for gay people. There is still a lot of prejudice about them.* (Lorena)

Everyone wears skinny pants. The higher the pants, the better. It is a symbol of masculinity; it is a way to showcase their intimate parts. (Alamo)

These quotes showcase that regional and cultural values define opposite perceptions of tight clothes. Specific characteristics of a region, however, may influence other regions in the same way. The "carioca" lifestyle influences menswear worldwide, where a more relaxed, chill image is part of the mood board presented by brands in this market. The casual, cool vibe of people who live close to the beach is appreciated in all Brazil regions, including areas that do not have any access to the beach, such as the countryside of São Paulo or the central area of Brazil.

This casual look of the surf wear is an important reference for designers in the Brazilian menswear market, even for the countryside. (Patricia)

The carioca lifestyle is a constant inspiration for menswear brands in Brazil. (Pedro)

Some regions are more traditional, and the image of a classic, masculine man is still the reference for the market. In the South of Brazil, men are more classic and more resistant to adhere to market changes. According to Marcelo, a cool hunter in the region, men in the South tend to buy pants one size larger, so the skinnies do not look so tight. At the same time, in the Northeast of Brazil, young men, even teenagers, are oversexualizing their way of dressing by adhering to a cultural phenomenon called Passinho (for reference, please see video http://bit.ly/passinhoBR).

Along with this casual, relaxed vibe, two other characteristics are relevant to design in the Brazilian menswear market: comfort and slim. Although these are often seen as opposite directions in fashion design, they are both present and essential in Brazil"s menswear. Comfort, experts say, is always a characteristic of garments that men appreciate. Men like comfortable clothes. This is a relevant feature of the garment. Men need to feel comfortable wearing clothes. But this does not necessarily mean a loose fit. Sometimes, a tight, slim fit can also be comfortable, especially if it highlights the features men want to display. According to the International Health, Racquet & Sports club Association, Brazil is the second country with more gyms and more gym members globally, which may help explain the value of being in shape in Brazil. Men are worried about having a good shape for their bodies and want the clothes to show that off:

> *Everything is slim in Brazil. You see tight, fitted clothes everywhere because Brazilian men like to exercise and be in shape.* (Pedro)
>
> *The excessive use of steroids, and the constant desire to be stronger, bigger, is something we see in Brazilian men.* (Alamo)

Most Men Dress to Belong, Not to Stand Out

The most common perception from the experts is that men dress to show status. The status they feel like they should have. It is not about the brand they wear but the brand they should be wearing because it translates to the lifestyle they value. In response to the question "When men dress, who do they dress for?" we have some different answers: "They dress inspired by the people they look up to", "Men dress to their peers", "Men dress to seduce". These are the three main variants in the answers. However, one commonplace amongst all the experts is that the rule of thumb is "men dress to belong. They do not like to stand out". This is a crucial characteristic of the market, explaining the low variety in colour charts and print designs. The following quote summarized this characteristic:

> *Men usually buy expecting the validation of others, different than women. He is always*
>
> *thinking about what others will think about it, they need to validate. (Leonardo)*

This, however, is not a unanimous characteristic, as some consumers dress to stand out, as it can be seen in the quotes from fashion designers João Pimenta and Igor Dadona:

Exclusivity is a key attribute to my clients. Over time, I feel like men changed from wanting to belong to a group to express themselves through their clothes. Instead of blending in, men now want to stand out. (João).

My client wants exclusivity. They want to have what others don't have. Sometimes they buy my clothes right after my fashion show. (Igor)

New Generations, Expressing Uniqueness

The new generation promises to promote significant changes in the behaviour of the menswear market in Brazil. Overall, this new generation is being considered by experts as much more open to change and less influenced by the established prejudices of gender and sexuality. WGSN predicts that the market is stratifying to offer men more individualistic options to dress, creating a narrative that goes hand in hand with the lifestyles they want to portray. Also, they see that the contemporary man is stepping away from the alpha model of behaviour, accepting more of his emotions and starting to dress to impress each other (WGSN, 2020): "the old ideas of what a man should look like or dress like have never been more open to interpretation. For the first time, guys are free to define the style for themselves" (WGSN, 2020, p. 3).

This is consistent with the literature: Shephard et al. (2016) found that men only seek fashion-related information when they embraced the role of fashion leaders, meaning that they are aware and actively look to play this role. The fashion market has seen "the rise of a male archetype interested in style, beauty, and esthetic values" (Lertwannawit & Mandhachitara, 2012; p. 1408). Cool hunter Alamo Bandeira says that Brazilian men are vain, and in the lower classes, they are even more vain, investing in cosmetics and grooming. Complementing this new pattern for men"s behaviour in fashion, journalist Pedro Diniz affirms that gender stereotypes do not restrict this new generation. The genderless promises to be a strong trend for the near future.

Fashion designer João Pimenta is known for releasing innovations in menswear fashion. He says the second most sold items in his collections are skirts. Male skirts. He thinks men like the skirts he designs because it resembles regular pants" structure, with a similar shape, but with more volume, a different take from the traditional skirt. Lately, he has been selling several dresses and using the perception. He learned that men are willing to explore when the garment"s structure resembles a previously known structure. The dress he sells is a mix of a sleeveless shirt with a structured skirt. One important thing to notice is that his clientele is older, between the late 30s and early 50s. He says this is because of his price target. As he sells more exclusive, tailor-made garments, his retail price is very high, typically not reachable for the younger consumer.

Changes After COVID-19

When asked about what COVID-19 may have changed in menswear, there is a consensus that there is an increase in more comfortable garments. Experts think that because of the time spent at home, men, that already value comfort, are going to be even more willing for clothes that make them feel comfortable:

> *The demand for more comfortable garments can already be seen in our stores. I think that they gain a new, different meaning now.* (Claudio)
>
> *With so much time spent at home, this will change the demands consumers will have in the future, including fashion.* (Patricia)

Besides comfort, the threat that the pandemic has imposed on consumers may also change their behaviour. Some experts think that now consumers will be more daring, willing to expose themselves more, adopting a more expressive, authentic style in fashion:

> *COVID has made people ponder about their real desires. I think people are now willing to take more chances to experience the threat of life that COVID presented. They are going to be bolder; they will want to experience more, to be more authentic.* (João)

Discussion and Further Research

This work aimed to discuss the main characteristics of the menswear market in an emergent country to help researchers and practitioners understand the characteristics of male buying behaviour in the fashion market. Brazil was chosen because it is the leading economy in Latin America, and it fits the definition of a cultural melting pot, showcasing the dynamic nature of the market. Challenged by the cultural concept of "machismo" present in this Latin American country"s culture, the menswear market still faces prejudice and barriers that hold back male consumers from engaging in a more pleasurable and hedonic shopping experience.

Our discussion with experts from the menswear market shows that barriers are being challenged and questioned by consumers in recent years. The new generation appears to have been disconnecting from the traditional roles assigned to male consumers in the fashion market, and young men are now adopting a more dynamic and relevant role as fashion buyers. But it progresses slowly and on a different rhythm in all the country, as some regions are more progressive than others. About 10 or 15 years ago, men were marginally involved in the process of buying clothes, with a great rejection of all things that were somehow related to the feminine world in fashion, including the pleasure of shopping for clothes. They also rejected the elastane in the clothes, the colours of the prints, and the clothes" shapes. These restrictions are changing but are still present in some parts of the country, and even with these advancements, men still present a more conservative behaviour in the market: buying clothes is still primarily rational, and the demand for a product with fashion trends information is still a small portion of the market.

There are several areas to be addressed in future studies related to the menswear market in emerging markets, such as Brazil. A phenomenological, qualitative study with male consumers that verify how they perceive these cultural influences in their shopping behaviour for fashion can shed some light on underlying mechanisms that interfere in adopting a more pleasurable, hedonic experience as a fashion buying behaviour. One other suggestion would be to investigate further the cultural differences of these barriers in different Brazil regions. Our findings indicate that the meaning of what is considered acceptable for men to wear varies from region to region; a study that focuses on exploring these differences would be helpful as it would allow researchers and practitioners to understand the dynamic nature of subcultural influences on consumer behaviour.

References

Barry, B., & Martin, D. (2015). Dapper dudes : Young men's fashion consumption and. *Critical Studies in Man's Fashion, 2*, 5–21. https://doi.org/10.1386/csmf.2.1.5

Brooksworth, F., Mogaji, E., & Bosah, G. (2022a). Fashion Marketing in Emerging Economies: An Introduction. In F. Brooksworth, E. Mogaji, & G. Bosah (Eds.), *Fashion Marketing in Emerging Economies (Volume 1) – Brand, Consumer and Sustainability Perspectives*. Springer.

Brooksworth, F., Mogaji, E., & Bosah, G. (2022b). Fashion Marketing in Emerging Economies: Conclusion and Research Agenda. In F. Brooksworth, E. Mogaji, & G. Bosah (Eds.), *Fashion Marketing in Emerging Economies (Volume 1) – Brand, Consumer and Sustainability Perspectives*. Springer.

Cova, B., Kozinets, R. V., & Shankar, A. (2011). *Consumer Tribes. Routledge Taylor & Francis Group*.

David, D. S., & Brannon, R. (1976). *The forty-nine percent majority: The male sex role*. Addison Wesley Publishing Company.

Euromonitor. (2020a). 'Jeans in Brazil,' *Passport*, (July).

Euromonitor. (2020b). 'Menswear in Brazil,' *Passport*, (December), pp. 1–28.

Gazzola, P., et al. (2020). Trends in the fashion industry. The perception of sustainability and circular economy: A gender/generation quantitative approach. *Sustainability (Switzerland), 12*(7), 1–19. https://doi.org/10.3390/su12072809

Gupta, S., & Gentry, J. W. (2016). Construction of gender roles in perceived scarce environments – Maintaining masculinity when shopping for fast fashion apparel. *Journal of Consumer Behaviour, 15*, 251–260. 10.1002/CB.

IBGE. (2018). 'Estatísticas de gênero: indicadores sociais das mulheres no Brasil', *Esudos e pesquisas: informação demográfica e socioeconômica*, (38), p. 12 p. Available at: https://biblioteca.ibge.gov.br/visualizacao/livros/liv101551_informativo.pdf.

Kang, M., Sklar, M., & Johnson, K. K. P. (2011). Men at work: Using dress to communicate identities. *Journal of Fashion Marketing and Management, 15*(4), 412–427. https://doi.org/10.1108/13612021111169924

Lertwannawit, A., & Mandhachitara, R. (2012). Interpersonal effects on fashion consciousness and status consumption moderated by materialism in metropolitan men. *Journal of Business Research, 65*(10), 1408–1416. https://doi.org/10.1016/j.jbusres.2011.10.006

Lorber, J. (1991). The Social Construction of Gender. *Sex and Gender, 1*, 111–117.

Manrai, L. A., et al. (2001). 'A cross-cultural comparison of style in Eastern European emerging markets. *International Marketing Review, 18*(3), 270–285. https://doi.org/10.1108/02651330110396479

Nielsen, M., et al. (2017). The persistent sampling bias in developmental psychology: A call to action. *Journal of Experimental Child Psychology, 162*, 31–38. https://doi.org/10.1016/j.jecp.2017.04.017

O'Cass, A. (2004). 'Fashion clothing consumption: Antecedents and consequences of fashion clothing involvement. *European Journal of Marketing, 38*(7), 869–882. https://doi.org/10.1108/03090560410539294

Otnes, C. C., & Zayer, L. T. (2012). *Gender, Culture, and Consumer Behavior, Routledge Taylor & Francis Group*. Routledge.

Rocha, M. A. V., Hammond, L., & Hawkins, D. H. (2005). 'Age, gender and national factors in fashion consumption. *Journal of Fashion Marketing and Management, 9*(4), 380–390. https://doi.org/10.1108/13612020510620768

Schofield, K., & Schmidt, R. Ä. (2005). Fashion and clothing: The construction and communication of gay identities. *International Journal of Retail & Distribution Management, 33*(4), 310–323. https://doi.org/10.1108/09590550510593239

Shephard, A., et al. (2016). Media influence, fashion, and shopping: A gender perspective. *Journal of Fashion Marketing and Management, 20*(1), 4–18. https://doi.org/10.1108/JFMM-09-2014-0068

Soetan, T. O., Mogaji, E., & Nguyen, N. P. (2021). Financial services experience and consumption in Nigeria. *Journal of Services Marketing, 35*(7), 947–961. https://doi.org/10.1108/JSM-07-2020-0280

Stevens, E. P. (1973). Machismo and marianismo. *Society, 10*(6), 57–63. https://doi.org/10.1007/BF02695282

Stock, K. (2014). Luxury brands are targeting global yummies: Young urban males. *Bloomberg Business Week*, 12–13.

Thompson, C., & Üstüner, T. (2015). Women Skating on the Edge : Marketplace Performances as Ideological Edgework. *Journal of Consumer Research, 42*, 1–54. https://doi.org/10.1093/JCR/ucv013

Tuncay, L., & Otnes, C. C. (2008). The Use of Persuasion Management Strategies by Identity-Vulnerable Consumers: The Case of Urban Heterosexual Male Shoppers. *Journal of Retailing, 84*(4), 487–499. https://doi.org/10.1016/j.jretai.2008.09.004

WGSN. (2020). 'Modern Men's Style Tribes,' *Think Tank, Consumer Insights.*

Workman, J. E. (2010). Fashion consumer groups, gender, and need for touch. *Clothing and Textiles Research Journal, 28*(2), 126–139. https://doi.org/10.1177/0887302X09356323

Workman, J. E., & Lee, S. H. (2012). 'Materialism, fashion consumers and gender: A cross-cultural study. *International Journal of Consumer Studies, 35*(1), 50–57. https://doi.org/10.1111/j.1470-6431.2010.00935.x

4

The Power of Neuromarketing: Taking Luxury Fashion Marketing in Southeast Asia Markets to a Whole New Level

Mamun Ala, Sumesh Nair, and Tareq Rasul

Introduction

Thanks to globalization and the rapid improvement in technology, fashion brands are increasingly facing strong competition in the global market. Tangible attributes including product design, packaging or store location are important; however, there needs to be an equal focus on understanding the impact of the brand on emotions and subconsciousness of consumers (Mukonza et al., 2021; Okonkwo, 2016). This chapter explores how the application of neuromarketing contributes towards the study of consumer behaviour in the Southeast Asia fashion markets. Southeast Asia includes 11 countries, namely Brunei, Cambodia, Indonesia, Laos, Malaysia, Myanmar, Singapore, Thailand, the Philippines, Timor-Leste and Vietnam. The region has unique diversity in history, cultural, ethnicity and religion. In recent decades, most countries in Southeast Asia have

M. Ala (✉) • S. Nair • T. Rasul
Australian Institute of Business, Adelaide, South Australia, Australia
e-mail: Mamun.Ala@aib.edu.au

F. Brooksworth et al. (eds.), *Fashion Marketing in Emerging Economies Volume II*, Palgrave Studies of Marketing in Emerging Economies,
https://doi.org/10.1007/978-3-031-07078-5_4

achieved considerable economic and social development, which is increasingly contributing towards the growing international significance of this region. This chapter will examine how the power of neuromarketing can effectively be used by marketers in Southeast Asia markets to take fashion marketing to a whole new level.

Neuromarketing is a relatively new knowledge area that studies the brain to predict and manipulate consumer behaviour (Mogaji, 2021). It relies on the premise that brain is the mediator of human behaviour (Murphy et al., 2008); as an interdisciplinary applied field, neuromarketing draws from biology, psychology, chemistry, mathematics, medical science and economics (Fugate, 2007; Madan, 2010). The advancement of neuroscience has enabled scientists to develop a map of the brain, learn the role of each part as well as how human brain responds to marketing stimuli (Couson & Vayssettes, 2013; Renvoisé & Morin, 2007; Sharma et al., 2010).

As suggested by Pine and Gilmore (1998), neuromarketing involves the application of a range of techniques of neuroscience to marketing to better understand customer requirements. Alternatively, neuromarketing allows marketers to explore how customers' brains are activated by their marketing activities, including advertising stimuli (Zaltman, 2003). Meyerding and Mehlhose (2018) argue that neuromarketing tactics assist marketers to better reflect on customer preferences with reduced biases. Thanks to neuromarketing, instead of depending on assumptions about consumer preferences and behaviour, marketers can now obtain clinical information about brain mechanisms and functions (Fugate, 2007; Kurtoglu & Ferman, 2020; Mull & Lee, 2014). This indicates that neuromarketing has the potential to take marketing to another level.

Neuromarketing analysis commonly includes the use of various technologies/methods to obtain brain-based information related to consumer preferences such as (1) *Eye tracking (ET)*—to monitor what catches and maintains consumers' attention; (2) *Galvanic skin response (GSR)*—to measure an individual's degree of emotional arousal; (3) *Electroencephalography (EEG)*—to measure the electrical activity in the brain relating to the levels of emotion, motivation and engagement with an advertisement or a product; (4) *Facial expression analysis*—to understand the type of emotion experienced by an individual while looking at a product or an advertisement;

(5) *Virtual reality (VR)*—a virtual store environment is created to measure respondents' reaction to store design. VR technology is also applied to inform outdoor advertising (consumer's response to billboard placement in a virtual environment helps marketers to identify appropriate locations for billboards) and (6) *Implicit association tests (IAT)*—to assess respondents' unconscious attitudes, beliefs and cognitive biases through measuring the level of association between brands and/or attributes. Generally, the aforementioned technologies scrutinize consumer's brain when they view products or brands to be able to accurately predict and/or influence consumer behaviour (Agarwal & Dutta, 2015; Chatterjee, 2015; Cîrneci et al., 2014; Fugate, 2007; Singh, 2020).

The key benefit of neuromarketing tools lies in the fact that they can help getting a reliable answer to the question: Why do people like or dislike something? The goal is to explore the objective information about how the inner brain works, not the subjective report (Cîrneci et al., 2014). Therefore, the use of neuroscience is economically more valuable than traditional marketing tools as the former can provide qualitatively superior information. It is argued that using neuromarketing can enable marketers better understand individuals' genuine emotional response/reaction to brand-related messages and thereby measure the impact of advertising and marketing approaches on consumers (Alsharif et al., 2020; Chatterjee, 2015; Fugate, 2007; Hamilton, 2020).

Many companies from various industries (e.g., automobile, film production and fashion) have already started exploring the possibilities of brain science to develop a modern consumer behaviour tracking technique capable of measuring reaction of the brain to marketing messages and/or products (Kurtoglu & Ferman, 2020; Mull & Lee, 2014; Okonkwo, 2016). More and more neuromarketing methods (such as EEG and eye tracking) are being used in fashion product design as they provide marketers with scientific insights regarding the impact of human psychology and behaviours on product appearance (Kurtoglu & Ferman, 2020; Mull & Lee, 2014).

Baldo et al. (2015) view that the fashion industry commonly faces challenges in terms of predicting new product performance, which leads to commercial failures. The research by Baldo et al. reports the validity of neuromarketing tools (such as brain scanning) in predicting the success of new shoes launched by a European shoe store chain. They argue that the same can be used in successful launching of other items in the fashion industry such as clothing, bags, accessories and watches. Thus, the application of neuromarketing would allow companies to offer customers with the products they genuinely desire and need. This will also enable them to achieve pleasurable shopping experience.

Scholars suggest that neuromarketing still largely remains an unexplored potential for marketers, although many firms are interested to learn about this marketing tool. Fugate (2007) infers that the use of neuromarketing can particularly help marketers to address considerable uncertainties relating to the marketing mix as the approach will enable them to get a clearer view of the consumer decision-making process. Ting, Goh and Isa (2018, p. 315) argue that six Southeast Asian countries (namely Malaysia, Singapore, Indonesia, Thailand, the Philippines and Vietnam) are 'driving Asian growth for luxury market in Asia.' On this premise, this chapter aims to highlight how luxury fashion brands in Southeast Asia markets in collaboration with neuromarketing research agencies can work out which part of the brain deals with purchase decisions and how to influence this action using appropriate marketing stimuli.

This chapter will first provide an overview of neuromarketing theories and trends that apply in the context of Southeast Asia and then present a discussion on the use of neuromarketing techniques and tools for advertising and marketing communication, market segmentation and product development, and the advantages and limitations of selected neuromarketing techniques and tools. This will be followed by an evaluation of effective neuromarketing techniques and tools for advertising and marketing communication, market segmentation and product development, and the advantages and limitations of selected neuromarketing techniques and tools. This chapter also includes a comprehensive analysis of the application of neuromarketing to support market research, product development and marketing communication associated with luxury fashion marketing in SE Asia markets. The use of neuromarketing has the potential to help marketers from developed countries to assess the cognitive and emotional experiences, interests and preferences of consumers in emerging economies and deliver products and services that are compatible with their preferences. A dedicated discussion on how neuromarketing tools and techniques can specifically be used to better understand consumer psychology and decision-making in the context of luxury fashion marketing in SE Asia markets. Since the use and misuse of neuromarketing draws a range of ethical questions, the chapter will also elaborate on legal and ethical aspects of neuromarketing and the importance of participants' privacy and trust.

Neuromarketing Techniques and Tools

Neuromarketing applies various methods to measure and understand the cognitive, affective activities in a customer's brain. Precisely, these methods measure the neural activities inside and outside of the brain and manipulate these neural activities to understand consumer behaviour in a better light (Lim, 2018). Some of the prevalent tools and techniques used in neuromarketing are discussed in this section.

Electroencephalography (EEG)

Electroencephalography (EEG) is a widely used neuromarketing tool for its simplicity and ease of use. EEG uses a network of electrodes that are fixed on the head to detect electrical waves or brainwaves (Madan, 2010; Solnais et al., 2013). EEG equipment is relatively lightweight and has been used in marketing research for understanding consumer reactions to advertisements and other marketing communications assessing the electrical waves in the brain regions (Lee et al., 2007). It generally measures consumers' attention to detail, engagement, boredom, excitement, emotional valence, cognition, memory encoding and recognition (Bercea, 2012).

Magnetoencephalography (MEG)

Magnetoencephalography (MEG) is similar to EEG, but MEG requires more elaborate preparation as it records the magnetic activity in the brain (Solnais et al., 2013). MEG, however, has some advantages over EEG. The magnetic field, unlike electricity, is not impacted by the brain tissues, and therefore, gives a much better picture of the cognitive activities of the brain (Sebastian, 2014). Sebastian (2014) also reiterated that MEG provides better spatial resolution compared to EEG. However, both the methods are incapable of measuring the subcortical brain activities. That is one of the significant limitations of these methods. Among other things, MEG can be used in testing new products, advertisements and packaging design (Bercea, 2012).

Steady State Topography (SST)

Steady State Topography (SST) is very similar to EEG in observing the electrical activities of the brain (Vialatte et al., 2010). SST is a specific application of EEG that observes the brain's electrical response called Steady State Visually Evoked Potential (SSVEP) (Vialatte et al., 2010). SST is used for testing advertisements, movie trailers, print advertisements and images, and brand communication (Bercea, 2012).

Positron Emission Tomography (PET)

Positron Emission Tomography is an invasive method. In this method, a 'positron-emitting radionuclide that is introduced' inside the body of the subjects of the study and then measures the 'gamma quants emitted' by the decay of the radioactive substance introduced (Plassmann et al., 2008, 2011). This method measures, among other things, blood flow, volume, glucose contents and oxygen consumption (Sebastian, 2014). PET could be effectively used to understand consumer sensory perceptions and emotions when testing new products, advertisements and packaging designs (Bercea, 2012). The method is not very popular due to the use of radioactive substances inside the body that might cause some side effects (Jelić, 2014).

Functional Magnetic Resonance Imaging (fMRI)

Functional Magnetic Resonance Imaging (fMRI) scans the thought process of the brain following the blood flow in various parts of the brain (Huettel et al., 2009). It precisely measures the oxygen contents in the blood (Zhang et al., 2019). fMRI results would provide a good understanding of the spatial and temporal resolution of the brain of the subject under study (Stanton et al., 2017). Specifically, fMRI identifies the brain regions that are turned on when the subject is exposed to some stimulus in a marketing test situation (Sebastian, 2014). It is not an invasive method, but the major disadvantage is the high cost of the fMRI machine (Stanton et al., 2017). fMRI machines can be used to measure brand loyalty, brand preference and brand recall of consumers (Bercea, 2012).

Galvanic Skin Response (GSR)

Galvanic Skin Response is a device to record the subject's cognitive loads, emotional state and stress levels (Nourbakhsh et al., 2012). GSR measures the electrical charges of the skin that changes depending on the moisture levels (Kumar & Singh, 2015). The GSR device is usually fixed on the fingers to measure the skin changes triggered by the sympaticus autonomic nervous system (Cuesta et al., 2018). GSR is used extensively in advertising research to understand consumers' responses, intellectual and mental responses to advertisements and other marketing communications (Ohme et al., 2009). It also could be used to understand the market performances of products and services (Bercea, 2012).

Eye Tracking (ET)

As the name suggests, eye tracking (ET) is a tool used to track the visual attention of the consumer that is rooted in cognitive and emotional reactions and responses to the visual stimuli (dos Santoset et al. 2015). ET measures eye movement patterns, excitement attention and pupil dilation of the subjects, to name a few (Bercea, 2012). One of the latest methods used is called 'corneal reflection' that tracts the exact location of eyes by the use of a high-resolution camera (Zamani et al., 2016). ET has been used very extensively in neuromarketing research (Solnais et al., 2013). Especially, eye tracking is useful in testing in-store reactions, packaging design, advertisements, prints, images and so on (Bercea, 2012).

Facial Coding (FC)

Facial coding (FC), as the name suggests, codes the micro facial expressions of the subjects (Bercea, 2012). A widely used guideline is established by a study that identified seven specific emotions combining 24 muscle movements on the face (Roth, 2014). The facial expressions of the test participants are observed and interpreted in this method by exposing them to the various stimulus (Kottier, 2014). FC is commonly used in neuromarketing, specifically to test advertisements and movie trailers (Bercea, 2012).

While the above-mentioned tools and techniques used in neuromarketing offer immense benefits to marketers in terms of understanding and measuring the cognitive and affective activities inside and outside of the brain to be able to further understand consumer behaviour, their application involves a number of challenges. As reported by Mileti et al. (2016), five key weaknesses of commonly used neuromarketing tools and techniques include the following:

1. High costs.
2. Large and immovable technologies.
3. Only a single research technology can be used at a time that limits the exploration into the interactions between multiple neurophysiological elements related to consumer behaviour.
4. The results obtained by fMRI do not conform to those found from other neuroimaging tools.
5. The use of neuromarketing tools raises considerable moral and ethical considerations.

Effective Strategies for Using Neuromarketing in e-Commerce and Social Commerce

It has been almost two decades since people all over the world started using a variety of e-commerce platforms for buying and selling products. According to Andrews and Currim (2004), e-commerce allows people to buy and sell online in a way that replaces physical sales and purchases in conventional stores such as supermarkets and department stores. Neuromarketing, which is based on neuroscience and marketing strategies, tends to play a key role in understanding customers' buying behaviour, not only in physical stores but also in the online space (Singh, 2020). Practitioners, especially marketers, have found neuromarketing useful in gaining competitive advantages over their rivals (Agarwal & Dutta, 2015; Hafez, 2019; Shaw & Bagozzi, 2018). In Southeast Asia, the expansion of the digital economy is phenomenal; it has influenced the steep growth of e-commerce-based businesses in the region, as well. In a study by Google and Temasek, it was estimated that by 2025, the e-commerce sector in Southeast Asia will surpass USD 100 billion (Anandan et al., 2018). In this region, fashion trends among people from almost every generation are contributing to the success of e-commerce. Competition is fierce among businesses, and to survive in the industry, some marketers have started using neuromarketing, to some extent, to retain existing customers and attract more (Kumar et al., 2016).

The literature suggests a high potential for neuromarketing in e-commerce. The use of neuroscience allows sellers to better evaluate online customers' complex behavioural perceptions about fashion brands, which has important implications for both customer satisfaction and profitability (Cherubino et al., 2019). Neuromarketing can help marketers to peep into the mind of tech-savvy customers in Southeast Asia, and therefore should be considered as part of critical marketing strategies for the brand (Zurawicki, 2010; Valaei & Nikhashemi, 2017: Ting et al., 2018). Kumar et al. (2016) discuss the emergence of neuromarketing in the context of India argue that Indian companies will be able to save huge amount of money through neuromarketing driven online advertising strategies.

Many scholars such as Agarwal and Dutta (2015) and Jordao et al. (2017) examine the application of neuromarketing in e-commerce. They suggest that a good combination of traditional marketing methods and neuromarketing will help e-commerce businesses understand customers' perceptions and live up to their expectations.

The relationship between non-traditional marketplaces such as e-commerce and neuromarketing's positive impact on them has been mentioned in many other studies (Uzbay, 2020; Stasi et al., 2018; Shaw & Bagozzi, 2018). Neuromarketing in e-commerce enhances marketers' ability to gain a competitive advantage over others for long-term business sustainability. In the online space, neuromarketing can achieve effective collaboration between buyers and sellers to their mutual benefits (Flavián et al., 2016; Singh, 2020).

Marketers have also been using neuromarketing techniques on a variety of social networking sites (such as Facebook or Twitter) as well, especially to advertise their products. Neuromarketing enables marketers to conduct social media analysis to understand the real reactions of their existing and potential customers; the identification and analysis of feelings lead to an increase in sales (Vences et al., 2020). Goh et al. (2013) conducted a study on the fashion industry, especially on clothing brand pages on Facebook, and the results confirmed that social interactions among users as well as with the administrator of these pages stimulated customers' buying behaviour. To simulate customers' buying behaviour, marketers took customers' emotions into account as part of the concept of neuromarketing. It indicates the fashion industry in Southeast Asia is likely to benefit by using social network sites.

Kumar et al. (2016) explore customers' awareness of neuromarketing in the Indian context. Their findings confirmed that Indian customers were aware of neuromarketing as Indian marketers had been using this technique to some extent to attract customers, win their confidence and meet their requirements. They also mentioned that in India, the incorporation of neuromarketing techniques in market research had been increasing to identify the needs of customers in almost every sector, especially in retail.

In a theoretical review study by Vences et al. (2020), a few key factors in the effectiveness of neuromarketing as a tool to maintain and build relationships between companies and customers on social networks are discussed. This is well-aligned with a study by Schultz (2017), in which fashion apparel and online social interactions are examined. From these, a few relevant factors are listed below:

- Neuromarketing has shown that emotion-based advertisements are more effective than rational advertisements (Hafez, 2019; Harris et al., 2019).

- Neuromarketing techniques allow users to fulfil their social needs based on the emotions and behaviours that they observe in others (Meshi et al., 2015; Turel et al., 2018).
- From the perspective of neuromarketing, posts that entertain develop better engagement between companies and customers (Cvijikj & Michahelles, 2013; Khan et al., 2016).
- On social networks, emotionally based messages, regardless of whether positive or negative, have a higher chance of going viral (Fan et al., 2018; Marbach et al., 2016).

Importantly, Vences et al. (2020) make some important recommendations for future trends in neuromarketing and social networking. Firstly, every product and service are different, so negative or positive reactions from customers on social network platforms need to be uniquely analysed. Secondly, changes in customers' behaviour on social network platforms through influencers could also be analysed in the future. Finally, it has been recommended that to gain organizational competitive advantage over others, businesses need to focus more on negative reactions on social network platforms.

Taken together, based on the above discussion, it can be asserted that neuromarketing has great potential in Southeast Asian industries, particularly in the fashion industry.

The Application of Neuromarketing in Fashion Marketing in Southeast Asian Markets

Southeast Asia is not only geographically diverse, but also a region with varied ethnicities, religions, cultures, traditions and lifestyles. At the same time, consumers are also characterized by a diversity of consumption habits (Otmazgin & Ben-Ari, 2013). In recent years, rapid economic development and urbanization have simultaneously taken place in most Southeast Asian countries. Many of the world's megacities (cities with a population of over ten million) are located in this region. With the increase in purchasing power of people in the Asian emerging economies and thanks to cultural globalization, there has been a dramatic increase in the demand for fashion products, which has created opportunities for many brands considering entering these markets (Populin, 2018; Ting et al., 2018). In this region, the possession of fashion products has become an important indicator of personal success and social status. In recent years, multi-cultural facets of many South Asian markets, namely Malaysia, Singapore, Indonesia, Thailand, the Philippines and Vietnam, have attracted many international luxury fashion brands into this region (Valaei & Nikhashemi, 2017: Ting et al., 2018).

However, the maturity of domestic markets for luxury goods poses considerable challenges in terms of growth opportunities, which is more problematic for foreign firms intending to expand into Southeast Asian markets. Therefore, to enhance their competitiveness, marketers need to acquire an in-depth understanding of fashion goods purchase intention among Southeast Asian consumers (So et al., 2013; Ting et al., 2018). As indicated already, neuromarketing has been used by marketers in the retail and fashion industry to better understand and influence customers' behaviour and to modify or develop effective marketing strategies accordingly (Adhikari, 2016). In the context of Southeast Asia, neuromarketing will be able to play an important role, especially in the fashion industry where customers have very diverse choices, which, from the marketers' viewpoint, are imperative to understand.

The literature suggests that neuromarketing offers more benefits over traditional marketing methods and tools to obtain an in-depth understanding of the effect brands, advertisements and logos have on consumers and their purchase decisions (Hafez, 2019; Harris et al., 2019; Khan et al., 2016). While many scholars view neuromarketing as a complementary method to traditional marketing methods in the retail and fashion industries (Ulman et al., 2015; Vences et al., 2020), Kurtoglu and Ferman (2020) argue that neuromarketing can be applied to every industry where human attitudes and emotions are present. This indicates its relevance in fashion marketing as people are interested in fashion brands and products not just for mere survival but rather to satisfy higher levels of psychological needs.

In recent years, having seen the effectiveness of neuromarketing in other countries (mainly in the Western developed countries), fashion marketers from emerging Asian economies have slowly started to take neuromarketing into account (Adhikari, 2016; Kumar et al., 2016). For example, fashion giant H & M has incorporated neuromarketing tactics in their campaigns in India to increase their sales and their market share (Adhikari, 2016). Other e-commerce giants such as Amazon and eBay are also applying neuromarketing tactics to sustain their position in the industry, especially in the fashion retail domain (Adhikari, 2016). Given that more and more Indian e-commerce companies (e.g., Myntra-Jabong) are following in their footsteps in implementing neuromarketing tactics (Kumar et al., 2016), neuromarketing appears to be a powerful means for new entrants and established fashion brands in Southeast Asian markets to precisely collect information about consumer characteristics and decision-making processes to identify as well as influence consumer needs. Specifically, neuromarketing techniques can be used in testing advertising effectiveness, product appeal, selection of celebrity endorsers, logo/brand selection and media selection (Couson & Vayssettes, 2013; Fugate, 2007).

Consumption being the last stage in the fashion marketing, maximizing sale is the prime goal of a fashion company. However, given the importance of the final consumer (who are essentially not just the passive recipients of the product), collection of rich information about consumers' very specific needs, desires and tastes (in other words, an in-depth exploration of the mystery of the consumer decision-making process) should be the first stage in the fashion marketing process (Fugate, 2007; Hamilton, 2020; Kumar & Singh, 2015; Lee et al., 2017). With the overwhelming digitalization of most aspects of life including shopping, the existence of shopping malls or superstores is constantly being challenged by online sales. The improvement of technology has also contributed to the competition in the media market; naturally, advertisers need novel ways to stand out in mass media and crowd advertisements to be able to reach the target audience (Kwiatkowska, 2008; Couson & Vayssettes, 2013). Studies suggest that there should be more use of neuromarketing in advertising research as various neuromarketing tools can be used to create innovative advertisements that would not only enhance consumer experience but will also save money (Couson & Vayssettes, 2013; Hamilton, 2020). The idea is to ensure a better use of creativity and media. Currently, a typical consumer is exposed to a large number of advertisements in different online and off-line media and often they are wrongly targeted leading to indifference, boredom and annoyance to the consumer. Every year companies end up wasting a huge amount of money on inefficient advertising. Neuromarketing can help advertisers to select appropriate content, media and location for advertisements. At the same time, it can help with the correct targeting of audience, minimize negative audience reaction and promote strong emotional responses (Hamilton, 2020). For example, if the aim of an advertisement is to generate excitement/humour for the brand, neuromarketing technique can be used to if the area of the consumer's brain that process excitement/humour is really affected when the consumer is exposed to the advertisement. In the event the advertisement stimuli fail to bring the expected organic change in the brain (through creating an attractive product image), the advertiser would need to alter the messages (Fugate, 2007).

EEG is used in many ways to test reactions to television advertisements, specifically to identify which moments within an advertisement catch the attention of the target audience and contribute to brand development (Hamilton, 2020). Brain scanning can reveal participants' emotional attachment to a brand, which has important implications for marketers as the brand success primarily depends on consumers' brand attachment. Overall, marketers can use brain-based tests to the effectiveness of product advertisement and promotional campaigns and create meaningful advertisements.

Importantly, as suggested by Cîrneci et al. (2014), functional magnetic resonance imaging (fMRI) may help advertisers address three important aspects relating to the effectiveness of a specific advertisement: whether it arouses the intended emotional reaction; if elements from it will at all be stored in consumers' long-term memory; and whether the ad will be processed attentionally? On the other hand, neuromarketing can help in celebrity branding. Marketers can use neuromarketing methods to connect and measure the impact of the auditory and visual stimuli of individual celebrities on consumers as they cause hormonal secretions into the brain leading to positive emotional responses and trust (Fugate, 2007; Hamilton, 2020; Kumar & Singh, 2015; Lee et al., 2017). In the same way, neuromarketing can also be used in logo/brand selection (Madan, 2010).

Neuromarketing can also help marketers identify the right products that should be offered in the Southeast Asian market. Traditional market research techniques often fail to accurately predict the potential response of consumers to new products or services as they largely depend on subjective data such as information spontaneously shared by respondents, which are subject to biases (Chatterjee, 2015; Sharma et al., 2010). Every year numerous new products are launched in the fashion market. According to Baldo et al. (2015), in the dynamic fashion market, a company's success in relation to brand image, customer loyalty and gross profit largely depends on the success of its new fashion product(s). Traditional market research methods (e.g. self-report, focus group) often fail to accurately predict customer preference and future market performance of the newly introduced products. Empirical evidence suggests that unconscious processes guide around 95 per cent of our purchases (Couson & Vayssettes, 2013). To deal with this problem, brain imaging can be used to minimize and eliminate subjective biases in information. The researcher can monitor consumers' real-time brain activity when seeing a product and can get accurate information about which products are most promising. This facilitates more efficient allocation of resources to develop those products (Chatterjee, 2015). In a study on the effectiveness of brain data over the self-report-based methods to forecast product performance and company gross profit of a European shoe store chain, Baldo et al. (2015) found that the accuracy in predicting the success using brain data was much higher than that of self-report-based methods (in the case of brain data, accuracy was 80 per cent). The study also revealed that while self-report-based prediction would increase company profit by 12.1 per cent, the prediction using brain data would increase it 36.4 per cent. The study concludes that innovative neuromarketing approach has the potential to bring considerable value for firms in terms of brand image, consumer satisfaction and shareholders' return.

Essentially, for fashion products, packaging is of utmost importance. Neuromarketing techniques can help in designing aesthetic packaging based on consumers' unconscious reactions and indicative preferences (García-Madariaga et al., 2019). Attractive packages create an impact on brain regions, namely the occipital lobe and precuneus that process visual stimuli and attention (Cîrneci et al., 2014). Aesthetic packaging can augment the emotions when the consumer is using the product; similarly, inappropriate packaging of a product may reduce its overall appeal to the consumer (Cîrneci et al., 2014; Couson & Vayssettes, 2013). Studies reveal that aesthetic packages considerably increase consumers' reaction time for choice responses; aesthetic packages result in increased stimulation in the ventromedial prefrontal cortex and nucleus accumbens; a customer is likely to choose a more expensive less-known product over a well-known brand with standard packaging (Reimann et al., 2012 cited in Cîrneci et al., 2014). As part of understanding consumers' packaging preferences, packaging designers commonly use eye-tracking technologies to examine consumers' reactions to the presence of images, text or brand elements on packages (García-Madariaga et al., 2019).

To sum up, neuroimaging techniques including the electroencephalography (EEG), functional magnetic resonance imaging (fMRI) and a range of other neuromarketing methods can go deeper into the brain and capture the hidden information regarding our true preferences, thus enabling marketers to understand the mystery of their decision-making process. Neuromarketing can offer cost-effective market research methods (Alsharif et al., 2020; Chatterjee, 2015; Couson & Vayssettes, 2013).

Legal and Ethical Aspects of Neuromarketing

Neuromarketing entices ethical concerns. For further insight, we evaluate a simple definition of neuromarketing. Lee, Broderick and Chamberlain (2007, p. 200) have defined neuromarketing as 'the application of neuroscientific methods to analyse and understand human behaviour in relation to markets and marketing exchanges.' The definition posits the aims of the neuromarketing process as logical and sound. However, it is the application of neuroscientific methods that evokes ethical apprehensions. The concern is that the methods applied in the process interfere with the free will and well-being of the subjects and consumers involved.

In one of the earlier works in marketing ethics, Bartels (1967, p. 21) has indicated that ethics are 'a standard by which business action may be judged "right" or "wrong."' Marketing ethics is obviously about doing the right things in the pursuit of marketing activities. In many instances, the terms right and wrong are hard to define and yield to diverse interpretations looking from lenses of different ethical theories and contexts (Donaldson & Dunfee, 1994). However, in a broader sense, neuromarketing should protect the rights and interests of the subjects and consumers involved in the process (Murphy et al., 2008).

As mentioned above, neuromarketing at the onset does not pose an ethical concern as it uses technology for research and commercial purposes (Eaton & Illes, 2007). The ethical concerns in neuromarketing (in other words, neuroethics) stem from two issues, according to Murphy, Ille and Reiner (2008, p. 293), '(1) protection of various parties who may be harmed or exploited by neuromarketing and (2) protection of consumer autonomy.' These two issues warrant further investigation to establish the ethical premises of neuromarketing.

The first issue is concerned with harming or exploiting the parties involved in the neuromarketing exercise, who are the subjects participated in the research and the end customers. As the case of harm or hurt, most of the neuromarketing methods are non-invasive as indicated in the previous section and, therefore, do not lead to physical damage. However, it could produce inevitable, though little, mental stress as it involves sophisticated machines, in the cases of EEG, PET and fMRI, to name a few. To this end, in all the studies, participants' consent is obtained before the start of the process. And the consent allows the participant to willingly leave at any stage of the research if feeling uncomfortable. Therefore, the harm and exploitation of the participant subject should not be a valid concern. In this connection, Murphy et al. (2008) suggest all neuromarketing studies should disclose all the goals, risks and benefits involved to all the participants. Complete disclosure of risks, if at all, would help the participants to provide informed consent and avoid discomfort.

Protection of consumer autonomy is more of a complex and less understood ethical issue related to neuromarketing. Many fear that neuromarketing experiments make consumer choices predictable (Stanton et al., 2017; Wilson et al., 2008) and, therefore, can be influenced (Stanton et al., 2017). Both the views are farfetched and without valid support. In reality, consumer choices are mostly autonomous, influenced by many internal and external factors (Wertenbroch et al., 2020). If consumer autonomy means no external influences on choices, then no consumer choice would be fully autonomous (Wertenbroch et al., 2020). However, if the external influences are manipulative, then it is both an ethical and legal problem (Sunstein, 2016). The neuromarketing research is not manipulative; it is trying to understand specific consumer choices under certain circumstances and influences in experiments using a small sample of consumers. The cognitive and affective functions of the brain could provide only some hinds of thought process when exposed to certain stimuli, and that cannot be an accurate prediction of future behaviour. Therefore, the argument that neuromarketing muddles with customer autonomy or free will is a misnomer.

Despite all the arguments for the neuromarketing's ethical orientation, this research approach should adhere to all acceptable good research practices, such as methodological rigour, transparency, privacy, validity, reliability and the like. Additionally, as Ulman, Cakar and Yildiz (2015, p. 1275) put it 'the concept of human dignity should be the ground for ethical principles such as autonomy, self-determination, privacy, confidentiality, protection of vulnerable groups, reliability and honest interpretation of research findings in line with the risk of manipulation by commercial actors.' An ethical approach in neuromarketing, like in any other human and social research, should be firmly rooted in respecting human dignity.

Suggestions for Future Research

As mentioned by Ulman et al. (2015), many developed countries are yet to get an appropriate legal framework to deal with the research and applications related to neuromarketing. To prevent any potential misuse of neuroimaging technology, the government in France has banned its commercial use except for human health and welfare. This study has largely explored the potential for neuromarketing tools and techniques to support fashion marketing in Southeast Asia where most countries lack adequate guidelines for ethical and responsible conduct of research involving human participants (Laothavorn et al., 2019). Therefore, we believe that more dedicated studies are required to understand the ethical and legal requirements and responsibilities relating to the use of such technologies in various countries of this region. Insensitive use of neuromarketing has the potential to endanger consumer rights, privacy and well-being. Future studies should explore the aspects of consumer rights, privacy and well-being associated with the use of neuromarketing as often it is argued that commercial research on emerging knowledge areas often compromises with ethical standards while dealing with human subjects, especially in the absence of well-defined regulations to govern such research. Additionally, future research should explore the implications of COVID for neuromarketing in SE Asian luxury fashion marketing environment, especially in the context of disrupted brick-and-mortar stores, cancelled or virtual-only fashion shows, and the global growth of luxury fashion e-commerce.

Conclusion and Implications

The chapter has explored neuromarketing as a modern and innovative field which has important potential for application in the luxury fashion marketing in Southeast Asia region. As discussed in the preceding sections, the application of brain science in marketing may provide a more efficient balance between costs and benefits to existing firms as well as the new entrants as marketers can avail hidden information regarding consumers' actual brand preferences. Arguably, traditional market research tools often rely on what consumers talk about—their needs and choices—it is difficult to ascertain if the response is genuine. Academic researchers and marketing practitioners claim that most of our thinking and emotions take place outside our level of awareness and that our purchase decisions are made in our subconscious minds. Neuromarketing techniques including the electroencephalography (EEG), Functional Magnetic Resonance Imaging (FMRI) and eye tracking can be used to go deeper into the brain and explore the hidden information relating to true consumer preferences, especially in the context of Southeast Asia, a region with varied ethnicities, religions, cultures, traditions, lifestyles and consumption habits. Scholars suggest that neuroscience can equally be used to understand the mystery of the decision-making process of online consumers (Brooksworth et al., 2022a, 2022b). However, the use of neuromarketing should be informed by ethical principles and considerations to ensure the protection of dignity, privacy, confidentiality and self-determination of each and every participant. Finally, given the ongoing disruption faced by physical stores and the unprecedented global growth of luxury fashion e-commerce, the implications of COVID-19 for neuromarketing in SE Asian luxury fashion marketing is worth examining.

References

Adhikari, H. (2016). *Limerence and neuro-marketing. Handbook of research on promotional strategies and consumer influence in the service sector*. IGI Global.

Agarwal, S., & Dutta, T. (2015). Neuromarketing and consumer neuroscience: Current understanding and the way forward. *Decision, 42*(4), 457–462.

Alsharif, A. H., Salleh, N. Z. M., Baharun, R. B. I. N., & Safaei, M. (2020). Neuromarketing approach: An overview and future research directions. *Journal of Theoretical and Applied Information Technology, 98*(7), 991–1001.

Anandan, R., Sipahimalani, R., Saini, S., Aryasomayajula, S., & Smittinet, W. (2018). e- Conomy SEA 2018 Southeast Asia's internet economy hits an inflection point. Diambil dari Think with Google APAC website: https://www.thinkwithgoogle.com/intl/en-apac/tools-resources/research-studies/e-conomy-sea-2018-southeast-asias-internet-economy-hits-inflection-point.

Andrews, R. L., & Currim, I. S. (2004). Behavioural differences between consumers attracted to shopping online versus traditional supermarkets: Implications for enterprise design and marketing strategy. *International Journal of Internet Marketing and Advertising, 1*(1), 38–61.

Baldo, D., Parikh, H., Piu, Y., & Müller, K. M. (2015). Brain waves predict success of new fashion products: A practical application for the footwear retailing industry. *Journal of Creating Value, 1*(1), 61–71.

Bartels, R. (1967). A model for ethics in marketing. *Journal of Marketing, 31*(1), 20–26.

Bercea, M. D. (2012, August). Anatomy of methodologies for measuring consumer behavior in neuromarketing research. In Proceedings of the LCBR European Marketing Conference, pp. 1–14.

Brooksworth, F., Mogaji, E., & Bosah, G. (2022a). Fashion Marketing in Emerging Economies: An introduction. In F. Brooksworth, E. Mogaji, & G. Bosah (Eds.), *Fashion Marketing in Emerging Economies (volume 1) – Brand, consumer and sustainability perspectives*. Springer.

Brooksworth, F., Mogaji, E., & Bosah, G. (2022b). Fashion Marketing in Emerging Economies: Conclusion and research agenda. In F. Brooksworth, E. Mogaji, & G. Bosah (Eds.), *Fashion Marketing in Emerging Economies (volume 1) – Brand, consumer and sustainability perspectives*. Springer.

Chatterjee, S. (2015). Neuromarketing-a path breaking approach to understanding consumer behaviour. *Journal of Management & Research, 9*(4/4), 2–10.

Cherubino, P., Martinez-Levy, A. C., Caratu, M., Cartocci, G., Di Flumeri, G., Modica, E., Rossi, D., Mancini, M., & Trettel, A. (2019). Consumer behaviour through the eyes of neurophysiological measures: State-of-the-art and future trends. *Computational Intelligence and Neuroscience, 2019*, 1–47.

Cîrneci, D., Angheluţă, A. V., & Gheorghe, D. (2014). The use of Neuromarketing in the study of brand related mental processes. Case study–Romanian food brands. *International Journal of Economic Practices and Theories, 4*(2), 331–342.

Couson, C., & Vayssettes, E. (2013). *How Neuromarketing has changed marketing?, dissertation in marketing*. Halmstad University School of Business and Engineering.

Cuesta, U., Niño, J. I., & Martínez-Martínez, L. (2018). Neuromarketing: Analysis of Packaging Using Gsr, Eye-Tracking and Facial Expression. In Paper presented at The European Conference on Media, Communication & Film.

Cvijikj, I. P., & Michahelles, F. (2013). Online engagement factors on Facebook brand pages. *Social Network Analysis and Mining, 3*(4), 843–861.

Donaldson, T., & Dunfee, T. W. (1994). Toward a unified conception of business ethics: Integrative social contracts theory. *Academy of Management Review, 19*(2), 252–284.

dos Santos, R. D. O. J., de Oliveira, J. H. C., Rocha, J. B., & Giraldi, J. D. M. E. (2015). Eye tracking in neuromarketing: A research agenda for marketing studies. *International Journal of Psychological Studies, 7*(1), 32–42.

Eaton, M. L., & Illes, J. (2007). Commercializing cognitive neurotechnology—The ethical terrain. *Nature Biotechnology, 25*(4), 393–397.

Fan, R., Xu, K., & Zhao, J. (2018). An agent-based model for emotion contagion and competition in online social media. *Physica A: Statistical Mechanics and its Applications, 495*, 245–259.

Flavián, C., Gurrea, R., & Orús, C. (2016). Choice confidence in the webrooming purchase process: The impact of online positive reviews and the motivation to touch: Choice confidence in the webrooming process. *Journal of Consumer Behaviour, 15*(5), 459–476.

Fugate, D. L. (2007). Neuromarketing: A layman's look at neuroscience and its potential application to marketing practice. *Journal of Consumer Marketing, 24*(7), 385–394.

García-Madariaga, J., López, M. F. B., Burgos, I. M., & Virto, N. R. (2019). Do isolated packaging variables influence consumers' attention and preferences? *Physiology & Behavior, 200*, 96–103.

Goh, K.-Y., Heng, C.-S., & Lin, Z. (2013). Social media brand community and consumer behavior: Quantifying the relative impact of user- and marketer-generated content. *Information Systems Research, 24*(1), 88–107.

Hafez, M. (2019). Neuromarketing: A new avatar in branding and advertisement. *Pacific Business Review International, 12*(4), 58–64.

Hamilton, N. (2020). Implications of Neuromarketing research in designing the marketing strategies. *International Journal, 8*(1), 1–8.

Harris, J., Ciorciari, J., & Gountas, J. (2019). Consumer neuroscience and digital/social media health/social cause advertisement effectiveness. *Behavioral Sciences, 9*(42), 1–25.

Huettel, S. A., Song, A. W., & McCarthy, G. (2009). Functional Magnetic Resonance Imaging, Sunderland, MA: Sinaur Associates. *Inc., January 16.*

Jelić, N. (2014). Behavioural economy, neuroeconomy, neuromarketing. In Croatian. *JAHR – European Journal of Bioethics, 5*(9), 193–208.

Jordao, I. L. D. S., Souza, M. T. D., Oliveira, J. H. C. D., & Giraldi, J. D. M. E. (2017). Neuromarketing applied to consumer behaviour: An integrative literature review between 2010 and 2015. *International Journal of Business Forecasting and Marketing Intelligence, 3*(3), 270–288.

Khan, I., Dongping, H., & Wahab, A. (2016). Does culture matter in effectiveness of social media marketing strategy? An investigation of brand fan pages. *Aslib Journal of Information Management, 68*(6), 694–715.

Kottier, W. G. (2014). The added value of neuromarketing tools in the area of marketing research (Bachelor's thesis, University of Twente).

Kumar, H., & Singh, P. (2015). Neuromarketing: An emerging tool of market research. *International Journal of Engineering and Management Research (IJEMR), 5*(6), 530–535.

Kumar, H., Mathur, N., & Jauhari, S. (2016). Role of emergengening Neuromarketing techniques in advertising with particular reference to Indian medical tourism industry: A discussion and agenda for future research. *Shodhaytan (AISECT University), 3*(5) http://aujournals.ipublisher.in/I/a/55439

Kurtoglu, A. L., & Ferman, A. M. (2020). An exploratory research among fashion business leaders and neuromarketing company executives on the perception of applied neuromarketing. *Journal of Management Marketing and Logistics, 7*(2), 72–80.

Laothavorn, J., Wongwai, P., Prakash Dumre, S., Kongjam, P., Na-Bangchang, K., & Karbwang, J. (2019). Ethical approval and informed consent reporting in ASEAN journals: A systematic review. *Current Medical Research and Opinion, 35*(12), 2179–2186.

Lee, N., Brandes, L., Chamberlain, L., & Senior, C. (2017). This is your brain on neuromarketing: Reflections on a decade of research. *Journal of Marketing Management, 33*(11–12), 878–892.

Lee, N., Broderick, A. J., & Chamberlain, L. (2007). What is 'neuromarketing'? A discussion and agenda for future research. *International Journal of Psychophysiology, 63*(2), 199–204.

Lim, W. M. (2018). Demystifying neuromarketing. *Journal of Business Research, 91*, 205–220.

Madan, C. R. (2010). Neuromarketing: The next step in market research? *Eureka, 1*(1), 34–42.

Marbach, J., Lages, C. R., & Nunan, D. (2016). Who are you and what do you value? Investigating the role of personality traits and customer-perceived value in online customer engagement. *Journal of Marketing Management, 32*(5–6), 502–525.

Meshi, D., Tamir, D. I., & Heekeren, H. R. (2015). The emerging neuroscience of social media. *Trends in Cognitive Sciences, 19*(12), 771–782.

Meyerding, S. G., & Mehlhose, C. M. (2018). Can neuromarketing add value to the traditional marketing research? An exemplary experiment with functional near-infrared spectroscopy (fNIRS). *Journal of Business Research, 107*, 172–185.

Mileti, A., Guido, G., & Prete, M. I. (2016). Nanomarketing: A new frontier for neuromarketing. *Psychology & Marketing, 33*(8), 664–674.

Mogaji, E. (2021). *Introduction to advertising: Understanding and managing the advertising process*. Routledge.

Mukonza, C., Hinson, R. E., Adeola, O., Adisa, I., Mogaji, E., & Kirgiz, A. C. (2021). Green marketing: An introduction. In C. Mukonza, R. E. Hinson, O. Adeola, I. Adisa, E. Mogaji, & A. C. Kirgiz (Eds.), *Green Marketing in Emerging Markets. Palgrave studies of Marketing in Emerging*

Economies (pp. 3–14). Palgrave Macmillan. https://doi.org/10.1007/978-3-030-74065-8_1
Mull, I., & Lee, S. E. (2014, January). Neuromarketing: A New Approach for Fashion Marketing?. In *International Textile and Apparel Association Annual Conference Proceedings* (Vol. 71, No. 1). Iowa State University Digital Press.
Murphy, E. R., Illes, J., & Reiner, P. B. (2008). Neuroethics of neuromarketing. *Journal of Consumer Behaviour: An International Research Review, 7*(4–5), 293–302.
Nourbakhsh, N., Wang, Y., Chen, F., & Calvo, R. A. (2012). Using galvanic skin response for cognitive load measurement in arithmetic and reading tasks. In Proceedings of the 24th Australian Computer-Human Interaction Conference, pp. 420–423.
Ohme, R., Reykowska, D., Wiener, D., & Choromanska, A. (2009). Analysis of neurophysiological reactions to advertising stimuli by means of EEG and galvanic skin response measures. *Journal of Neuroscience, Psychology, and Economics, 2*(1), 21–31.
Okonkwo, U. (2016). *Luxury fashion branding: Trends, tactics, techniques*. Springer.
Otmazgin, N., & Ben-Ari, E. (Eds.). (2013). *Popular culture and the state in east and Southeast Asia* (Vol. 35). Routledge.
Pine, J. B., & Gilmore, J. H. (1998). Welcome to the experience economy. *Harvard Business Review, 76*, 97–105.
Plassmann, H., O'Doherty, J., Shiv, B., & Rangel, A. (2008). Marketing actions can modulate neural representations of experienced pleasantness. *Proceedings of the National Academy of Sciences, 105*(3), 1050–1054.
Plassmann, H., Ramsøy, T. Z., & Milosavljevic, M. (2011). Faculty and Research Working Paper: Branding the Brain - A Critical Review. INSEAD The Business School of the World 2011/15/MKT.
Populin, A. (2018). *Sustainable fashion and its possible developments in the Japanese fashion industry, dissertation*. Università Ca'Foscari Venezia.
Reimann, M., Castaño, R., Zaichkowsky, J., & Bechara, A. (2012). How we relate to brands: Psychological and neurophysiological insights into consumer–brand relationships. *Journal of Consumer Psychology, 22*(1), 128–142.
Renvoisé, P., & Morin, C. (2007). *Neuromarketing: Understanding the buy buttons in your customer's brain*. HarperCollins Leadership.
Roth, V. A. (2014). The potential of neuromarketing as a marketing tool (Bachelor's thesis, University of Twente).

Schultz, C. D. (2017). Proposing to your fans: Which brand post characteristics drive consumer engagement activities on social media brand pages? *Electronic Commerce Research and Applications, 26*, 23–34.

Sebastian, V. (2014). Neuromarketing and evaluation of cognitive and emotional responses of consumers to marketing stimuli. *Procedia-Social and Behavioral Sciences, 127*, 753–757.

Sharma, J. K., Singh, D., Deepak, K. K., & Agarwal, J. P. (2010). *Neuromarketing: A peep into customer S minds*. PHI Learning Pvt. Ltd.

Shaw, S. D., & Bagozzi, R. P. (2018). The neuropsychology of consumer behavior and marketing. *Consumer Psychology Review, 1*(1), 22–40.

Singh, S. (2020). Impact of neuromarketing applications on consumers. *Journal of Business and Management, 26*(2), 33–52.

So, T. J., Parsons, G. A., & Yap, S. F. (2013). Corporate branding, emotional attachment, and brand loyalty: The case of luxury fashion branding. *Journal of Fashion Marketing and Management: An International Journal, 17*(4), 403–423.

Solnais, C., Andreu-Perez, J., Sánchez-Fernández, J., & Andréu-Abela, J. (2013). The contribution of neuroscience to consumer research: A conceptual framework and empirical review. *Journal of Economic Psychology, 36*, 68–81.

Stanton, S. J., Sinnott-Armstrong, W., & Huettel, S. A. (2017). Neuromarketing: Ethical implications of its use and potential misuse. *Journal of Business Ethics, 144*(4), 799–811.

Sunstein, C. R. (2016). Manipulation, welfare, and dignity: A reply. *Journal of Marketing Behavior, 1*(3–4), 351–361.

Ting, M. S., Goh, Y. N., & Isa, S. M. (2018). Inconspicuous consumption of luxury fashion goods among Malaysian adults: An investigation. *Global Business & Management Research, 10*(1), 313–330.

Turel, O., He, Q., Brevers, D., & Bechara, A. (2018). Delay discounting mediates the association between posterior insular cortex volume and social media addiction symptoms. *Cognitive, Affective, & Behavioral Neuroscience, 18*(4), 694–704.

Ulman, Y. I., Cakar, T., & Yildiz, G. (2015). Ethical issues in neuromarketing:"I consume, therefore I am!". *Science and Engineering Ethics, 21*(5), 1271–1284.

Uzbay, T. (2020). Importance of brain reward system in Neuromarketing. In D. Atli (Ed.), *Analyzing the strategic role of Neuromarketing and consumer neuroscience*. IGI Global.

Valaei, N., & Nikhashemi, S. R. (2017). Generation Y consumers' buying behaviour in fashion apparel industry: A moderation analysis. *Journal of Fashion Marketing and Management: An International Journal, 21*(4), 523–543.

Vences, N. A., Díaz-Campo, J., & Rosales, D. F. G. (2020). Neuromarketing as an emotional connection tool between organizations and audiences in social networks. A theoretical review. *Frontiers in Psychology, 11*, 1787–1798.

Vialatte, F., Maurice, M., Dauwels, J., & Cichocki, A. (2010). Steady-state visually evoked potentials: Focus on essential paradigms and future perspectives. *Progress in Neurobiology, 90*, 418–438.

Wertenbroch, K., Schrift, R. Y., Alba, J. W., Barasch, A., Bhattacharjee, A., Giesler, M., et al. (2020). Autonomy in consumer choice. *Marketing Letters, 1*, 1–11.

Wilson, R. M., Gaines, J., & Hill, R. P. (2008). Neuromarketing and consumer free will. *The Journal of Consumer Affairs, 42*, 389–410.

Zaltman, G. (2003). *How consumers think*. Harvard Business School Press.

Zamani, H., Abas, A., & Amin, M. K. M. (2016). Eye tracking application on emotion analysis for marketing strategy. *Journal of Telecommunication, Electronic and Computer Engineering (JTEC), 8*(11), 87–91.

Zhang, X., Huettel, S. A., O'Dhaniel, A., Guo, H., & Wang, L. (2019). Exploring common changes after acute mental stress and acute tryptophan depletion: Resting-state fMRI studies. *Journal of Psychiatric Research, 113*, 172–180.

Zurawicki, L. (2010). *Neuromarketing: Exploring the brain of the consumer*. Springer Science & Business Media.

5

Afloat in a Changing COVID-19 World: The Rise of Artisanal Fashion in India for Brand Story Relevance in Challenging Times

Pandora Kay and Caroline Young

Introduction

COVID-19 presented many challenges to the fashion industry worldwide in 2020/2021 (The Business of Fashion and McKinsey & Company, 2020b) and will not be over until a widely available vaccine is discovered (Mladenović et al., 2021). Face masks emerged as one unlikely fashion hero in 2020 as the COVID-19 pandemic developed (Edwards, 2020). Lebanese fashion designer Eric Ritter was one of the first designing artisanal masks and writing about them on Instagram in January before the virus spread (Ritter, 2020). Eleven months later, a Google search of 'face masks' produces more than 1 billion results. For some fashion brands, face masks became a fashion accessory that also served as a marketing tool which will be explored in this chapter.

P. Kay (✉)
Freelance Consultant, Melbourne, VIC, Australia

C. Young
Freelance Creative Director, Delhi, India

F. Brooksworth et al. (eds.), *Fashion Marketing in Emerging Economies Volume II*, Palgrave Studies of Marketing in Emerging Economies,
https://doi.org/10.1007/978-3-031-07078-5_5

Most other brand-related activities undertaken by fashion brands as the pandemic developed were in many instances, already under consideration or development in the years prior to the pandemic, but were accelerated either during, by or in response to the rapid global changes associated with pandemic and varied regional and country responses.

This chapter traces the story of fashion-related initiatives by entities such as fashion designers and other fashion-related philanthropic charities, foundations and social enterprises, for 20 artisanal fashion brand cases from India. As will be seen in the following discussion, India is an emerging market of significance for multiple reasons that will be firstly considered as well as India as a fashion market of significance, yet only a few published research exceptions exist (e.g., Gupta et al., 2017; Khaire, 2011; Khan & Khan, 2017). Some of these artisanal fashion cases have been the focus of theses (e.g., Goldsmith, 2018; Varma, 2015). Mostly, these artisanal fashion cases are well documented on their own Internet sites and other online sources with such secondary sources used as the primary data source in this chapter.

In all instances, the 20 focal cases collaborate with artisans of traditional Indian handcrafts (e.g., handloom weaving; block-printing; embroidery; natural dyes, leatherwork and metalwork are just a few examples) and as such are considered to be part of artisanal fashion which will then be defined from an overview of the literature. Most of the brand cases have manufacturing operations which have been a limited area of study within the literature (Guercini & Runfola, 2019). Some also have their own retail outlets domestically and internationally. These brand cases range in size from major corporations with multiple brands to smaller-scale single brand labels described elsewhere as small-scale artisanal fashion design entrepreneurs who are of growing importance, but for which there is very little research to date (Ott & Cukier, 2013). Foundation spans a 40-year period from the early 1980s for the brand Lecoanet Hemant (founded in Paris 1981, but now in Delhi since 2000), to the early 1990s (House of Anita Dongre; James Ferreira) through to the younger brands founded 2015 (PELLA; Kaleekal) and the youngest in 2017 (Akihi; Buna). Not-for-Profit social enterprise fashion brands are also included (i.e., Nila House founded 2016 in Delhi and its artisan support projects in Rajasthan, Northern India through the Lady Bamford Charitable Trust (2001) and Foundation (2013); the Rehwa Society founded 1979 and WomenWeave since 2002 both in Indore, Central India, with their first artisan weaving and spinning support projects in the ancient temple village of Maheshwar; and the IOU Project in 2009/2010 collaborating with artisans of the classic Madras check fabric in Chennai/Madras, Southern India).

Branding is the dominant logic of the marketing lens (Mogaji, 2021) to be applied in the analysis of these artisanal fashion cases in India, particularly the brand story for understanding fashion production and marketing initiatives within the specific fashion context of artisanal fashion in India during the challenging times of the humanitarian, health and economic crises associated with the COVID-19 pandemic. This brand story is underpinned partly by other branding elements and decisions, namely, brand architecture and portfolio for the brand, and partly by collaborations between the brand and other brands that often result in co-branding.

A primary research question explored in this chapter will be: What is artisanal fashion, and for those within artisanal fashion production and marketing in the COVID-19 crisis for contemporary Indian fashion as an emerging market, what are the branding implications?

This chapter makes several contributions to an understanding of Indian contemporary fashion and its relationship with artisanal fashion principles at a time defined universally as a global crisis due to COVID-19. Firstly, the consumer market in India as an emerging market for contemporary fashion is considered. The second contribution considers the current production system perspective and its long heritage of artisan textiles and hand embellishments with a focal interest in the branding perspective implications. Thirdly, a new contribution to contemporary artisanal fashion considers its associations with a range of richly diverse associated fields including art, craft, architecture, Eastern spiritual philosophies and meditation, and a final contribution concludes with a framework for analysing artisanal fashion in India that could be of relevance to artisanal fashion elsewhere in other developing and emerging markets as well as high income, industrialised countries.

India as an Emerging Market for Contemporary Fashion

The ascent of India as a focal point in the fashion industry has been widely highlighted both for its rapidly growing middle class and for increasingly powerful manufacturing sector (e.g., Guercini & Runfola, 2019; The Business of Fashion and McKinsey & Company, 2019). They forecast that this should see India by 2022 move from being an increasingly important sourcing hub to being an attractive consumer market with more than 900 million Indian consumers online by 2021.

India's middle class is growing fast and probably moved to third spot globally overtaking Japan in 2016 (Kharas, 2017). By 2022, it could become the second-largest middle-class market in the world overtaking the United States and second to China (Kharas, 2017). Developments in two of the largest economies of the world—India and China—will contribute to their middle-class expansion. However, there are structural challenges in the Indian fashion market and consumption differences in the middle-class market that make India a "whole different ball game" to China (Darshan Mehta cited in The Business of Fashion and McKinsey & Company, 2019). One significant difference is that the emerging middle-class Indian market is largely first-generation wealth with different luxury consumption habits that present opportunities as well as challenges as observed by fashion industry leaders such as Darshan Mehta, CEO of the fashion division, Reliance Industries, but this topic has been seldom covered in academic research. One exception is research of India's luxury market that identifies five key customer types including the New Money Consumer and the globe-trotting Non-Resident Indians (NRIs) who are an important market abroad, but also domestically when they make their way back to resettle in India (Gupta et al., 2017). When buying luxury apparel, two hot product categories in India today are bridalwear and the festive category (Kamath, 2021), sometimes described as occasion wear. Another difference is that traditional clothing is still the choice of Indian women and is expected to account for more than half of the market share by 2023 (The Business of Fashion and McKinsey & Company, 2019). These consumption characteristics represent huge markets whereby India becomes a frontier where consumers in tier-two cities like Indore and Aurangabad have deep pockets, even though buying luxury items is often a once-in-a-lifetime purchase (Kamath, 2021).

The supply side is also deemed robust with India's average labour cost significantly lower than China's and comparable with Vietnam's combined with high availability of raw materials (such as cotton, silk and jute) which bodes well for the entire fashion value chain (The Business of Fashion and McKinsey & Company, 2019). There are, however, structural challenges in the Indian fashion industry that could offset these opportunities. The Indian apparel business is considered largely "unorganised" with formal retail a relatively low proportion of sales, despite new retail ecosystems with large-scale luxury malls in Delhi, Mumbai, Kolkata and Chennai (The Business of Fashion and McKinsey & Company, 2019). Some 60 million people depend on the fashion industry for their livelihood in India, some of whom have been left without livelihood following the cancellation of orders with Indian suppliers during India's lockdown due to COVID-19 starting 23 March 2020 (Jay, 2020a). Furthermore, women are the most vulnerable segment in supply chains as those often employed as informal, short-term or piece-rate workers (Mark Anner cited in Jay, 2020a). The plight of vulnerable workers and procurement partners in fashion value chains is acknowledged in the State of Fashion Report 2021, as a theme that started in 2020 and is expected to continue in 2021 and beyond (The Business of Fashion and McKinsey & Company, 2020c).

In 2019, India experienced the strongest absolute growth globally in the number of Internet users and saw social media use expanding at around 25 per cent annually, with nearly 70 per cent of users active on Instagram (The Business of Fashion and McKinsey & Company, 2020a). These platforms are becoming the dominant way for consumers to be introduced to fashion brands and make online purchases, especially during COVID-19 when foot traffic in stores has fallen dramatically. As tech giants develop new social media platforms and functions, CEO of the new Indian messenger app Hike, Kavin Bharti Mittal expects "the rise of social niches" as the future of social media (cited in The Business of Fashion and McKinsey & Company, 2020a, p. 38).

The focus of this fashion research is the emerging market of India for local fashion brands from a branding and production perspective that occupy a market associated with a variety of terms including artisanal fashion, slow fashion or sustainable fashion to name a few, as will be discussed in the next section. Many of these are considered by some as niche markets or niche fields and communities of practice, which often intersect with luxury apparel which is sometimes also categorised as a niche market (e.g., Beard, 2008; Mukendi et al., 2020). From a branding perspective, these are dynamic categories with some of the case study brands launching sub-brands they describe as "affordable luxury". For example, Anita Dongre's fashion house taps both bridal and affordable fashion categories and Urvashi Kaur includes a new line of festive/occasion wear and an affordable diffusion line. At least two of the Indian case brands have received outside investment from India's luxury conglomerates who continue tapping the bridal couture, occasion wear markets (Kamath, 2021). Anita Dongre's fashion house was one of the first back in 2009 from Kishore Biyani's Future Group, and again in 2013, from General Atlantic, while the Sabyasachi brand founded on the enduring appeal of tradition and Indian culture and bridal couture, attracted a 51 per cent stake from Aditya Birla Fashion and Retail Limited (ABRFL) in January 2021. The product portfolio of the Sabyasachi brand positions it as a balanced luxury brand including clothing, jewellery, bags and accessories creating "at times a resonance of brand that is larger than its size and economics" (Kamath, 2021).

Artisanal Fashion Within the Indian Context

This research is concerned primarily with artisanal fashion which is synonymous with artisan fashion and is often viewed in the fashion marketplace as a subset of so-called slow and/or sustainable fashion. It can mean anything from Haute Couture to basement craft (Goldsmith, 2018), and what it means in this study, adopts a definition similar to Goldsmith's whereby it is both the material product(s) and the system(s) that employ artisans to make them (p. 25). It also adopts Aakko's (2016) understanding whereby the bridge between fashion and artisanship integrates "skilful materiality", which signifies qualities of the design and production processes such as skilfulness, craftsmanship quality, aesthetics (artistic quality of design), provenance (with in-house or local or regional provenance preferred), materiality and origin of fabrics often playing a significant role, as well as the role of the artisanal designer themselves. Hence, the discussion of artisanal fashion in this study will include immaterial qualities and values of artisanal work as well as tangible elements. It also includes couture brands where craftsmanship is essentially associated with the creation of "exclusive custom-made garments constructed with the finest artisanal methods from luxurious fabrics" (Aakko, 2016, p. 2), through to small-scale, designer-led fashion brands by micro-organisations where limited finances encourage the use of free social media platforms, such as Twitter and Facebook, to communicate brand messages to a wider audience (Henninger et al., 2017).

Like the movements from which artisanal fashion departs such as slow fashion (Clark, 2008; Fletcher, 2010) and slow design (Beverland, 2011), producers can be considered to have values in common: they often value local resources and distributed economies; transparent production systems; and sustainable and sensorial products that have a longer usable life and are more highly valued than typical "consumables" (adapted from the Slow + Design Manifesto 2006 cited in Clark, 2008). Many are also providing models for more socially aware design (Clark, 2008) or "socially beneficial" fashion (Liya Kebede cited in Goldsmith, 2018).

As a system for production, artisanal fashion can be considered to share some confusion with slow fashion and slow culture. As Fletcher (2010) insightfully argues, slow culture confusion derives from "lock in" to the current fashion model's growth-focus worldview and conception of the way things are done and so becomes a marketing angle or alternative distribution channel in the current model and a tool for material throughput and continual economic growth rather than being allowed to seed a radical new approach (p. 263). Furthermore, fashion supply chains globally can be long and complex "with different risks at different stages" (Peter Keegan cited in Gorman, 2020, n.p.). A recent COVID Fashion Report by Baptist World Aid Australia of 428 brands in Australia, New Zealand and international companies, which looked at six key areas of worker protection throughout the pandemic in conjunction with garment workers' organisations, reported "no company could fully assure that their actions extended to every worker at every tier of the supply chain" (cited in Gorman, 2020, n.p.). In India, protecting the craft ecosystem that Indian fashion is built on is one key learning to come out of the pandemic (Jay, 2020b). Sabyasachi, one of India's most coveted bridal brands and one of the 20 cases in this study, has emphatically commented about this:

> *Money lost over a season or two can always be recovered eventually but it's very important to protect the ecosystem that has made us who we are. Every single employee on the payroll has been looked after in the past few months.* (Sabyasachi Mukherjee cited in Jay, 2020b)

As a material product, the contemporary Indian aesthetics surrounding artisanal fashion in India come into play and range from 'minimalism' to 'royal chic'. Varma's (2015) thesis on contemporary Indian aesthetics by fashion designers sheds light on these two aesthetics, which this current study proposes form opposing endpoints on an artisanal fashion spectrum. Varma further associates the former with "new more prosperous middle-class identity" and the latter with "old pre-liberalization middle class and elite producers". Minimalism fashion design is characterised by "aesthetic acts of toning, paring down and embracing minimalism by showing less 'work' or embroidery" (p. 19). This minimalism aesthetic has been described as "chill but edgy" and an aesthetic "intelligent but reflective position" in post-liberalised India (Varma, 2015, p. 210). In characterising the 'royal chic look', Varma draws on Vuldova's work whereby another contemporary Indian luxury market depends on a "specific kind of 'work' or embroidery that invokes the craft of the Mughal period to gain value" (Varma, 2015, p. 86).

While there are strong links between artisanal fashion design, the slow fashion movement and sustainability, with sustainability identified as one of the biggest challenges and opportunities facing the global fashion industry (The Business of Fashion and McKinsey & Company, 2020a, p. 14), the growing body of literature examining the many related concepts and issues is largely beyond the scope of this study. Rather, sustainability is considered here in this study from a branding perspective, even though, presenting brands as fulfilling an ecological need is still considered controversial as acknowledged by Joy et al. (2012) in their study, but they argue in favour of the leadership potential of luxury brands on issues of sustainability and ethical appeal. For nearly a decade though, many luxury fashion brands already see ecologically sustainable fashion clothing and accessories as part of their brand with examples in Joy et al. (2012) such as Stella McCartney and Vivienne Westwood doing so. The branding concepts that will be applied in this study are outlined next.

The Relevance of Branding Within a Fashion Context in Crisis

This study adopts the relevance of branding as the primary dominant logic that drives many fashion marketing initiatives in an increasingly competitive global marketplace (Kim & Sullivan, 2019). This builds the brand story, for fashion brands globally as well as within the specific fashion context of interest in this study, that is, artisanal fashion in India during the challenging times of the humanitarian, health and economic crises associated with the COVID-19 pandemic (Adeyanju et al., 2022). Storytelling is a powerful marketing strategy that uses narratives to appeal to or inspire consumers (Kaufman, 2003; Silverstein & Fiske, 2003), and through its emotional influence, storytelling creates a holistic brand image (Mossberg, 2008). From the growing body of scholarly literature on sustainable fashion and luxury brand storytelling, at least seven fashion sustainability issues have been identified for understanding innovative behaviour by a growing number of firms in the fashion industry and segments of fashion consumers (Woodside & Fine, 2019). Two issues relate to a scale for measuring sustainable slow fashion developed by Jung and Jin (2014), which appear to overlap with some key characteristics of artisanal fashion, namely social equity issues including working conditions and fair compensation of the apparel producers, and authenticity issues including craftsmanship, traditional techniques and the value of handcrafted clothes relative to mass-produced ones.

Brand story in artisanal fashion as in other industries is also underpinned partly by other branding elements and decisions, namely brand architecture and portfolio for the brand, and partly by collaborations between the brand that can result in co-branding. The brand architecture concept first appeared in the literature in 1987, but has gained considerable attention in the last decades among practitioners, despite only a few academic studies conducted in field (Brandão et al., 2020). In a conceptual article on luxury fashion branding (Keller, 2017), ten defining characteristics of luxury brands are identified and include brand architecture for luxury brands which must be managed very carefully by developing an appropriate brand portfolio and sub-brands. Brand stories are also discussed in terms of brand points of parity and points of difference (Keller et al., 2002).

Brand values and propositions are higher-level concepts that many fashion brands have yet to articulate or formalise which is in contrast to many other major brands and corporations across other industry sectors. Take telecommunication brand Oppo—world-leading smart device manufacturers and innovators—who recently collaborated with one of the 20 fashion brands in this study, PELLA, by featuring her as one of six artists in their 2020 Reno Stories. Their brand vision, mission and values are clearly stated on their website (Oppo, 2020). Of course, one explanation for why some fashion brands do not provide content on their fashion label vision, mission and values may be that many artisanal fashion entrepreneurs or designers see themselves as the founders and leaders of fashion labels, houses, social enterprises or some other entity but not founders of brands. This study explores the concept of branding for artisanal fashion for the first time which is a significant contribution.

Brand value has been recognised as a high-level concept in an evolving brand spectrum that adds value to customers' lifestyles through customer valued relationships at every point of contact and is beyond the brand identity-image nexus and the branding role of minimising customers' perceived risk (De Chernatony, 2009). As an evolving entity, adding value through brands has been seen in the literature as a concept that blends "input" creations by manufacturers with "outputs" that exist in consumers' minds (De Chernatony & Dall'Olmo Riley, 1997). While brand value is ultimately a blended input/output concept, in this study, the brand values are only considered from the brand creators' perspective using existing secondary brand communication data sources from which the brand values will be deduced.

When considering the brand value proposition in artisanal fashion, the central tenant of classical brand management still seems relevant—"as a result of augmenting the core offering with consumer relevant added values consumers will be prepared to pay a price premium" (De Chernatony & Dall'Olmo Riley, 1997, p. 45). In the context of artisanal fashion, this value proposition presents a specific social benefit value of providing artisans with a livelihood which is an important value proposition for many fashion brands involved in artisanal fashion in the Indian context as seen in this study.

Academic studies on the use of branding and marketing in the sustainable luxury fashion sector are also scarce, fragmented and sometimes conflicted. In their synthesis of sustainable luxury and its marketing, Athwal et al. (2019) compare luxury with non-luxury, noting that the former is synonymous with superior quality, uniqueness and going beyond need; it is uncompromisingly extravagant in terms of effort and material and often exhibits craftsmanship and expertise, and it is enduring. Other authors acknowledge the marketing of luxury goods that has become increasingly complex as it needs to convey an image of quality, performance and authenticity, but also attempts to sell an experience by relating it to consumer lifestyle constructs (Atwal & Williams, 2017). The distinguishing characteristics of luxury goods including fashion suggest that marketing within the sector would be different from many other industries, but discriminating differences in approaches between luxury goods marketing from other consumer products is often difficult (Atwal & Williams, 2017). Furthermore, while there is a diversity and complexity of sustainable practices from all manufacturing stages in textile, apparel and fashion (TAF) industry contexts, there is less research in developing country contexts where most TAF production takes place (Islam et al., 2021).

Branding for sustainable fashion is rarely considered with only scarce reference from a social retail marketing perspective (Mukendi et al., 2020), with the authors noting that advice on sustainable fashion branding is, at best, conflicted. Consumer brand schemas are important in influencing how consumers perceive the fit between sustainability and the brand, but consumers may also be more open to sustainable fashion by fast brands than previously conceptualised (Nguyen & Mogaji, 2022a). Another dimension is that consumers do not consider sustainability when shopping for clothing despite the brand stories of impending climate disaster, and ill-treatment of garment workers (Mukonza et al., 2021). While there are various continuums for where a brand is positioned on a variety of dimensions (Pedersen & Andersen, 2015) or a matrix of possible sustainable activities a brand could undertake (Henninger et al., 2016), dedicated sustainable fashion consumers may need more specific marketing claims about the sustainability of the product (Kim et al., 2012) than discussion of donations to a cause (Phau & Ong, 2007). This discussion strongly supports Mukendi et al.'s (2020) summation on branding and sustainable fashion that different segments need to be approached using different marketing methods to speak to heterogeneous consumer needs.

Although scholarly research on how luxury organisations communicate about their sustainability practices is scant and rationale for engaging in particular sustainable practice is often unproven, (Athwal et al., 2019), luxury conglomerates and individual luxury fashion brands document numerous sustainable initiatives in annual Corporate Social Responsibility (CSR) and sustainability reports. For example, there is strong industry evidence from luxury brand *Stella McCartney* that the brand is putting sustainability, vegetarianism and eco-friendly garments at the core of the brand (Athwal et al., 2019) and is a successful sustainable fashion brand (Mukendi et al., 2020). The fashion brand's 2020 Eco Impact Report (Stella McCartney Ltd, 2020) reflects on their sustainability journey since the brand's establishment in 2001 as well as recent updates. They saw 2020 as a monumental year, with a new deal for nature needed and the global pandemic and international human rights movements forcing them to pause and rethink their priorities for the future. With an overarching goal "of bringing a conscience to the fashion industry", they constantly explore innovative ways to become more sustainable, from designing to product manufacturing and retail practices (p. 5) and a key to creating change in complex supply chains is more collaborative initiatives (p. 31). They partner with numerous key sourcing countries of which India provides some raw material extraction and 5 per cent of their Tier 1 and 2 productions (p. 26). Small networks of highly skilled workers making handcrafted products have been studied to ensure these workers felt respect and recognition for their dedication and artistry. Such collaboration involving partnerships with other brands and suppliers to develop tailor-made programmes focused on improving the lives of workers in specific contexts is "the most impactful way to work in supply chains where we have limited influence" (p. 28).

Method

This study documents recent branding developments for 20 artisanal fashion brands in India. As early exploratory research in this field, a multiple comparative qualitative case study approach (Yin, 1994) was used with the data for each case drawn from existing secondary sources. The multiple case study approach allows a contemporary phenomenon to be examined in its real-life context (Mogaji et al., 2021; Yin, 1981). It also enables isolated factors within particular case studies to receive substantive attention, and the number of cases was deemed large enough to warrant cross-case comparisons (Yin, 1981). Brands were firstly selected intentionally by one of the authors who is a Creative Director based in Delhi and has collaborated with the Indian fashion industry for the past 15 years. Other cases were included in the data set using a triangulation approach whereby leads emerged from cross references to them in the other relevant secondary sources that were used. Case selection criteria were based on key characteristics of artisanal fashion as identified in the literature of relevance to artisanal fashion in a luxury brand context as discussed earlier in the chapter. All cases collaborate with artisans using contemporised traditional techniques to produce premium quality products at the high-end of their product category.

Data collection for all cases, initially started with collecting content from the brand's websites, and for many their social media sites on Facebook and Instagram. Fashion magazine articles on each brand were an important secondary source some of which were sourced from the brand's websites, others by results from online searches via Google search engine. Other important secondary sources were fashion industry trade reports and relevant academic journal articles and theses, which were identified through Google Scholar searches of key terms. Other online sources such as videos and blogs were also used to build the data set in a couple of cases. Globally, the role of technology in fashion marketing has been expanding at a rapid rate for consumers as well as suppliers, which has only increased during COVID-19. This was further justification that any research on fashion marketing and branding would need to start with data from these sources as the first stage in the research process.

This study focuses on the narrative branding story that can be gleaned from the content available on these existing secondary sources. Data analysis used a content analysis approach to explore the data, and code it into domains developed from the fashion branding and marketing literature with regard to our dominant branding logic. Our approach was based on identifying "discrete passages of text … that … exemplify the same theoretical or descriptive data" (Gibbs, 2002) in order to illustrate relationships and patterns in the data (Bazeley, 2009). The data was then analysed using an analytical framework for fashion creation and production adapted from Payne (2014) with details outlined in the next section. Analysis of the actual websites and other social media as used by the 20 fashion brands for marketing and e-commerce purposes is beyond the scope of this chapter, but would be another fruitful topic for future research.

Findings and Discussion

The narrative brand story for each artisanal fashion case was analysed by several branding characteristics and dimensions. Firstly, brand-related company characteristics in three specific branding areas were identified: (1) the brand portfolio as seen by the range of apparel and other product categories in which the case was involved, (2) the brand architecture adopted by each case (i.e., number of brands and sub-brands) and (3) artisanal collaborations in recent years and associated co-branding. Secondly, the brand messages, narratives and stories were grouped into three types of activity of relevance to artisanal fashion creation and production (adapted from Payne, 2014): (1) product related which included tangible brand associations (e.g., aesthetic style of the apparel) as well as more intangible abstract brand qualities (e.g., vision, philosophy), (2) systems related (e.g., design processes, production techniques and role of the designer), and (3) wider community related which for all cases included working with artisans. Table 5.1 (in the appendix) presents the analysis of the brand story data for each artisanal fashion case, and Table 5.2 presents a summary for some of these brand dimensions. Key findings will be discussed under each of these branding dimensions.

Brand Portfolio and Brand Architecture for Artisanal Fashion in India

In terms of brand portfolio and the product range covered by each of the cases (see Appendix Table 5.1, Column 5; Table 5.2 Columns 2–6) during 2020, all cases continued their well-established signature artisanal apparel and/or accessories which involve varying levels of handcrafted embellishments and details. Many of the cases, however, expanded into new product lines or categories either in response to new demand associated with COVID or because COVID provided an opportunity for increased demand for product categories that were new to the case organisation but had been planning and so existing plans were accelerated. Six cases added face masks to their brand (Cases 2, 9, 12, 15, 18 and 20). All of these face masks were inspired by traditional Indian handcrafts and designs, and some were part of a collaborative project that directed profits to vulnerable groups (Cases 2 and 15). A further case created an apron series that was commissioned in response to demand because of increased home cooking during COVID (Case 19). Other cases had been planning new product categories that were accelerated during COVID such as demand for homeware and décor (Case 10). Sometimes though, the extension of product category marked a significant milestone anniversary of their label which resulted in one case (Case 16) adding handcrafted artisanal objects.

Analysis of the brand architecture and the structure and hierarchy of brands for each of these cases shows that half are single brand name labels, but the others have multiple brands (see Appendix Table 5.1, Column 5 and Table 5.2 Columns 5, 7 and 8). Two cases have five brands (Cases 2 and 17), four have three brands (Cases 9, 12, 15 and 20) and three have two brands (Cases 10, 16 and 19). This highlights a variety in brand architecture by artisanal brands. While the cases with more brands in the hierarchy tend to reflect larger, longer-established cases, two of these cases have a brand distinctly positioned as a sustainable or organic brand (Cases 2 and 9). One case includes Haute Couture (Case 9), but most other cases, both single brand name and multiple brands, would offer bespoke one-off fashion for special occasion wear which includes Diwali and wedding bridal parties, all of which have been severely curtailed by lockdowns and other gathering size limitations during COVID. Limitation on large social gatherings during COVID is a global phenomenon with particularly dire consequences for the fashion industry, as noted in the latest State of Fashion 2021 report where planning for a post-COVID world includes:

> *ensuring that they will be able to capitalise on the excitement that is unleashed once the pandemic is over, as consumers return to long-haul destinations and large social gatherings such as weddings, festivals and cultural events.* (The Business of Fashion and McKinsey & Company, 2020c, p. 54)

Some cases attained notoriety from having garments featured in Indian reality TV shows and feature movies (Cases 9 and 17). Featuring bespoke even haute couture in these situations brings high-end artisanal fashion from a more niche market to the attention of a mass audience and further influencer opportunities for reaching new upper middle-class markets. With the garments copied by neighbourhood tailors and sold cheaply to a wider market, this is not a negative, but carefully planned.

> *I told her, let's make something very relatable. So relatable it gets furiously copied. Otherwise, what's the point.* (Sabyasachi Mukherjee cited in Thakur & Ghosh, 2019)

Artisanal Brand Story for Product

Analysis of the artisanal brand story for product in each of the cases (see Appendix Table 5.1, Column 6) reveals many rich themes and influences. All cases elaborate their signature style with reference to Indian artisan handcraft, and many make further reference to the importance of the cloth. More sustainable fabrics are a part of the value proposition either through revival of handloom weaving and contemporising it (e.g., cases 3, 6, 11, 13 and 20) or initiatives to produce the ancient Ramie fibre in Meghalaya (Case 9). These signature styles for artisanal fashion are a complex combination of aesthetics, philosophies, fashion genres and design. While each signature style is unique and so constitutes a compelling brand Point of Difference (PoD) (Keller et al., 2002), self-described aesthetics range from minimalism (e.g., Cases 3, 4, 8 and 11) to Royal Chic by some of the occasion wear brands (e.g., Case 17). In several cases (13, 15 and 17), the designers perceive their roles in artisanal fashion as different to that of a fashion designer and often discussed it in relation to design values and philosophy:

> *I don't see myself as a fashion designer. I am more of a textile designer. I stick to my core value: quality craftsmanship.* (Sabyasachi Mukherjee cited in Tewari, 2019)
>
> *Aneeth still does not like to be tagged as a 'Fashion Designer' and would rather be called a "Textile and Dress Maker". …. She strives to balance fashion with tradition, making every day dressing fun and trendy. The foundation of her design philosophy is that Less is More.* (Arora/péro in Strand of Silk, n.d.)
>
> *As a painter, … I use line, proportions and colour to achieve an initial idea. So, in that respect, it is simply a shift in canvas for me. … the way I approach dressmaking is what sets our clothes apart. The prism with which I see clothes is our primary differentiator.* (Payal Khandwala cited in Dabral, 2017)

In other cases, the designers discuss how Eastern spiritual philosophies, mediation and architecture (e.g., Cases 3 and 14) influence their artisanal fashion design and brands:

Priyanka Ella Lorena Lama launched her debut collection under the label PELLA … in 2015. She is influenced by the Wabi-sabi school of thought – she believes imperfections make us appreciate the beauty of natural objects and processes which is also a key foundation for the brand PELLA. A simple experience like breathing or a complex one like meditation is expressed through the designs she creates - hoping to inspire someone somewhere. (British Council, 2016)

My approach has most often been called minimalist, still, its deeper nuances resonate with the modernism of post-independence India, with the strong Bauhaus influences the architecture of that time expressed. (Sachdeva/ BODICE cited in Dezeen, 2019)

As seen from this analysis of product and influences, a complex combination of aesthetics, philosophies, fashion genres and design influences artisanal fashion and underlies brand story and core values—art (e.g., Case 13), architecture (e.g., Case 3), meditation and Eastern spiritualism (e.g., Case 14). The role of the artisans and the designer is integral to the brand story for artisanal fashion, as encapsulated in one brand story quote (Case 4):

Our story is a collective narrative of all the makers whose shared efforts culminate in a beautiful legacy. (Buna, 2020)

Artisanal Brand Story for Systems Involved Product Production

Analysis of the artisanal brand story for the systems involved in product production in each of the cases (see Appendix Table 5.1, Column 7) reveals several rich themes. The process is as important as the product in artisanal fashion. All of the cases work closely with artisans that are either in-house or in craft clusters in regions of India historically renowned for particular indigenous crafts and techniques. Designers work closely with the artisans, and in most cases, this collaborative approach involves artisan handwork and design interventions that add value to the finished product. Design interventions range from contemporising the indigenous crafts and techniques (e.g., Cases 3, 4, 7, 9, 16 and 20) to design that strives to reduce waste and devise eco-friendly methods of production (e.g., Case 5) or achieve environmental and social responsibility across the value chain (e.g., Case 2). Both the artisan handwork and design interventions have sustainability principles at their heart, which form an important part of the artisanal fashion brand story in most of the cases. The range of design interventions and handwork involved in artisanal fashion ensures these Points of Parity (PoP) (Keller et al., 2002) become the essence of each brand and thereby an important part of the brand story which constitutes another compelling brand Point of Difference (PoD).

On the other hand, artisanal fashion shares these calls for sustainability principles and strategies, design interventions and supply chain transparency with the global apparel industry in general. The pandemic has heightened awareness of exposure to risks in the apparel value chain which could alter global sourcing strategies (The Business of Fashion and McKinsey & Company, 2020c). These important issues and practices are largely beyond the scope of this study, other than the extent to which they are evident in brand story. Sustainability principles and strategies, and design interventions, are highly evident in the brand story for all of the artisanal fashion cases in this study. It would seem that artisanal fashion systems have many similarities with other fashion genres and systems, but also some differences which warrant further research.

Artisanal Brand Story in the Wider Systems of Company and Community Engagement

Analysis of the artisanal brand story for the wider systems of company and community engagement in each of the cases (see Appendix Table 5.1, Column 8) reveals further rich themes. Working with artisans is undertaken for a complex combination of aesthetic and other reasons as already discussed in the analysis of product and production systems. Some of the cases do so for pro-social principles and actions of reviving and advocacy for indigenous crafts and techniques and empowering artisans with skill training and other resources, thereby giving them a source of livelihood. This becomes an integral part of their brand story (e.g., Cases 2, 12, 13 and 20). These cases have systems for supporting the artisans with training and work, collaborations with designers and additional support for the artisan communities in forms of housing, health, childcare and education. In these cases, the brand story is inextricably linked with socio-political causes and involves a range of stakeholders.

Artisanal Fashion Collaborations and Co-branding

Analysis of recent artisanal fashion collaborations and co-branding in each of the cases (see Appendix Table 5.1, Column 4; Table 5.2, Column 9) reveals further rich themes of relevance to artisanal brand story and co-branding.

Some artisanal fashion collaborations are undertaken for cause-related reasons, such as the two cases who participated in face masks projects in 2020 with the profits directed towards vulnerable groups (Cases 2 and 15). Other cause-related collaborations also directed profits to causes (e.g., Case 17 Save the Saree initiative) or participated in cause-related events (e.g., Case 17 participation in the Fashion for Peace group presentation of conscious designers in NY in association with the Isha Foundation). Other collaborations are more pro-social oriented involving collaborations with Foundations and Charitable Trusts that have either been set up to support specific artisanal fashion initiatives or are pro-social artisanal projects supported through such entities (e.g., Cases 2, 12 and 20).

Many of the cases have participated in co-branding collaborations, but some recent examples feature artisanal fashion *per se* (e.g., Case 14 inclusion in the Oppo Reno stories 2020). Another form of artisanal fashion collaborations is with architecture and art (e.g., Case 11 collaborating with architect Anupama Kundoo to make special panels of upcycled denim which are included in the architect's monographic exhibition at the Louisiana Museum, Denmark and an installation for Levi's 501 Day).

Other artisanal fashion collaborations are more sustainability related (e.g., Case 2 joining the Sustainability Apparel Coalition, using certified sustainable fibres, and PETA approved cruelty-free materials).

One other example combines artisanal fashion, art and branding (e.g., Case 15). péro's 'Time to Love' exhibition, in collaboration with India Art Fair held in Delhi 2020, celebrates the brand's first decade in fashion and its sustainable manufacturing process.

> *The purpose of the exhibit is to involve people in the process of our garment making. We want them to be a part of the journey, hence we haven't used a lot of garments. Instead, you will find hanging textiles and buttons. It's all about [raising awareness] of the effort that goes in making the clothing. Over time I have realised that we get so caught up in the rut of crafting a collection every six months, that we stop enjoying and embracing the process. So, this whole concept is about the time that you give to make something, and the process that goes into it.* (Arora/péro in Chopra, 2020)

Conclusion

This exploratory study of 20 cases of Indian artisanal fashion provides answers to the primary research question: What is artisanal fashion, and for those within artisanal fashion production and marketing in the COVID-19 crisis for contemporary Indian fashion as an emerging market, what are the branding implications? As the first study to explore the concept of branding for artisanal fashion in any context, but specifically the rich Indian context with its extensive history of artisanal fashion and embellishment, this study makes several significant contributions.

Firstly, the significance of India as an emerging market for contemporary fashion is considered. India is moving from being an increasingly important sourcing hub to being an attractive consumer market as one of the two largest economies in the world—second to China—with its fast-growing middle class and strongest absolute growth globally in the number of Internet users which during the pandemic has become the dominant way for consumers to be introduced to fashion brands and make online purchases (Kaur et al., 2022). All bodes well for India as a significant market for contemporary fashion in the immediate future.

Definitions and characteristics of artisanal fashion are then considered, where many similarities, but also some departures, from other fashion movements such as slow fashion and sustainable fashion are another contribution of this study. India's long heritage of artisanal fashion and embellishment is acknowledged with a fashion genre continuum proposed ranging from 'minimalism' to 'royal chic'.

Branding is the dominant logic applied in the analysis of these artisanal fashion cases in India, particularly the brand story for understanding fashion production and marketing initiatives. The brand story is firstly considered, that is, underpinned by other branding elements and decisions such as brand architecture, portfolio for the brand, points of parity and points of difference. Brand values and propositions are considered higher-level concepts that many fashion brands have yet to formalise or articulate in contrast with many other brands and corporations across other industry sectors. Brand collaborations are also evident which can lead to brand extensions and sometimes co-branding (Mogaji & Nguyen, 2021). All companies have a brand story that they craft and prior to social media used to control, but these days are also co-created by consumers. This study looks at the brand story from the company's existing secondary sources only which is an appropriate place to start, but also a limitation suggesting fruitful avenues for future research that are identified.

What did we find? All brand stories incorporate some sustainable fashion principles, but in doing so this is a brand point of parity unless the brand can truly evidence brand sustainability initiatives (Nguyen & Mogaji, 2021a, 2022b). All 20 cases have wonderful brand stories as Indian fashion brands that are making their way in the current competitive market of artisanal fashion which is their point of difference but have been also innovating, initiating and growing during COVID. A framework for analysing brand story by three further characteristics is also presented for grouping brand messages, narratives and stories into three types of activity of relevance to artisanal fashion creation and production (adapted from Payne, 2014): (1) product related which often include tangible brand associations (e.g., aesthetic style of the apparel) and more intangible abstract brand qualities (e.g., vision, philosophy); (2) systems related (e.g., design processes, production techniques and role of the designer) and (3) wider community related which for all cases included working with artisans and, thereby, pro-social actions of providing a livelihood for vulnerable groups in the community (Nguyen & Mogaji, 2021b), while simultaneously contemporising and advocating for indigenous crafts and techniques—social enterprise that is powerfully summarised as "to make things better" (Goldsmith, 2018, p. 206). This framework for analysing artisanal fashion in India is a contribution of this study that could be of relevance to artisanal fashion elsewhere in other developing and emerging markets as well as high income, industrialised countries (Brooksworth et al., 2022a, 2022b). Across all of these fashion branding areas, optimal strategies for artisanal fashion brands are found with implications for artisanal fashion brand architecture, portfolio, points of difference, innovation, sustainability and collaboration that is another contribution with implications for fashion practice in India and other emerging markets as well as elsewhere.

Artisanal fashion definitions, characteristics and strategies are considered, but whether artisanal fashion is a subset, sibling or cousin of slow fashion and/or sustainable fashion or something entirely unique in its own right remains unclear. One clear finding from the research is that artisanal fashion is a compelling brand story with points of difference and value propositions which seem to meet growing consumer needs and values for sustainability and mindful consumption in the emerging markets of India and elsewhere in the recovery from the uncertain and challenging COVID world.

Appendix

Table 5.1 Indian fashion cases: company and brand details

(Case) Fashion label/founder (geographic location)	Flagship stores and locations	Year founded	Artisanal brand collaborations	Brand portfolio and architecture
(Case 1) **Akihi** by Srishti Arora (originally from Jaipur, now **Chandigarh**)	Studio/atelier in Chandigarh	Label in 2017.	Ramie project 2018	**Akihi:** bronze threadwork and textile jewellery for men and women; **Bold moves:** jewellery collection using Ramie fabric for Ramie project
(Case 2) **Anita Dongre (HQ Mumbai/Bombay)**	Flagship stores in New York and Notting Hill, London	Label in early 1990s Foundation in 2015 COVID fund in 2020 to support artisanal workforce with medical and financial requirements.	Behind the Masks project 2020 with *Pichhwai* craft inspired masks	**House of Anita Dongre:** men and women's couture/ bespoke bridalwear/ occasionwear; fine jewellery; **Boho-chic:** wear; **AND:** western wear; **Grassroot:** sustainable luxury
(Case 3) **Bodice** by Ruchika Sachdeva **(Delhi)**	Studio/atelier and store in Delhi	Label in 2011.	Ramie project 2018	**Bodice**: womenswear apparel; cloth bags (as packaging)

Brand story (including artisans)		
Product and influences	Systems around product	Wider company
Brand ethos is designs with a medley of textures using metal wires and threads twined together with intricate stitches which is then mounted onto a frame and adorned with subtle embellishment or bold pattern detail.	Employs artisan workforce with each piece passing through several hands from the silk dyer, to the embroiderer to the metalsmith.	Works with Indian artisans
Signature style shows an affinity for indigenous craft tradition, coupled with a modern aesthetic to create beautiful timeless pieces. Cruelty-free fashion: all accessories are made from cruelty-free, PETA-approved materials. Source sustainable fabrics such as TENCEL™ fibres.	Works with highly skilled artisans in traditional Indian arts and crafts from Rajasthan (embroidery weaving). Often designs collections with sole aim of uplifting particular artisans. Joined Sustainable Apparel Coalition (SAC) beginning 2019 as "Brand & Retailer" Member to measure and assess sustainability performance and further drive environmental and social responsibility across the value chain.	**Anita Dongre Foundation** works with local government and village Panchayat to train rural women and create self-help groups to bring employment back to Indian villages. Has set up five Community Tailoring Units in rural Maharashtra, India, wherein marginalised tribal women are trained professionally to make garments. Units have been operating at Charoti since 2015, Jawhar, Dhanevari, and Modgaon, since 2018, and Kawada since 2019, with more than 276 women trained or in training and 134 women working at these centres. They are also provided with sustained livelihood opportunities, thereafter resulting in positive socio-economic impact.
Signature aesthetic is a representation of the chaos and order of India, an ode to and symbolic representation of our intimate connections to nature and expresses fashion's capacity to create art. Meditative and communal elements of Eastern philosophy are an influence. Brand philosophy is comfortable, yet structured pieces.	Signature aesthetic explores the indigenous fabrics and time-honoured weaving traditions of India with a contemporary approach.	Works with Indian artisans to explore indigenous fabrics and weaving traditions of India.

(*continued*)

Table 5.1 (continued)

(Case) Fashion label/founder (geographic location)	Flagship stores and locations	Year founded	Artisanal brand collaborations	Brand portfolio and architecture
(Case 4) **Buna** by Pallavi Shantam **(Delhi)**	Studio in Delhi	Label in 2017.	Not listed	**Buna:** womenswear apparel; cloth bags (as packaging)
(Case 5) **Huemn** by Shyma Shetty and Pranav Misra **(Delhi)**	Studio in Delhi	Label in 2012.	Ramie project 2018 Huemn x Ramie—A photo-story of India's streets "Within this project, we explore the maiden journey of one of the oldest textile fibres in the world through one of the oldest civilisations of the world, effectively throwing open the windows to life on Indian streets in 2018. If you look carefully, you will find our protagonist—a square piece of fabric."	**Huemn:** Gender-fluid and socially responsible luxury street style apparel Artworks (installation panels)

Brand story (including artisans)		
Product and influences	Systems around product	Wider company
Brand story is a collective narrative of all the makers whose shared efforts culminate in products with a global and timeless appeal. Uses high-quality, natural raw materials and organic processes to create soft, breathable handwoven fabrics like cotton, muslin, cotton silk, silk, organza, and linen. These are then made into fluid, relaxed, and contemporary shapes.	Has in-house team of hand embroiderers. The process is as important as the product and both have slow living with sustainability at their heart. Uses handwoven textiles, natural materials and has contemporised artisanal techniques of *Jamdani* (loom embroidery with intricate, opaque motifs woven over a fine muslin base) and *Chanderi* printed by slow-process hand block printing. Consciously strives towards reducing waste and devising eco-friendly methods of crafting garments. Majority of textiles are handloom and then develop the rest of their natural fabrics on small-scale automated looms. Repurpose their textile waste through handloom weaving, creating **upcycled** fabrics with a unique character and texture to them. The textile scraps from previous collections get cut into strips to make the yarn. It is then inserted in the weaving process to create a patterned fabric inspired by nature.	Works with artisans from Rajasthan, India.
Huemn projects: Huemn x Ramie; Huemn x D Shave (barber shops); Huemn x shirts (gorilla); Huemn x shirts (deconstruction); Huemn x Bukowski (limited edition T-shirts with messages). New initiative of embroidered art installation panels. Brand vision stresses equally on **relevance** of product as it does on **responsibility** in action.	Some limited edition garments and art installation panels are one-offs. Consciously strive towards reducing waste and devising eco-friendly methods of crafting garments. Huemn project Edition 3 (August 2017). Today's waste is tomorrow's biggest resource. (All upcycled pieces were created using waste material from Indian designers' labels such as Antar-Agni, Bodice, Dhruv Kapoor, DRVV, and Ikai.)	Works with embroidery workers.

(continued)

Table 5.1 (continued)

(Case) Fashion label/founder (geographic location)	Flagship stores and locations	Year founded	Artisanal brand collaborations	Brand portfolio and architecture
(Case 6) **The IOU project** by Kavita Parmar (formerly from **Chennai/Madras)**	E-commerce social network built as a meeting place for a like-minded community	Project in 2009–2010.	With Luskentyre Harris Tweed weavers, Isle of Harris, Scotland, since 2011.	**The IOU project**: handmade apparel and e-commerce social network.
(Case 7) **James Ferreira (Mumbai/Bombay)**	Studio in Mumbai; production unit in iconic 47-G Bungalow at Khotachiwadi, which is one of the last surviving heritage villages of Bombay	Label in 1992.	Diamond jewellery with Gehna Jewellers in 2013.	**James Ferreira:** apparel for men and women; bridalwear; jewellery design.
(Case 8) **KALEEKAL** by Alan Alexander (Thiruvananthapuram/ Trivandrum capital of Indian state of **Kerala)**	**RAHEL**: multi-brand artisan concept store/fashion and design studio/ library/art gallery in a 100-year-old heritage building near Napier Museum	Label in 2015.	Ramie project 2018	**KALEEKAL**: gender neutral apparel.

Brand story (including artisans)		
Product and influences	Systems around product	Wider company
Brand concept is the uniqueness of each item that allows traceability from weaver to consumer. The stories of how that item was created, of the people involved, and of the customers who purchased them are the essence of the e-commerce social network.	Using technology creates mass market potential for an easy-to-wear line of clothing, where each piece is handmade and completely unique.	Works with artisan weavers in India who make classic Madras check fabric and Harris Tweed weavers in Scotland.
Is considered a master draper whose garments in predominantly natural fabrics seamlessly blend Western silhouettes with Indian crafts and technique. Every pattern of his is unique, as each design is intended to suit a particular lifestyle, with emphasis on comfort and ease of movement. Personal challenge is to do something unique every time.	Hand looms, hand embroidery, block printing.	Works with Indian artisans. In 1994, he started the Khotachiwadi welfare and heritage trust, a charity organisation, which protects the heritage precinct he lives in. 1999 to 2002—conducted finishing and cutting classes for the workers of Lucknow-based NGO "SEWA" run by Runa Banerjee and Sahiba Hussain.
Employs traditional Indian handloom fabrics in conceptualising a subversive take on wardrobe staples. "My design sensibilities are a reflection of my Kerala roots. While the rest of India is known for their riot of colours and embroideries, Kerala stands apart in the fact that our traditional garments feature simple off-white cottons and plain gold *zari* borders. This minimalism is largely reflected in my design aesthetics and the strictly functional detailing of my clothes."	Regularly works with weaving societies to handwoven natural fabrics like organic cotton, silk, wool, and linen and is aware of the value design interventions add. Explores zero-waste manipulation during pattern cutting to reduce the wastage of fabric during garment production. Opts for organic cotton, hemp, and jute instead of regular cotton to help reduce the impact of pesticides and chemicals on the soil and also reduce the amount of natural resources consumed. Post-production techniques of sustainability have also been employed at times where we work with fabric/yarn wastes and upcycling of consumer/production wastes for detailing and surface development.	Works with local weavers in craft clusters in Koothali, Kannur, Kunjipalli, and Maniyur, with many having own looms at home. Through his store, helps local designers collaborate with weavers and craft clusters around the country, adding a new facet to their design and bringing a pan-India appeal to their work. Curates local brands that each have an authentic story and selling point that makes up the brand identity. A contemporary design aesthetic and a relevant design narrative are key elements.

(*continued*)

Table 5.1 (continued)

(Case) Fashion label/founder (geographic location)	Flagship stores and locations	Year founded	Artisanal brand collaborations	Brand portfolio and architecture
(Case 9) **Lecoanet Hemant (LH)** by Hemant Sagar and Didier Lecoanet **(HQ Delhi)**	**Lecoanet Hemant Couture** fashion house in Gurugram, Haryana, India; **Genes Lecoanet Hemant** stores in Delhi, Kolkata, Lucknow, and Madras **Ayurganic** online at www.ayurganic.com Store in Chennai	Label founded in Paris 1981, now in Delhi since 2000.	Curated the first Ramie fibre project produced in Meghalaya, India, for the Indo-French government Ramie project 2018 Haute Couture gown featured in Netflix TV series *Fabulous Lives of Bollywood Wives* (2020)	**Lecoanet Hemant Couture:** includes high-end, bespoke masks; **Genes Lecoanet Hemant:** ready-to-wear for men and women includes artisanal masks encrusted with pearls and embroidered with sequins and masks featuring prints from the collection; **Ayurganic:** sustainable/organic range of garments and accessories includes masks with herbs and restorative oils/essences woven into the fabric, and names of the herbs in the masks are included as calligraphy on the masks, for example Tosi/Basil.
(Case 10) **Nappa Dori (Delhi)**	Store with café in Delhi; flagship store in Seven Dials, Covent Garden London; Well-established e-commerce channel	Label in 2010 by Gautam Sinha.	Not listed	**Nappa Dori:** leather bags, satchels, and accessories; **Dori Living** focusing on homewares—soon to launch as a pivot that was long in planning, but fast-tracked due to 2020 event.

Brand story (including artisans)		
Product and influences	Systems around product	Wider company
Combines fluid silhouettes with intricate detailing—giving the spirit of Haute Couture to their collections. The designs are architectural, with pure clean lines and sleek tailoring. **Genes Lecoanet Hemant**, made entirely in India for India, is a lifestyle collection of garments and accessories offering a modern alternative and affordable luxury. **Ayurganic:** stay-at-home collection of garments or Ayurvastra (*Ayur* and *vastra* meaning health and cloth, respectively, in Sanskrit) is permeated with special herbs and oils, making it free of synthetic chemicals and toxic irritants. Wearing these garments helps restore balance within the body and strengthens the immune system.	Every piece is designed and produced in-house, ensuring impeccable quality. **Ayurganic** (sustainable/organic range made of Ayurvedic fabrics exclusively using GOTS-certified cotton) is hand–treated, following the century-old Ayurvedic recipes; Fair Trade; No child labour.	Based in Delhi, following the call of the exquisite textiles, beading, and embellishment which India's heritage has to offer.
Finely crafted products made by artisans.	Not available.	Works with artisans in North Delhi.

(continued)

Table 5.1 (continued)

(Case) Fashion label/founder (geographic location)	Flagship stores and locations	Year founded	Artisanal brand collaborations	Brand portfolio and architecture
(Case 11) Naushad Ali (Pondicherry/ Puducherry)	Studio Liam in Auroville	Label in 2014.	In 2020, made special panels of upcycled denim for monographic exhibition of Indian architect Anupama Kundoo, "Taking time", at Louisiana Museum, Denmark (Oct 8, 2020–Jan 31, 2021). Textile meets architecture meets art! Recycling and giving a new life to waste as building elements. In 2020, planning soft furnishings range with architectural design firm in Copenhagen. *In 2019, created art installation for Levi's 501 Day, exhibited in Mumbai, showcasing a sustainability philosophy and celebrating the greener future of fashion.*	**Naushad Ali:** hand-crafted apparel. Art Installations. Before COVID lockdown in Feb 2020 it was adding home furnishings to the collection.

Brand story (including artisans)		
Product and influences	Systems around product	Wider company
Minimalistic silhouettes that customise their classic styles in their signature fabrics. Motto since conception is to revisit to adapt, rather than add.	90% of creating collections is about working on the fabric in close quarters with traditional weavers, so that the brand's USP became one where the design process starts with the designing of the fabric rather than the garment. By producing own fabric, is dedicated to sustainability—operates on a zero-waste policy and works towards the economic sustainability of handloom weaving. Brand vision is creating a space where the family of artisans can work together; a place to do weaving, dyeing, and garment production under one roof, a single space where fashion is celebrated from loom to fashion.	Works with weavers across India and develops new fabrics initially with weavers from Bengal, and then later weavers in the south such as Madurai and Chettinad.

(continued)

Table 5.1 (continued)

(Case) Fashion label/founder (geographic location)	Flagship stores and locations	Year founded	Artisanal brand collaborations	Brand portfolio and architecture
(Case 12) **Nila House (Delhi)** and **Project Utpal (Rajasthan)** as part of the Lady Bamford Foundation **(Jaipur)**	**Nila House** is a 1940s home in Delhi converted into a craftsmanship centre of open studios, collection showrooms, archive and research library, exhibition gallery, textiles vault, and artists-in-residence rooms	Nila House in 2016. The Lady Bamford Charitable Trust in 2001 has three objectives: to improve education, help promote economic growth, and support women and children. The Lady Bamford Foundation in 2013 works with communities around Jaipur and Udaipur—recently launched Project Utpal.	The Lady Bamford Foundation: works with communities with the goal of enhancing sustainable production and business efficiency in 100 artisan units across five districts—Bagru, Kaladera, Jahota, Jairampura, and Akola. The Foundation also works with like-minded NGOs across remote parts of India, building on the local farm-to-textile economies of rural communities.	**Nila House/Studio:** apparel; face masks. **Nila House:** supports creative development to conserve, promote, and strengthen traditional artisanal communities in Rajasthan, with a particular focus on natural dyes and handloom textile; annual capsule in-house clothing collection. Nila hopes to encourage and establish more traditional and sustainable craft value chains, from seed to stitch.

Brand story (including artisans)		
Product and influences	Systems around product	Wider company
Nila Studio: collaborates annually with a designer on an in-house clothing collection. By working with creators who are pushing the boundaries of excellence in hand-craftsmanship and contemporary design, the Nila Studio team builds knowledge base and exchanges ideas with an extensive community of crafters and designers. These capsule collections will be available at Nila House. Nila's first designer is Anna Valentine who with Nila House team explores the hues of true indigo in a collection of 20 shapes that are contemporary, while the techniques used are dense with Indian tradition. "Each piece exemplifies the principles of slow fashion—timeless designs made to last, crafted from handmade textiles and celebrating skills that have been passed down through generations."	**Navrang Challenge**: nationwide competition ending August 2020 inviting all artists, artisans, and designers for creating hand-crafted posters to communicate health and safety measures that prevent the spread of the Coronavirus and also about awareness around physical and mental health, or your own personal experience during COVID. Posters were to be made using any craft technique (example embroidery, appliqué, hand painting, collages) and available materials at home. The three winning posters will become part of Nila's communication strategy for building awareness around the preventive measures of the Coronavirus in the rural communities.	**Project Utpal**, in Rajasthan, supports artisan income growth while enabling environmentally sensitive production processes. With a strong focus on education, it will run regular workshops and artisan consultations, empowering 5000 artisans with information on plant dyes and sustainable practices, as well as furthering knowledge on local craft.

(continued)

Table 5.1 (continued)

(Case) Fashion label/founder (geographic location)	Flagship stores and locations	Year founded	Artisanal brand collaborations	Brand portfolio and architecture
(Case 13) Payal Khandwala (Mumbai/Bombay)	Studio (bespoke) and retail store in Mumbai; also stores in Delhi and Bangalore; and official online store	Label in 2012 by *Payal Khandwala* and Vikram Ramchandani.	Ramie project 2018	**Payal Khandwala:** women's apparel; metal jewellery.

Brand story (including artisans)		
Product and influences	Systems around product	Wider company
Signature style sensibility has not shifted since the inception of her eponymous label. "The prism with which I see clothes is our primary differentiator: as a painter, I use composition, colour and line to communicate an idea and when I design clothes it's not that different. I use line, proportions and colour to achieve an initial idea. So in that respect, it is simply a shift in canvas for me. I'm inspired by the same formal elements when I paint or when I'm patterning something new, and because I don't really care about fashion, as much as I do about style, the way I approach dressmaking is what sets our clothes apart." "I don't blindly follow trends; I wouldn't want to fit someone into something that doesn't complement their body. This is where the real challenge lies I believe—in maintaining the DNA of the brand. Colour is also a significant element since I have painted all my life." With silhouettes that work for women of all ages, sizes, shapes, and personalities. Clothes that are simple yet dramatic; priced well and had a certain India modern spirit—wanted clothes that were rooted in India but transcended our cultural and geographical boundaries. "My exposure to street style, art school, amongst other popular culture triggers inform many of the choices I make design wise and it definitely shapes my aesthetic. I find that it is deeply rooted in India but has a spirit that is more global." Believes in making clothes that are functional, but still luxurious. "I love the simplicity and fuss-free clothing that empower women. This is why my focus is always personal style over fashion because trends can enslave you."	Handloom fabrics are a big part of her design aesthetic. "I've always loved the poetry of a handwoven textile. Just the idea that it is woven by man, the process, the time, the love and skill it takes to weave the simplest of textiles. The romance of that is unparalleled in my eyes." "I love them with all their imperfections and their possibilities." "I find they feel more real, more tactile and they are deeply rooted in our tradition, but they are so versatile and in a different context can be so global in their spirit too. India is singular in this area, with the length and breadth of our craft belts across our country." Personally prefers silks because the yarn takes colour so well, especially when the hues are saturated, and loves to play with colour. Also *Benarasi* brocades because its beauty lies in the fact that they are so intricate and the gold thread makes them so luxurious but also light and comfortable. Uses zero-waste pattern-making. "I use geometry as a tool to simplify. To cut a garment in the simplest way to achieve a certain result is akin to solving a math problem. It requires logic and process. And I enjoy that. I find it is also a challenge to start draping from humble beginnings, a square, a circle and then to build with pleating, tucking, folding. It is a great way to resolve ideas and stumble upon new ones."	Uses handloom fabrics and *Benarasi* silk brocades. We try to support women that can work with handlooms from their homes once their daily duties end. We try our best to support them in a more well-rounded way. We have a system where they and their families are covered in terms of health and education.

(*continued*)

Table 5.1 (continued)

(Case) Fashion label/founder (geographic location)	Flagship stores and locations	Year founded	Artisanal brand collaborations	Brand portfolio and architecture
(Case 14) **PELLA** by Priyanka Ella Lorena Lama **(Bangalore)**	Studio in Bangalore	Label in 2015.	Oppo Reno Stories: Ep 2 PELLA (Priyanka Ella) To Create is to Live 2020 Ramie project 2018	**PELLA:** women's apparel.

Brand story (including artisans)		
Product and influences	Systems around product	Wider company
Label PELLA is an acronym for her full name. Brand ethos is its innovative and imaginative take on garments that present an emotive quality. Brings in elements of the more traditional Indian clothing such as the sari, but adds her own twist with monochromatic colour schemes. Robe like silhouettes, mostly cinched at the waist in cotton silks with fluid hints which came in the form of sleeves or trails, made up the collection. Tessellated patterns extended into exaggerated sleeves which cast a dramatic effect with pieces coming as close as to the ankle and others embracing the concept of infinite sleeves that don't end—just meet each other near the belly. Is influenced by the Wabi-sabi school of thought—she believes imperfections make us appreciate the beauty of natural objects and processes which is also a key foundation for the brand PELLA. A simple experience like breathing or a complex one like meditation is expressed through the designs she creates—hoping to inspire someone somewhere.	PELLA is an artisanal label conceptually driven towards slow fashion incorporating zero-waste creative pattern-making in garment construction and design. It is a 100% hand-stitched label creating designs without any use of machines. Zero-waste designs often using a "CELLA", which involves a single block of fabric and minimum sewing and measurements, to create a limitless potential in silhouettes and ensure minimal wastage. Thread work coupled with hand-painting techniques create a blurred visual appeal that sits well with the designers' constructional genius of creating a whole garment out of a single block of fabric. Unstructured free-flowing silhouettes featuring elements like pleats and layers, teamed up with details like rolled and blind hems created exquisite ensembles in handwoven fabrics.	Uses handwoven fabrics such as pure Eri silks, *jamdani*, cashmere, pashmina, and *tassar* fabrics. Recycled wood from shipping containers came out in details on certain garments to highlight the sustainable idea behind the collection.

(continued)

Table 5.1 (continued)

(Case) Fashion label/founder (geographic location)	Flagship stores and locations	Year founded	Artisanal brand collaborations	Brand portfolio and architecture
(Case 15) **Péro (Delhi)** by Aneeth Arora (from **Udaipur, Rajasthan)**	Studio in Delhi	Label in 2009.	Péro's "Time to Love" exhibition, in collaboration with India Art Fair held in Delhi on Feb 1 –Mar 13, 2020, celebrates the brand's first decade in fashion and its sustainable manufacturing process. Invites the public to experience the brand's production practice and showcase it as an art form. "We are about to repeat over 42 days what we have done over the last ten years: labour over one garment with all our love and attention" (Péro Facebook 2020). Péro's "Time to Love" exhibition includes a doll house reference to Péro's collaboration with performance artist Princess Pea. Hand-crafted masks, for Moonriver **Masks 4**. All raising funds for charities such as @goonj and @ karwanemohabbat who are supporting the invisible and marginalised. Ramie project 2018. In 2014, one of India's few designers commissioned for inclusion in Indian fabrics and textiles exhibition London's Victoria and Albert Museum 2015–2016.	**Péro:** men and women's wear; jewellery; other accessories (scarves, bags, shoes, limited edition socks, face masks). **Chhota Péro:** kid's wear. **Lazy Péro:** women's wear.

Brand story (including artisans)		
Product and influences	Systems around product	Wider company
Péro sensibility is androgynous clothing that is playfully light and feminine summer collections; winter collections are masculine. Always a message underlying each collection. The Indianness of Péro rests in the textile process, where materials pass through the hands of one craftsperson to the other, carrying forward the Indian tradition of hand-crafting and creating pieces that are at once unique. The resulting garment evokes some sense of culture from where it originates. This culture communicates internationally in a way that the wearer looks equally at ease in the streets of Paris or London, as she does here in India. The look is not about an age group or season, it is about a mindset—a willingness to incorporate the effortless style of the locals. Creates apparel that is crazy enough to surprise people, but wearable and stylish at the same time. She strives to balance fashion with tradition, making every day dressing fun and trendy. Calls herself a "textile and dress maker" and what fascinates and inspires her most is the clothing and dressing styles of the local people, which makes them so effortlessly stylish and trendy, therefore making them real trend-setters of our time. Personalises garments and emphasises her "love" for the craft of dressmaking by hand-stitching a heart on to every garment before packaging. A symbol for clients to discover either immediately or after a few wears, depending on where it was stitched (Varma 2015:195). Foundation of her design philosophy is that "Less is More", which reflects in her designs as well, with clothes exuding versatility and comfort, but also carrying a keen attention to detail.	Develops surfaces using different hand embroidery techniques incorporating threads and the fibres to create pompoms, tassels, and flowers. Incorporating hand techniques not only adds value to the woven textile surfaces but also makes every garment unique in itself as it is passed through the hands of various craftspeople. Sustainable manufacturing and production process that is also an art form as showcased in the "Time to Love" exhibition, held in Delhi on Feb 1–Mar 13, 2020. Each season changes the form of distributing "love" at her fashion week shows, for example heart-shaped cookies to anyone who walked by or pinning tiny velvet hearts on the audience. It only took one or two seasons for most people to know that the heart, even without the label name Péro written on it, was from Arora's brand (Varma 2015: 198). Hand-crafted masks are a conscious attempt to create reusable, plastic-free, rubber free biodegradable masks of love, hand-crafted from recycled pure cotton textile scraps from seasons past, with adjustable strings to avoid the use of elastic.	Works with Indian craftspersons. For collaboration with Grounds—Japanese shoe label, Péro's strength of hand-crafting and upcycling, they hand embroidered the shoes with sequin and glitter, fitted lights in their transparent soles making them glow in the dark, and together created a pair of perfect dancing shoes.

(continued)

Table 5.1 (continued)

(Case) Fashion label/founder (geographic location)	Flagship stores and locations	Year founded	Artisanal brand collaborations	Brand portfolio and architecture
(Case 16) **Raw Mango** by Sanjay Garg **(Delhi)**	Retail stores in Delhi, Mumbai, and Bangalore	Raw Mango in 2008; Sanjay Garg in 2014.	Raw Mango included in TEXTO 2020 in Mexico, a global gathering organised by Kavita Parmar of 45 heritage craftspeople and designers from 23 countries. A **Raw Mango** sari with a particular crow motif is displayed at London's Victoria and Albert Museum.	Women's apparel; **Raw Mango** is strongly connected with the handloom saris, but brand has expanded into music and objects. Founder Sanjay Garg wants his brand to embody "a lived experience". As a design house it continues to create new conversations in textile, culture, and politics through a range of saris, garments, and objects. **Sanjay Garg** showcased a line of stitched *Banarasi* garments, shown on runways for the first time in 2014.

Brand story (including artisans)		
Product and influences	Systems around product	Wider company
Raw Mango uses century-old skills and innovation to create its designs in order to define a new aesthetic collection of clothes. Over recent years, a new fashion movement has steadily gained ground in India. Seasonal trends are being linked intrinsically with local, sustainable resources; handloom is being reinterpreted in contemporary designs; forgotten craft traditions are being revived; and the saree is being reclaimed as a bona-fide style statement. "But working in *Chanderi* [in 2006] motivated me to think more deeply on the subject—why was handloom in such crisis, why didn't women want to wear sarees any more, and why was there this great divide between fashion and craft?" "I was just doing it out of passion and love, and because I strongly felt that there was a need to simplify the traditional designs." "We've woven bird motifs like parrots and sparrows into *Chanderi*. I've also worked flowers like roses and marigolds, and wildlife like deer and flamingos into my collections, and our design experiments continue to this day. We were also the first to get silver, gold and copper *zari* woven into *Chanderi*. Silver *zari* was always used but in very small quantities, so we increased the amount of silver and added copper too." "The traditional weave patterns were *nal pherwa*, dandidar border, *chatai, jangla, bundi, ganga jamuni, ashrafi booti* etc. But at Raw Mango, we have experimented over the last 11 years with colours and design. Our success with this contemporary interpretation of *Chanderi* saris and dupattas has had an impact on the entire industry. In terms of colours, the shades used earlier were red, purple, pale blue, pistachio green, white and black. We introduced a palette of new colours like yellow, lime green, midnight blue and sharbati pink, which had never seen before in *Chanderi*."	"We must support weavers, but, instead of worrying about the plight of crafts, we must encourage our children to engage in these crafts and create an ecosystem where a profession like weaving is lucrative." Raw Mango is part of a wave that has reclaimed traditional handloom as a luxurious style statement. Prices for saris and stitched garments can be more aspirational than affordable, but Garg is keen to find ways to make this luxury more accessible to India. "There are many reasons why everyone can't wear handlooms. If I could harness technology to make an improvement, I would make handlooms easier to wash and dry, lighter and cheaper too, without compromising on quality." In terms of the time taken, it depends on the complexity of the sari. A *Chanderi* sari with a plain weave will take approximately three days, but depending on the level of detail in the design, it can go up to 15 days.	To sustain the essence of its brand idea, Raw Mango works with tailors and weavers across India that are famous for their history in handwoven clothing such as block prints from Rajasthan, *Chanderi* from Madhya Pradesh, and silk work from Varanasi. "Since then, the wages of my artisans have increased fivefold, which is rare for India. The Scindia family, who have unconditional love for the craft, were able to bring infrastructure like electricity and water to their villages. Most importantly, I've always treated them as true collaborators, because frankly, weaving is in their heritage and their DNA. They could do things with their eyes closed and at the end of the day, I'm an outsider. Perhaps I look at things differently, and they may not see what I see. But the success comes from a combination of both." His vision for the next ten years is for India to have the best textile infrastructure and designers in the world. "Like the world looks to the West for fashion, they must look to us for the best in textiles in the future", he says.

(continued)

Table 5.1 (continued)

(Case) Fashion label/founder (geographic location)	Flagship stores and locations	Year founded	Artisanal brand collaborations	Brand portfolio and architecture
(Case 17) **Sabyasachi** Mukherjee (from **Kolkata/ Calcutta**)	Five stores in Mumbai, Delhi, Hyderabad, and Kolkata, including a jewellery store in Mumbai Flagship store in New York planned to open in 2020	Label in 1999.	In 2020, uniform initiative—designs block print uniforms for under-privileged girls in Jaisalmer, Rajasthan. For Manhattan's iconic luxury department store Bergdorf Goodman, an exhibition of exclusive hand-crafted pieces of fine and bohemian jewellery collections in Jan 30–Mar 21, 2020, but extended due to lockdown of Bergdorf Goodman. February 2019, showed in NY as part of Fashion for Peace, a group presentation of conscious design in association with the Isha Foundation. Designed costumes for movie, *Black*, where involvement was integral to the visual narration. NDTV channel's popular reality television show *Band Baaja Bride*. In season five, Sabyasachi was one of the show hosts. In each episode, he designed elaborate, bespoke couture for the selected couples from across India, irrespective of social status, who were given a "Sabyasachi makeover". Close-up camera shots of the bride's *lengha*—feature yards of hand-worked embroidery.	**Sabyasachi** men and women's couture bridalwear; **Sabyasachi** fine jewellery; **Sabyasachi** accessories; **Sabyasachi** sarees (basic to bridal); **Sabyasachi** beauty and fragrances. "The only thing that I have learnt in these 20 years is that it's only through repetition that you can create iconism and I want the brand to be iconic. I want people to remember." Transitioning from a clothing brand to a lifestyle brand.

Brand story (including artisans)		
Product and influences	Systems around product	Wider company
Indian handloom and embroidery have been his forte. With his signature look—a marriage of regal and bohemian styles—using traditional fabrics, heritage, and culture, he brought to the fashion scene a renewed sense of Indian opulence. His style is about old-world luxury: think Sabyasachi and you think rich *Benarasi* silks and brocades, delicate *zardozi*, and outfits with traditional Indian prints. Sabyasachi brought a new idea of beauty—dark shades, dull gold embroidery, mismatched patchwork, tea-stained hues, and a knowledge of textiles. His subversive aesthetic made him a disruptor, a badge he has worn with great pride in recent years. "I don't see myself as a fashion designer. I am more of a textile designer", says Mukherjee. "I stick to my core value: quality craftsmanship."	"Mass couture" is another fashion disruption by the designer. "I decided early on what my role at the label would be. If I need to sell myself to sell my clothes, what's the point", he says. "I don't believe in customisation. You can't come in with a piece of jewellery and tell us to draw inspiration from it and embroider it onto a lehenga or a sari. We won't do that. We only offer some colours and some combinations, and some changes in arm-length and neckline. My staff has been personally trained by me and they can take care of brides themselves. Other than that, I'm just there to take selfies with them." "This TV show opened a new world for me", he says. "Wide reach and access, yes, but more importantly, it made high-fashion more democratic."	Opulent handloom fabrics by artisans. Over the years, he has employed close to 4500 artisans across India—in West Bengal, Bihar, Orissa, Tamil Nadu, Gujarat, Kashmir—to make exquisite handicrafts with artisanal techniques, the legacy of his brand. In his design factory in New Delhi, Sabyasachi has an in-house team of 900 artisans. "Save the Saree" initiative started by Sabyasachi focuses on giving the saree weavers the price that they deserve. The sarees produced by the weavers are sold under his name and are reasonably priced between INR 2000 and 4000. The funds collected directly go to the weaver's pockets.

(continued)

Table 5.1 (continued)

(Case) Fashion label/founder (geographic location)	Flagship stores and locations	Year founded	Artisanal brand collaborations	Brand portfolio and architecture
(Case 18) **SavioJon** by Savio Jon Fernandes (**Goa**)	The Village Studio Goa	Label in 2000s.	Ramie project 2018	**SavioJon:** womenswear with strong reference to menswear and the deconstruction of the classic shirt; face masks: 100% cotton. Madras Checks Masks S/S 2017 Collection followed a ten-year hiatus.
(Case 19) **Urvashi Kaur** (**Delhi**)	Studio in Sultanpur, Delhi	Label in 2008.	Tatacliq series of aprons in 2020. BoAt consumer electronics brand collaboration during a show at Lakme Fashion week in 2019. Urvashi Kaur designed special accessories of backpacks and suspended head phones.	**Urvashi Kaur:** non-binary, ready-to-wear for women and men, including a new line of festive/ occasion wear. **Kapda:** affordable diffusion line.

Brand story (including artisans)		
Product and influences	Systems around product	Wider company
Likes to blend street wear with avant-garde to make "anti-fit", functional garments. "My design philosophy has always been a nod towards the classic shirt, which is to me: a most simple and complex construction all at once. My fascination with the shirt has led me to explore variations of the t-shirt, tunic and shirt dress whether I am constructing or deconstructing them, or elevating them to some kind of theatrical status." To Savio clothes are not just clothes. They are an emotional understanding between texture, colour, and detail. A bridge between art and fashion that is quite conceptual. "I have always loved the simplicity and clean lines of a sharp collar and cuff. I like to take that and mess it up a bit; manipulate it, deconstruct it." Details like the vintage buttons and trimmings are rare finds from his travels that make each garment feel like a limited edition piece.	Lack of any formal training has helped Savio break the rules of fashion with more ease giving room to further experimentation without compromising on technique. Maintains absolute control by still cutting every piece from his collection. It's about fashion from an organic source using natural cottons, silks, and wax cottons.	Fabrics from organic sources.
The design aesthetic is based on comfort and cosmopolitanism. Re-imagined *salwars*, asymmetric tunics, *kurta* dresses, and cropped blouses are constants in a palette of earthy, muted tones. "The label is tied around versatile separates. When I ideate, I am thinking of the wearer. In how many ways can the clothes be worn? How comfortable are they?" Constant promotion and revival of indigenous Indian weaves and age-old techniques define her design philosophy. The brand has a genre-inclusive philosophy: "I don't follow trends. Doing that is an easy way of getting featured in one publication or another. The fact that there are no rules is beautiful." Her clothes are underscored by airy silhouettes and unconventional shapes. Her travels have been a catalyst in developing a complex body of work that goes beyond fashion and draws inspiration in art and culture.	Use of handwoven textiles is a constant, "Textile is a medium and source, but the aim is fashion. ... It is fashion that excites me." "The creativity in the label is not about what we do, but how we do it." The designs are global in their construction, but defiantly Indian in their sensibility. It attempts to create an economically sustainable and culturally influential brand. She endorses an alternate fashion movement by embracing heritage handwoven, organic textiles and natural dyes.	Long-time collaboration with artisans in Kota, Rajasthan. Frequent incorporation of *leheriya* (traditional Rajasthani tie-dye) and *Ajrakh* (block printing) in the collections. Increasingly establishing relationships with various NGO's by providing employment opportunities to women and promoting the development of handloom.

(*continued*)

Table 5.1 (continued)

(Case) Fashion label/founder (geographic location)	Flagship stores and locations	Year founded	Artisanal brand collaborations	Brand portfolio and architecture
(Case 20) Women Weave (WW) (Indore)	Maheshwar 3 production units: Gudi Mudi; Itawdi; Dindori cottage-production Project (where many weavers work from home)	WomenWeave Charitable Trust in 2002 was established by Sally Holkar with an all-woman board of directors and trustees. Founding vision to help local women lead better lives by ensuring that handloom weaving is a profitable, sustainable, fulfilling, and dignified form of livelihood for them. The Handloom School, established in Maheshwar in 2015 and since extended to other small clusters in Madhya Pradesh and elsewhere in India.	Grew from **REHWA Society** co-founded by Sally Holkar in 1979 to revive Maheshwar's weaving community. Formed on three ideals: to sustain the handweaving traditions of the town of Maheshwar; to empower women weavers by giving them a source of livelihood; to provide housing, healthcare, and education to the weavers and their families. Today, 85% of the weavers working with REHWA Society and WW are women. WW collaborates with freelance designers who in the early days of WW were board members or friends. Also with BioDye natural dye enterprise and native block printers in Bagh.	Handloom textile fabrics and garments including soft cotton handspun, handwoven masks. Each location uses somewhat different techniques and is branded as different collections, for example Dindori products are branded as the **Khat Kata collection** and feature indigenous techniques.

Brand story (including artisans)		
Product and influences	Systems around product	Wider company
WW is dedicated to support slow and sustainable growth; to create a sensitive awareness of handloom's potential; and to continue to build a bright future for our weavers by unlocking handloom's enormous potential in local and global markets. Collections are developed when WW leadership and management team decide they are needed to keep up customer interest and stay fresh. For some years, collections were twice annually, following a spring and fall convention. Brand mission is the "make things better" enterprise; to keep handloom relevant by design developing products that are appealing to fashion consumers and creating a functioning system of making and managing.	The design process—prototyping with combinations of weight, fibre, yarn, colour, pattern, denting, texture, drape, and hand—is normal other than consideration of the low technology and the skills of the weavers. The designers, with the help of the artisans, use a variety of hand tools to visualise designs, but also employ "soft mechanisms" that go with "the textile designer typology". These include sensitivity to and ability to interpret materials, style, trend, and the broad cultural forces that influence taste, and the emotional intelligence to work collaboratively with a range of individuals (Goldsmith 2018:202). "The designers share a similar dedication to WW or admiration for its mission, and *love* handloom: the process, the products, working with weavers, the idea of it" (Goldsmith 2018:132).	While one pillar of WW is the demonstration of production units and projects for spinning and weaving, and a second pillar is education (i.e., The Handloom School), a third pillar is advocacy for handloom weaving, which includes talking with potential clients, but also means being part of a national network of similarly engaged people.

Table 5.2 Indian fashion cases: branding summary

	Brand portfolio				
Case	Occasion-wear	Apparel	Access-ories	Sustain-able sub-brand	Other
1			X		Jewellery
2	X	X	X	X	Jewellery; face masks
3		X	X		Cloth bags (as packaging)
4		X			Cloth bags (as packaging)
5		X			Artworks (embroidered installation panels)
6		X			E-commerce social network
7	X	X			Jewellery
8		X			

Brand architecture		Co-branding	Brand values as proposed by the authors
House of brands (No.)	Single brand		
	X		Hand-crafted; mindful designs
5		Anita Dongre Foundation; Sustainable Apparel Coalition (SAC) beginning 2019 as "Brand & Retailer" Member; Behind the Masks project 2020	Indigenous craft tradition; eco-conscious; sustainability; compassionate; pro-social actions
	X		Indigenous fabrics; Eastern philosophy; contemporised traditional Indian techniques (weaving); mindful design; minimalism
	X		Artisans' collective narrative; slow processes; slow living; sustainability; handwoven textiles; contemporised traditional Indian techniques; sustainable design; minimalism
	X		Eco-friendly crafted; individuality; sustainability; inclusivity; mindful design and buying
	X	With Luskentyre Harris Tweed weavers, Isle of Harris, Scotland since 2011	Hand-crafted; uniqueness; supply chain transparency; social and environmental responsibility
	X	Diamond jewellery with Gehna Jewellers in 2013	Hand-crafted; unique; contemporised traditional Indian crafts and techniques
	X		Minimalism; sustainability; hand-crafted; mindful design

(continued)

Table 5.2 (continued)

	Brand portfolio				
9	X	X	X	X	Curated the first Ramie fibre project produced in Meghalaya, India, for the Indo-French government; face masks
10			X		Homewares
11		X			Art Installations; soft furnishings range
12		X	X		Face masks
13		X	X		Jewellery
14		X			
15		X	X		Jewellery; face masks; cloth bags (as packaging) Péro's "Time to Love" exhibition, in collaboration with India Art Fair held in Delhi in 2020; Inclusion in Indian fabrics and textiles exhibition in London's Victoria and Albert Museum in 2015–2016

Brand architecture		Co-branding	Brand values as proposed by the authors
3			Hand-crafted; quality; unique; contemporised traditional Indian crafts and techniques; sustainable fibres
2			Hand-crafted
	X	Inclusion in monographic exhibition of Indian architect Anupama Kundoo "Taking time" at Louisiana Museum, Denmark (2020–2021); soft furnishings range with architectural design firm in Copenhagen in 2020; *created art installation for Levi's 501 Day, exhibited in Mumbai in 2019*	Ethical; sustainable; hand-crafted; minimalism
3		The Lady Bamford Charitable Trust; The Lady Bamford Foundation; Project Utpal	Hand-crafted; slow fashion; sustainable craft value chains
	X		Painter's prism of colour, line, and proportions; mindful design; holistic sustainability by sourcing and manufacturing responsibly and conscious consumption; pro-social actions
	X	Oppo Reno stories 2020	Hand-crafted; slow fashion; mindful design
3		Grounds—Japanese shoe label; Moonriver Masks 4 All 2020; with performance artist Princess Pea; India Art Fair 2020	Labours of love; attention to detail; Less is More; androgynous; fun; playful; local, effortless Indianness style; wearable; sustainable manufacturing processes; hand embroidery

(*continued*)

Table 5.2 (continued)

	Brand portfolio			
16	X	X		Music; Objects A Raw Mango sari with a particular crow motif is displayed at London's Victoria and Albert Museum; Included in TEXTO 2020 in Mexico, a global gathering organised by Kavita Parmar of 45 heritage craftspeople and designers from 23 countries
17	X	X	X	Jewellery; beauty and fragrances; February 2019, showed in NY as part of Fashion for Peace, a group presentation of conscious design; Designed costumes for movie, *Black*; NDTV channel's popular reality television show *Band Baaja Bride*
18		X	X	Face masks
19	X	X	X	Aprons for increased home cooking due to COVID-19; backpacks and suspended head phones
20		X	X	Handloom fabric lengths; face masks

Brand architecture	Co-branding	Brand values as proposed by the authors
2		Hand-crafted; contemporised traditional Indian crafts and techniques
5	Save the Saree initiative; Bergdorf Goodman-Manhattan's iconic luxury department store in 2020; Isha Foundation in Fashion for Peace NY 2019	Quality craftsmanship; Indian opulence; royal chic (a marriage of regal and bohemian styles); pro-social actions
X		Organic sources; mindful design; contemporised classic shirts; anti-fit
2	Tatacliq series of aprons in 2020; BoAt during a show at Lakme Fashion week in 2019	Hand-crafted; contemporised traditional Indian crafts and techniques; mindful design; sustainable; culturally influential
3	WomenWeave Charitable Trust; REHWA Society; The Handloom School; BioDye natural dye enterprise	Artisanal and sustainable luxury; Indianness; hand-crafted; contemporised traditional Indian crafts and techniques; pro-social actions to make things better

(*continued*)

References

Aakko, M. (2016). *Fashion In-between: Artisanal design and production of fashion*. Aalto University.

Adeyanju, S., Ajilore, O., Ogunlalu, O., Onatunji, A., & Mogaji, E. (2022). *Innovating in the Face of the COVID-19 Pandemic: Case Studies from Nigerian Universities* (pp. 104–120). STAR Scholar Book Series.

Athwal, N., Wells, V. K., Carrigan, M., & Henninger, C. E. (2019). Sustainable luxury marketing: A synthesis and research agenda. *International Journal of Management Reviews, 21*(4), 405–426.

Atwal, G., & Williams, A. (2017). Luxury brand marketing–the experience is everything! In J.-N. Kapferer, J. Kernstock, T. O. Brexendorf, & S. M. Powell (Eds.), *Advances in Luxury Brand Management* (pp. 43–57). Springer.

Bazeley, P. (2009). Analysing qualitative data: More than 'identifying themes. *Malaysian Journal of Qualitative Research, 2*(2), 6–22.

Beard, N. D. (2008). The branding of ethical fashion and the consumer: A luxury niche or mass-market reality? *Fashion Theory, 12*(4), 447–467.

Beverland, M. B. (2011). Slow design. *Design Management Review, 22*(1), 34–42.

Brooksworth, F., Mogaji, E., & Bosah, G. (2022a). Fashion Marketing in Emerging Economies: An Introduction. In F. Brooksworth, E. Mogaji, & G. Bosah (Eds.), *Fashion Marketing in Emerging Economies (Volume 1) – Brand, Consumer and Sustainability Perspectives*. Springer.

Brooksworth, F., Mogaji, E., & Bosah, G. (2022b). Fashion Marketing in Emerging Economies: Conclusion and Research Agenda. In F. Brooksworth, E. Mogaji, & G. Bosah (Eds.), *Fashion Marketing in Emerging Economies (Volume 1) – Brand, Consumer and Sustainability Perspectives*. Springer.

Brandão, A., Sousa, J. C. C., & Rodrigues, C. (2020). A dynamic approach to brand portfolio audit and brand architecture strategy. *European Business Review, 32*(2), 181–210.

British Council. (2016). 'PELLA by Priyanka Ella Lorena Lama'. Retrieved November 24, 2020, from https://design.britishcouncil.org/blog/2016/jan/19/pell-priyanka-ella-lorena-lama/.

Buna. (2020). *About Us*. Retrieved November 20, 2020, from https://www.bunastudio.com/.

Chopra, Y. (2020). 'Aneeth Arora of Péro marks 10 years in fashion with an endearing exhibition', *Vogue India*. Retrieved November 28, 2020, from https://www.vogue.in/fashion/content/aneeth-arora-pero-10-year-anniversary-exhibition-fashion.

Clark, H. (2008). SLOW+ FASHION—an Oxymoron—or a Promise for the Future…? *Fashion Theory, 12*(4), 427–446.

Dabral, A. (2017). In conversation with Payal Khandwala. Retrieved November 26, 2020, from http://www.anupamdabral.com/in-conversation-with-payal-khandwala/.

De Chernatony, L. (2009). Towards the holy grail of defining brand. *Marketing Theory, 9*(1), 101–105.

De Chernatony, L., & Dall'Olmo Riley, F. (1997). Brand consultants' perspectives on the concept of the brand. *Marketing and Research Today, 25*(1), 45–52.

Dezeen. (2019). 'Bodice clothes are for the women "challenging conventions" in Indian society', *Dezeen*. Retrieved November 24, 2020, from https://www.dezeen.com/2019/11/06/bodice-ruchika-sachdeva-fashion-design-india/.

Edwards, L. (2020). 'Friday essay: vizards, face gloves and window hoods - a history of masks in western fashion', *The Conversation*. Retrieved September 13, 2020, from https://theconversation.com/friday-essay-vizards-face-gloves-and-window-hoods-a-history-of-masks-in-western-fashion-143994.

Fletcher, K. (2010). Slow fashion: An invitation for systems change. *Fashion Practice, 2*(2), 259–265.

Gibbs, G. R. (2002). *Qualitative data analysis: Explorations with NVivo*. Open University Press.

Goldsmith, D. (2018). *WomenWeave Daily: "Artisan Fashion" as "Slow and Sustainable Fashion"*. Doctoral Dissertation, University of Borås, Sweden.

Gorman, A. (2020). 'Covid crisis fashion report: 'workers' rights, wellbeing and dignity should not be put on hold', Available: The Guardian. Retrieved October 29, 2020, from https://www.theguardian.com/global-development/2020/oct/28/covid-crisis-fashion-report-workers-rights-wellbeing-and-dignity-should-not-bc-put-on-hold.

Guercini, S., & Runfola, A. (2019). Developing fashion retail operations to growth in emerging markets. *Journal of Global Fashion Marketing, 10*(2), 145–162.

Gupta, A., Purohit, T., & Kapoor, N. (2017). Creating & Managing Customer Value, Satisfaction & Loyalty: An Introspective into India's Luxury Market. In S. K. Reddy & J. K. Han (Eds.), *The Essence of Luxury: An Asian Perspective: LVMH-SMU Luxury Research Conference 2016* (pp. 148–165). Singapore Management University.

Henninger, C. E., Alevizou, P. J., & Oates, C. J. (2016). What is sustainable fashion? *Journal of Fashion Marketing and Management: An International Journal, 20*(4), 400–416.

Henninger, C. E., Alevizou, P. J., & Oates, C. J. (2017). IMC, social media and UK fashion micro-organisations. *European Journal of Marketing, 51*(3), 668–691.

Islam, M. M., Perry, P., & Gill, S. (2021). Mapping environmentally sustainable practices in textiles, apparel and fashion industries: a systematic literature review. *Journal of Fashion Marketing and Management: An International Journal, 25*(2), 331–353.

Jay, P. (2020a). 'Fashion Workers Left Destitute in India', *Business of Fashion Intelligence* [Online article], Available: Business of Fashion. Retrieved October 21, 2020, from https://www.businessoffashion.com/articles/professional/fashion-workers-left-destitute-in-india.

Jay, P. (2020b). 'India's Fashion Industry at a Crossroads', *Business of Fashion Intelligence* [online article], Available: Business of Fashion. Retrieved October 21, 2020, from https://www.businessoffashion.com/articles/intelligence/indian-fashion-makes-its-crisis-pivot.

Joy, A., Sherry, J. F., Jr., Venkatesh, A., Wang, J., & Chan, R. (2012). Fast fashion, sustainability, and the ethical appeal of luxury brands. *Fashion Theory, 16*(3), 273–295.

Jung, S., & Jin, B. (2014). A theoretical investigation of slow fashion: Sustainable future of the apparel industry. *International Journal of Consumer Studies, 38*(5), 510–519.

Kamath, A. (2021). 'The brewing battle between India's two luxury conglomerates', *Vogue Business*. Retrieved March 12, 2021, from https://www.voguebusiness.com/companies/the-brewing-battle-between-indias-two-luxury-conglomerates.

Kaufman, B. (2003). Stories that sell, stories that tell: Effective storytelling can strengthen an organization's bonds with all of its stakeholders. *Journal of Business Strategy, 24*(2), 11–16.

Kaur, J., Mogaji, E., Wadera, D., & Gupta, S. (2022). "Sustainable consumption practices in Indian households: a saga of environment management linked to Indian ethos and generational differences", Society and Business Review, Vol. ahead-of-print No. ahead-of-print. https://doi.org/10.1108/SBR-08-2021-0132

Keller, K. L. (2017). Managing the growth trade-off: Challenges and opportunities in luxury branding. In J.-N. Kapferer, J. Kernstock, T. O. Brexendorf, & S. M. Powell (Eds.), *Advances in Luxury Brand Management* (pp. 179–198). Springer.

Keller, K. L., Sternthal, B., & Tybout, A. (2002). Three questions you need to ask about your brand. *Harvard Business Review, 80*(9), 80–89.

Khaire, M. (2011). The Indian fashion industry and traditional Indian crafts. *Harvard Business History Review, 86*, 345–366.

Khan, S., & Khan, B. M. (2017). Marketing Indian Haute Couture Brands. In S. K. Reddy & J. K. Han (Eds.), *The Essence of Luxury: An Asian Perspective: LVMH-SMU Luxury Research Conference 2016* (pp. 205–228). Singapore Management University.

Kharas, H. (2017). *The unprecedented expansion of the global middle class: An update*. Brookings Institution.

Kim, H., Lee, E.-J., & Hur, W.-M. (2012). The normative social influence on eco-friendly consumer behaviour: The moderating effect of environmental marketing claims. *Clothing Textiles Research Journal, 30*(1), 4–18.

Kim, Y.-K., & Sullivan, P. (2019). Emotional branding speaks to consumers' heart: The case of fashion brands. *Journal of Fashion Textiles, 6*(2), 1–16.

Mladenović, D., Rrustemi, V., & Mogaji, E. (2021). Using COVID-19 vaccination as a resilience strategy for the tourism sector–evidence from Serbia. Current Issues in Tourism, Vol. ahead-of-print No. ahead-of-print. Pp. 1-5. https://doi.org/10.1080/13683500.2021.2018407

Mogaji, E. (2021). *Brand Management*. Palgrave Macmillan.

Mogaji, E., Adeola, O., Hinson, R. E., Nguyen, N. P., Nwoba, A. C., & Soetan, T. O. (2021). Marketing bank services to financially vulnerable customers: evidence from an emerging economy. *International Journal of Bank Marketing, 39*(3), 402–428. https://doi.org/10.1108/IJBM-07-2020-0379

Mogaji, E., & Nguyen, N. P. (2021). Can we brand a pandemic? Should we? The case for corona virus, COVID-19 or SARS-CoV-2. *Journal of Public Affairs, 21*(2), e2546.

Mossberg, L. (2008). Extraordinary experiences through storytelling. *Scandinavian Journal of Hospitality and Tourism, 8*(3), 195–210.

Mukendi, A., Davies, I., Glozer, S., & McDonagh, P. (2020). Sustainable fashion: Current and future research directions. *European Journal of Marketing, 54*(11), 2873–2909.

Mukonza, C., Hinson, R. E., Adeola, O., Adisa, I., Mogaji, E., & Kirgiz, A. C. (2021). Green Marketing: An Introduction. In C. Mukonza, R. E. Hinson, O. Adeola, I. Adisa, E. Mogaji, & A. C. Kirgiz (Eds.), *Green Marketing in Emerging Markets. Palgrave Studies of Marketing in Emerging Economies* (pp. 3–14). Palgrave Macmillan. https://doi.org/10.1007/978-3-030-74065-8_1

Nguyen, P. N., & Mogaji, E. (2022a). Emerging Economies in Fashion Global Value Chain: Brand Positioning and Managerial Implications. In F. Brooksworth, E. Mogaji, & G. Bosah (Eds.), *Fashion Marketing in Emerging Economies – Strategies, Tools and Insights for Fashion Brands* (pp. 234–345). Springer.

Nguyen, N. P., & Mogaji, E. (2022b). A Theoretical Framework for the Influence of Green Marketing Communication on Consumer Behaviour in Emerging Economies. In E. Mogaji, O. Adeola, I. Adisa, R. E. Hinson, C. Mukonza, & A. C. Kirgiz (Eds.), *Green Marketing in Emerging Economies. Palgrave Studies of Marketing in Emerging Economies* (pp. 253–274). Palgrave Macmillan. https://doi.org/10.1007/978-3-030-82572-0_11

Nguyen, P., & Mogaji, E. (2021a). Brand Development through Sustainability Certifications in Emerging Markets: Adoption of B Corporation Certification in Vietnam. In O. Adeola, R. Hinson, & A. Sakkthivel (Eds.), *Marketing Communications and Brand Development in Emerging Markets* (pp. 34–45). Palgrave.

Nguyen, N. P., & Mogaji, E. (2021b). Financial Inclusion for Women in the Informal Economy: An SDG Agenda Post Pandemic. In O. Adeola (Ed.), *Gendered Perspectives on Covid-19 Recovery in Africa*. Palgrave Macmillan. https://doi.org/10.1007/978-3-030-88152-8_12

Oppo. (2020). *oppo.com*: OPPO. Retrieved November 23, 2020, from https://www.oppo.com/en/about/.

Ott, R., & Cukier, W. (2013). 'Artisanal fashion design: Entrepreneurs on thinking, process, and decision making'. *International Textile and Apparel Association (ITAA) Annual Conference Proceedings*.

Payne, A. (2014). Spinning a sustainable yarn: Environmental sustainability and brand story in the Australian fashion industry. *International Journal of Fashion Studies, 1*(2), 185–208.

Pedersen, E. R. G., & Andersen, K. R. (2015). Sustainability innovators and anchor draggers: A global expert study on sustainable fashion. *Journal of Fashion Marketing and Management, 19*(3), 315–327.

Phau, I., & Ong, D. (2007). An investigation of the effects of environmental claims in promotional messages for clothing brands. *Marketing Intelligence and Planning, 25*(7), 772–788.

Ritter, E. (2020). 'On masks and wearing them', *Instagram*. Retrieved September 13, 2020, from https://www.instagram.com/p/B7CDivfJPZJ/?utm_source=ig_embed.

Silverstein, M. J., & Fiske, N. (2003). Luxury for the masses. *Harvard Business Review, 81*(4), 48–59.

Stella McCartney Ltd. (2020). 'Eco Impact Report 2020'. Retrieved March 12, 2021, from https://www.stellamccartney.com/cloud/smcwp/uploads/2020/09/EcoImpact_2020.pdf.

Strand of Silk. (n.d.). 'Pero by Aneeth Arora'. Available: Strand of Silk. Retrieved November 23, 2020, from strandofsilk.com/designer/pero-aneeth-arora.

Tewari, B. (2019). 'Sabyasachi Mukherjee: King of India's Bridal Market', *Business of Fashion*. Retrieved November 20, 2020, from https://www.businessoffashion.com/articles/global-markets/sabyasachi-mukherjee-king-of-indias-bridal-market.

Thakur, A., & Ghosh, D. (2019). 'In Sabyasachi Mukherjee's lab of luxury', *Fortune India*. Retrieved November 20, 2020, from https://www.fortuneindia.com/people/in-sabyasachi-mukherjees-lab-of-luxury/103095 (Accessed 20 November 2020).

The Business of Fashion and McKinsey & Company. (2019). *The State of Fashion 2019.*

The Business of Fashion and McKinsey & Company. (2020a). *The State of Fashion 2020.*

The Business of Fashion and McKinsey & Company. (2020b) *The State of Fashion 2020: Coronavirus Update.*

The Business of Fashion and McKinsey & Company. (2020c) *The State of Fashion 2021 Report: Finding Promise in Perilous Times.*

Varma, M. (2015). *Making Designs on Fashion: Producing Contemporary Indian Aesthetics.* Doctoral Dissertation, UCLA (University of California, Los Angeles).

Woodside, A. G., & Fine, M. B. (2019). Sustainable fashion themes in luxury brand storytelling: The sustainability fashion research grid. *Journal of Global Fashion Marketing, 10*(2), 111–128.

Yin, R. K. (1981). The case study crisis: Some answers. *Administrative Science Quarterly, 26*(1), 58–65.

Yin, R. K. (1994). *Case study research: Design and methods* (2nd ed.). Sage.

Part III

Fashion Marketing in Emerging Economies: African Perspectives

6

Towards Understanding How Nigerian Fashion Brands Influence Customer Purchasing Behaviour. A Case Study of Nigerian Fashion Brands

Damilola Joseph

Introduction

In Western countries, the fashion industry has witnessed changes in the buying behaviour of consumers based on trends and fads seeing as fashion consumption has been based on fashion seasons (Tyler, Heeley, and Bhamra, 2006), and fast fashion (Christopher et al., 2004). However, in heterogeneous and ethnically fragmented societies like Nigeria, consumer buying behaviour is influenced by a myriad of factors because of cultural and ethnic diversity and religious differences (Farrag & Hassan, 2015; Briliana & Mursito, 2017; Islam & Chandrasekaran, 2019), and the dynamic macro-environmental factors like changes in the political and economic environment. As such, it is imperative to study the Nigerian fashion industry and how fashion brands influence consumer buying behaviour within a highly fragmented society.

D. Joseph (✉)
Lecturer in Business, Teesside University, Middlesbrough, UK
e-mail: D.Joseph@tees.ac.uk

F. Brooksworth et al. (eds.), *Fashion Marketing in Emerging Economies Volume II*, Palgrave Studies of Marketing in Emerging Economies,
https://doi.org/10.1007/978-3-031-07078-5_6

In recent years the Nigerian fashion industry has grown rapidly over the years in size and sophistication, attracting global attention. Euromonitor International suggests that the sub-Saharan fashion market is worth $31 billion, with Nigeria alone accounting for 15% of that ($4.7 billion) (Akinsola, 2019; Chege, 2019). Also, Nigerian designs have received increased global presence and exposure over the years, having been featured in fashion shows and designs across the world (Akutu, 2019). For instance, the GT Bank Fashion Week focuses on showcasing African fashion to a more global audience and succeeded accordingly in that regard. The textile, apparel, and footwear sub-sectors remain the second largest contributor to Nigeria's manufacturing sector (after food, beverages, and tobacco). It posted the total output of N799 bn (US$2.6 bn) in Q3 2018 or 22% of the country's manufacturing GDP. Although Nigeria has a huge appetite for fashion, textile manufacturers struggle with limited capacity in clothing production, poor patronage, and meagre purchasing power (FBNQuest, 2019).

Although some research on the purchasing behaviour of fashion consumers exists, important gaps still remain. While studies have examined the impact of the physical environment on consumer purchasing behaviour (Chang & Chen, 2008; Sherman et al., 1997), the impact of emotional components on purchasing behaviour is yet to be fully explored (Martin et al., 2008; Shaw & Ivens, 2002; Smith & Wheeler, 2002; Yalch & Spangenberg, 2000). Research on consumer purchasing mostly outlines purchasing behaviour from the consumer perspective, the customer cognitive psychology, and the decision-making process (Dias, 2003; Foxall, 2004; Loken, 2006; Perry & Kyriakaki, 2014; Schmitt, 2012; Zhong & Mitra, 2020). Very few studies have examined fashion brands and their role in influencing consumers' buying decisions. Studies have highlighted the limitation of the customer psychology perspective because of its focus on the overall consumption and acquisition processes (Nguyen & Mogaji, 2022b; Parker et al., 2016; Pham, 2013). This chapter intends to contribute to research by examining how fashion brands influence consumers' purchasing behaviour (Brooksworth et al., 2022a, 2022b).

Specifically, this study provides new insights into consumer buying decisions in the fashion industry in Nigeria. In doing so, it explores how fashion brands develop their marketing mix and how it affects their marketing strategies in the sub-Saharan African country. We address how Nigerian fashion brands influence consumer buying behaviour, an important area that needs to be explored. This study contributes to the literature by investigating how Nigerian fashion brands influence the consumer buying behaviour of female consumers. The novelty of this study lies in the Nigerian context that is utilized. Attention is drawn to the contextual influences (Elsner & Schwardt, 2015; Ojong & Simba, 2020; Smallbone et al., 2014; Welter, 2012) in the country and its impact on the influence Nigerian fashion brands have on consumer buying behaviour. This study contributes to the literature on consumer buying behaviour by exploring a non-mainstream context and acknowledging a fragmented and heterogeneous context (Ojong & Simba, 2020; Welter, 2012, p. 193).

In the following sections, we will consider the factors that can influence consumer purchasing decisions as well as previous studies conducted in the literature. We will then discuss the methods and specifics of the case that was evaluated. We will conclude by assessing the findings of the study concerning the literature.

Literature Review

Nature of the Nigerian Fashion Industry

The Nigerian fashion industry has been influenced by political, economic, and socio-cultural factors. In the 1960s, the Nigerian fashion industry was heavily swayed by the European style of fashion; women's fashion particularly consisted of fitted and oversized silhouettes and miniskirts. Nigeria was under colonial rule at the time and striving for cultural and economic independence from the British Rule (Langevang, 2016). The use of local fabrics and dress practices to express African pride and cultural identity was common (Rovine, 2010). For instance, the Yoruba women wore *iro* and *buba*, tied *gele* on their heads with *ipele* over their shoulders (Adeleke, 2018). A prominent designer during that time who was credited with the introduction of ready-to-wear clothes in Nigeria was Shade Thomas Fahn (Jennings, 2015). She was a

'Western-trained African designer'; who trained at Central Saint Martins, London (Langevang, 2017; Jennings, 2015; Rovine, 2010). She launched the *Shade's Boutique* chain where she modernized traditional African garments. Her designs consist of pre-tied *gele,* turning *iro* and *buba* into a zip-up wrapper skirt and turning men's *agbada* into women's embroidered *boubou*" (Jennings, 2011, p. 7), in which she catered to the Nigerian elites, royalty, and professional women (Jennings, 2011).

In the 1970s, Nigeria had transitioned from colonial rule to military rule. Under the administration of General Olusegun Obasanjo, protectionist policies were introduced and implemented, like the ban on the importation of ready-made clothes, to give room for local production and consumption (Oyejide, Ogunkole, and Bankole, 2005). This led to the rise of designers like Lanre Ogunlesi of *Sofisticat* (Kreglex, 2016). This ban also drove the demand for indigenous wears like *oleku,* oversized sleeves with high-waist wrappers that stopped at knee length (Kreglex, 2016).

The 1980s also witnessed the influence of European style on West African fashion; people began to sew English-styled dresses from *aso-oke*: skirt suits for ladies, trousers with a short-sleeved jacket for men, and a host of other atypical styles (Agbadudu & Ogunrin, 2006; Kreglex, 2016). The popular designers around these times were Folorunsho Alakija of *Supreme Stitches* and Princess Abah Folawiyo of *Labenella Creations.* Alakija's fashion brand catered for up-scale and elites of Nigeria, like wives of politicians, royals, and wives of the military officers (Siun, Akinyoade & Quaye, 2017; Kreglex, 2016). Princess Abah Folawiyo created designs that clothed top celebrities in Nigeria; she was famous for designing President Olusegun Obasanjo's agbada (Daigbare, 2016). Labella's creations targeted clothing for plus-sized African women, and these designs include kaftans, culottes, and many others (Kreglex, 2016).

In the 1990s, Nigeria witnessed a crisis in its political and military landscapes. There was a power shift from the 21-year military rule to a democratically elected government (Sesay and Ukeje, 1997; Onishi, 2001). This period was a tumultuous time for Nigerians as there was the annulment of the 1993 election, the death of the winner Moshood Abiola, and the hanging of activists like Ken Saro Wiwa and nine others under the administration of General Abacha (Sesay and Ukeje, 1997).

The civil unrest during this period led to a high rate of emigration of Nigerians including many fashion designers such as Ade Bakare Coutour and Deola Sagoe who were then in their prime. Ade Bakare's designs displayed his use of historic Yoruba textiles and design techniques to complement gowns and dresses, making them more African in style than Western (Jean, 2015), while Adeola Sagoe's haute couture designs cater to the needs of Nigerian elites. The former operated from abroad and the latter worked in Nigeria. In the 2000s, the Nigerian political system had successfully transformed from military rule to democratic rule.

In 2015, the Nigerian economy, like many others, was greatly affected by the fall in global oil prices, being an oil producer and exporter of crude oil. In turn, the stock market lost $10.5 billion as investors were wary of the "heightened risk environment" and dumped their stocks (Kazeem, 2016). According to the National Bureau of Statistics, the constant basic price of the Nigerian GDP reduced in the second quarter of 2016 by 2.06% after shrinking by 0.36% in the first quarter of 2016. Annual inflation reached 17.1% in July 2016 from 16.5% in June, while food inflation witnessed an increase from 15.3% to 15.8% (National Bureau of Statistics, 2016; Gabriel et al., 2016). In addition to this economic downturn, the Naira fell drastically to an abysmal rate of 423 Naira to 1 dollar. This only further fuelled the rapid devaluation of the Nigerian currency (Omoh et al., 2016).

The crippling oil prices caused by reduced demand together with the diminishing foreign exchange earnings prompted President Buhari to respond by introducing 'unorthodox' fiscal policies such as restricting the use of Nigerian debit cards abroad to prevent the depletion of Dollar reserves (Kazeem, 2016). Due to the limited success of these policies, Nigerian lawmakers and government officials led a social media campaign with the Twitter hashtag *#BuyNaijaToGrowTheNaira*, aimed at encouraging Nigerians to patronize local products to save the Naira and the Nigerian economy and in turn, stir patriotism amongst the Nigerian populace (Kazeem, 2016). As a consequence, the campaign encouraged people to wear Nigerian brands as a means of promoting the local fashion industry. For example, Nigerian author, Chimamanda Ngozi Adichie, posted on her Facebook page that she intended to wear Nigerian designs to most of her public appearances to actively promote made-in-Nigeria products in support of the 'Buy Nigeria to grow Nigeria' campaign. This campaign resulted in increased collaborations and partnerships between Nigerian fashion designers, artists, actors, and fashion influencers to promote the Nigerian Economy and encourage a sense of national pride.

Consumer Purchase Behaviour

Scholars have conceptualized various definitions of consumer behaviour. Some definitions have examined consumer behaviour as a process (Cai & Xu, 2006; Foxall, 1993; Harrison et al., 2006; Swarbrooke & Horner, 2007) while others examine its outcome (Armstrong et al., 2020). Consumer buying behaviour refers to the "buying behaviour of final consumers—individuals and households that buy goods and services for personal consumption" (Armstrong et al., 2019). From a European perspective, "consumer behaviour is the study of the processes involved when individuals or groups select, purchase, use or dispose of products, services, ideas or experiences to satisfy needs and desires" (Bamossy et al. 2006, p. 6).

There are multidisciplinary perspectives of consumer purchasing behaviour in psychology, sociology, and economics. According to neoclassical economic theory, consumers are rational and, as such, maximize their utility based on a cost–benefit analysis of price and product scarcity (or availability) (Tversky & Kahneman, 1980; Baines et al., 2016). In line with this school of thought, consumers make purchases when the functional benefit of an offering outweighs the costs (Baines et al., 2016). However, this perspective has been criticized by other scholars who argue that consumers' actions are inconsistent with economic theory (Foxall, 2009; Thaler, 1980). Other scholars have alluded to the individualistic approach of the rational perspective of consumer behaviour as it is based on a consumer's mental state and the impacts it has on their actions (Satz & Ferejohn, 1994). In contrast, the socio-psychological school of thought is based on the assumption that buying behaviour is influenced by the emotions and feelings of the consumers (Baines et al., 2016). Several empirical studies have alluded to the role of emotions in consumer behaviour (Bagozzi et al., 1999; Cohen et al., 2006; Erevelles, 1998; Escalas & Stern, 2003; Laros & Steenkamp, 2005; Peck & Wiggins, 2006; Watson & Spence, 2007).

Several factors influence consumer purchasing behaviour. These factors consist of cultural, social, personal, and psychological characteristics (Kotler & Armstrong, 2020). Culture can be defined as a set of beliefs, values, and behaviours that are learned from and conditioned by family and society to guide the way of life of a group of people (Kotler & Armstrong, 2020). Hofstede defined culture as the collective programming of a group of people. The concept of culture is a broad and encompassing concept that requires demystification for further understanding. Within a culture, there exist sub-cultures and ethnic groups, which consist of a group of people who share a similar language, religion, and an ontological perspective in how they view the world. Empirical studies (Cakanlar & Nguyen, 2019; He & Wang, 2015; Kacen & Lee, 2002; Kim et al., 2002; McCort & Malhotra, 1993; Miao et al., 2019; Sethi & Chawla, 2014) have alluded to the role of culture on consumer behaviour.

Another factor that influences consumer purchasing behaviour is social class. Social class is defined as "society's relatively permanent and ordered divisions whose members share similar values, interests and behaviour" (Armstrong & Kotler, 2020, p. 164). Social factors have been argued to influence consumer purchasing behaviour such as consumer groups and social networks, family and social roles, and status. Reference groups "consist of direct or indirect points of comparison or reference in forming a person's attitude or group" (Armstrong & Kotler, 2020, p. 165). Organizations employ the use of influencers, opinion leaders, and word-of-mouth influence on consumer purchase behaviour.

Review of Previous Research on the Nigerian Fashion Industry

Over the last decade, there has been a dearth of research examining the Nigerian fashion industry and consumer behaviour. However, in recent years, a few scholars have begun to examine the design and development of Nigerian brands (Adelaja et al., 2016; Agbadudu & Ogunrin, 2006); fashion consumption behaviour of Southeast Nigeria (Agu & Onuoba, 2016); Entrepreneurship (Fasinu, 2020) and distribution channels and internalization (Ogunrin & Inegbenebor, 2015). Due to the significance of the Nigerian fashion industry to the country's economy and to the global market, it is important to examine the Nigerian fashion industry and contribute to research on fashion in the developing economy.

A few studies have begun to examine the purchase decision of Nigerian customers in the fashion industry. For example, Uzo et al.'s (2018) study examined the characteristics of African buyers purchasing behaviour in Nigeria, Kenya, and South Africa. Findings from their research revealed that African buyers purchase mainly consumables for household consumption, price bargaining, and local culture. Similarly, Agu and Onuoba's (2016) study measures the extent of the relationship between psychological influences and fashion consumption behaviour of consumers in Southeast Nigeria. Findings from the study revealed fashion consumers value product fitting in a fashion purchase decision.

Previous studies examining purchasing decisions of fashion customers have also employed diverse research designs in an attempt to answer their research questions. For instance, Anu and Onuoha (2016) employed the use of quantitative research and multiple regression analysis as a data analysis technique to investigate the purchase decisions of fashion customers. Other studies also employed the use of qualitative research to investigate purchasing behaviour (Uzo et al., 2018). This study has contributed to the literature on customer purchasing behaviour in Nigeria. However, the use of the case study approach of Nigerian fashion brands like *Lisa Folawiyo*, *Lanre Da Silva*, and *Grey Velvet* will reveal new knowledge and provide a new perspective towards understanding how fashion brands in Nigeria influence the purchasing decisions of Nigeria female consumers between the ages of 18 and 35. A case study analysis provides in-depth analysis, interpretation, and discussion of the research problem and provides recommendations for improving existing problems.

To answer the research question, a plethora of studies have applied various methodological approaches. Studies have adopted quantitative research methods (Ünal et al., 2019; Valaei & Nikhashemi, 2017; Choi et al., 2012; O'cass, 2020); mixed methods (Morgan & Birtwistle, 2009); and qualitative research methods (Grant & Stephen, 2005; Nash, 2019). Although these studies have laid a foundation towards understanding consumer purchasing behaviour, a case study analysis will reveal a new way of approaching the research problem and offer a perspective that points to the need for additional research.

Within the literature, gaps can be observed. Firstly, studies analysing consumer purchasing behaviour have examined the perspective of the customers methodologically towards answering the research question. Understanding how fashion brands influence the purchasing behaviour of women will offer a new dimension to the literature from a developing country's perspective. The literature on fashion marketing and purchasing behaviour has focused on more developed economies like the UK and the US—countries that have a high purchasing power due to customers with disposable income. Understanding how fashion brands influence the purchasing behaviour of millennials within the 21–35 age group in emerging economies will contribute towards an understanding of the research problem from a different macroeconomic context.

Methodology

The nature of the social reality of this study is relativist ontology. Relativist Ontology is based on the assumption that there exist multiple socially constructed realities ungoverned by natural laws (Guba & Lincoln, 1994; Kaur et al., 2022). Relativist ontology excludes the possibility of a 'true' construction. There is no objective world or truth; everything is relative and created by social beings (Eisenhardt, 1989; Guba & Lincoln, 1994).

The epistemological position of this research is an interpretive paradigm. This paradigm emphasizes the need for social context, human complexity, and how people understand their social phenomenon (Orlikowski & Baroudi, 1991). The interpretive view suggests that meanings are constructed by human beings as they engage with the world they are interpreting (Orlikowski & Baroudi, 1991). This study adopts the interpretivist stance because this research does not aim to test hypotheses and is not involved in law-like generalization.

This study adopts the qualitative research method to answer the research questions. Case studies tend to focus on qualitative data using methods such as interviews, observations, and analysis of primary and secondary sources (e.g., newspaper articles, photographs, and official records). In this study, qualitative data sources consist of multiple case study analyses of interviews, websites, and social media of Nigerian fashion brands like *Jewel by Lisa*, *Orange Culture*, and *Nkwo Onwuka*.

The sampling strategy adopted in this study is the Theoretical/Purposive sampling strategy. This study is not interested in randomly selecting case studies or samples that do not allow us to answer the research question. Thus, "the goal of theoretical sampling is to choose cases which are likely to replicate or extend the emergent theory. In contrast, traditional, within-experiment hypothesis-testing studies rely on statistical sampling, in which researchers randomly select the sample from the population" (Eisenhardt, 1989, p. 537). The data analysis technique that is employed in this research is the thematic analysis technique by Braun and Clarke (2006).

Findings

Product

A consistent theme that has emerged from the analysis of the case studies was that Nigerian fashion brands when designing clothes incorporate the African design and their own cultural identity and philosophy into the product development process. In the development of their clothes, a lot of these products are sourced, inspired, and designed from the culture, ethnicity, and hometown of the fashion brand owners. The culture and history of the designer are also deeply embedded in the creation and development of the fashion brand.

> *When I'm designing a collection, it's usually what I know, who I am. I have lived in Nigeria, grown up in Nigeria even though my father is from Ogbomosho and my mother is from West Indian, this is who I am. Everything I put into what I make, is all of me, it's my culture, it's my history and everything that I am. (Lisa Folawiyo).*

There has been an increased interest and trend for Africans, both within the continent and in the diaspora, to connect with their roots and use fashion to express their identity, support local entrepreneurs, and increase export and production. In Nigeria, consumer fashion choices have been heavily influenced by European fashion and style, and this has, in effect, influenced consumers' purchasing behaviour over the years. However, changes in the political, economic, and socio-economic environment have led to an increase in demand for fashion with bold African prints and designs. For example, the release of the movie Black Panther in 2019 led Africans across the globe to express a deep sense of pride in their identities and roots rather than the eurocentric outlook that has long been embedded in the psyche of Africans and people of African descent. This renaissance led to an increased interest in clothes with African designs, prints, and jewellery as a form of self- and political expression. As a result, the consumption of African fashion has gone beyond fashion consumption as a fad or trend but one that connects to the ideology, philosophy, and sense of self and how they construct their reality, which will influence how they think, feel, and perceive, thus influencing their purchasing behaviour.

Culture can be defined as the total way of life of a group of people. Culture has a role in how individuals construct their reality and how they view themselves (Geertz, 1996). Ethnic identity, on the other hand, is defined "as the shared identity of people based on a common historical background, ancestry, and knowledge of identifying symbolic elements such as nationality, religious affiliation, and language" (Chattaraman & Lennon, p. 520). Several studies on consumer research have investigated the relationship between ethnicity and consumer consumption (Deshpande et al., 1986; Stayman & Deshpande, 1989; Koslow et al., 1994; Donthu & Cherian, 1994; Kim & Kang, 2001; Ogden et al., 2004; Chung & Fischer, 1999; Burton 2010; Huang et al., 2013).

The identity theory involves the reflexivity of self, a situation whereby an individual sees themselves as an object that can be categorized or classified about a social group (Stets & Burke, 2000). Social identity perspective occurs when individuals categorize themselves as part of a group and form their perspectives in alignment with the norms of the group (Hogg, 2016). These cognitive processes individuals go through are segmented into depersonalization and self-verification (Hogg, 2016; Stets & Burke, 2000). Depersonalization is the cognitive process whereby individuals do not see themselves as people, but rather as part of a group and follow the norms and act following those norms. Self-verification is a situation whereby individuals try to ensure consistency in maintaining the standards of the group via role-playing and acting to portray their identity (Hogg, 2016; Stets & Burke, 2000).

Consumers have moved from consuming fashion as part of a trend to developing deep ideological meaning and relationships with fashion that is a part of their self-identity and self-philosophy. This identity and philosophy could be based on psychological factors like ethnicity, religion, and sustainability, which give an individual a sense of purpose, self-actualization, and acceptance within a particular society (Nguyen & Mogaji, 2021a). Identity can be defined as "any category label to which a consumer self-associates either by choice or endowment" (Reed II et al., 2012, p. 312). Identities can be categorized based on "objective membership groups", "culturally determined membership groups and abstracted role ideas" (Reed II et al., 2012).

Empirical studies have examined the influence of identity on fashion purchase and consumption. For instance, Grine and Saeed's (2017) study analysed the motivation influencing women to wear a hijab. Findings from the study revealed that women wore the hijab for religious obligations rather than for fashion purposes (Lindridge, 2005; Saeed et al., 2020). This is in alignment with the literature on ethical and sustainable fashion where purchasing behaviour is made based on ethical commitment and ethical values (Joshi & Rahman, 2015; Joy et al., 2012; Khare, 2015; Niinimäki, 2010). Other studies have examined the role of cultural identity on fashion purchasing behaviour (Miller-Spillman et al., 2016; Noble & Ang, 2018). For example, Chattaraman and Lennon's (2008) study in the US investigated whether ethnic consumers' consumption of cultural apparel and attributional responses related to their consumption is predicted by their strength of ethnic identification. Findings from their analysis revealed that ethnic identification was a significant predictor of cultural apparel consumption. Similarly, a qualitative study by Gbadamosi (2015) in the UK showed the role of cultural and psychological factors in the consumption decision of ethnic minority consumers and highlighted the role of symbolic consumption for acceptance. This is in line with previous research on the impact of ethnic identification on the consumption of ethnic-inspired apparel (Forney & Rabolt, 1985–1986; Kim & Arthur, 2003).

Price

One of the critical challenges that Nigerian fashion brands face is pricing which, in effect, influences the purchasing behaviour of customers in Nigeria. Several internal and external factors influence pricing amongst fashion brands. The first internal factor is the cost of production. Secondly, the sector is also plagued by institutional constraints and a lack of government in the form of grants, funds, and loans. Despite the impact of the Nigerian fashion industry on the GDP and the high level of demand for luxury fashion in Nigeria, a lack of support and institutional factors also influence the increase in price and the lack of accessibility to luxury fashion brands by Nigerian women.

The lack of institutional support implies that Nigerian fashion brands embrace the use of cost-based pricing, 'which involves setting prices based on the costs of producing, distributing, and selling the product plus a fair rate of return for the company's effort and risk'. This however affects customers' decision-making because of a lack of disposable income and low purchase behaviour, which could affect customer acquisition and retention (Shin et al., 2012).

Promotion

Nigerian fashion brands effectively advertise their products through fashion shows like the *Lagos Fashion and Design Week* and the *GTBank Fashion Weekend* where they engage in competitive advertising and showcase their brand's features, originality, and functionality to their target audience. Though this is effective in ensuring market penetration and showcasing the features and distinctiveness of the brand, the market penetration might not be effective for the Nigerian middle and lower class.

Secondly, Nigerian fashion brands employ the use of social media influencers to promote their fashion designs. For instance, fashion designer Lanre Da Silva utilized popular Big Brother Nigeria contestant, Erica, as her fashion brand ambassador. Also, Nigerian fashion brands employ the use of existing fashion influencers based in Nigeria as part of their social media marketing. For instance, Nigerian ready-to-wear brand *Myt5s*, a contemporary female apparel brand *Adey Soile*, a custom-made womenswear brand *Fablanebyderin*, and a women's wear fashion designer *Toju Foye* collaborate with millennial fashion influencer/actress Ini-Dima Okojie to promote their brand to young millennial and gen Z women.

Nigerian designers also promote their designs across the domestic shores using Hollywood actors, writers, and politicians to pay tribute to the African heritage, promote Nigerian brands across the domestic shores, and influence the buying decisions of consumers across Nigeria. For instance, Rihanna was the first celebrity to wear an Ankara-printed shirt in 2014 during President Obama's second term (Toure, 2019). Similarly, we have Nigerian writer, Chimamanda Ngozi Adichie collaborating with Nigerian designers like *Fia Factory*, *Grey*, and *Ladunni Lambo* to wear Nigerian-made clothes for identity and political reasons. She states, "this project is an act of benign nationalism, a paean to peaceful self-sufficiency, a gesture towards what is still possible; it is my uncomplicated act for complicated times" (Financial Times, 2017). These collaborations and partnerships could influence consumer buying behaviours of female consumers who aspire to be like Chimamanda and Ngozi Okonjo Iweala in Nigeria and across the domestic shores.

The use of influencers and opinion leaders have been employed by various organizations because of their exposure to relevant media, being peer groups of the target market, they aim to influence (Baines, 2019). Chan and Misra's (1990) discriminant analysis revealed the varied characteristics of an opinion leader, as public individuation, product familiarity, and personal involvement. They are also referred to as influencers; Enke and Borchers (2019, p. 261) define a social media influencer as "third-party actors who have established a significant number of relevant relationships with a specific quality to influence organizational stakeholders through content production, content distribution, interaction, and personal appearance on the social web".

People who are publicly individuated differ from others based on their actions and behaviour, which results in public attention (Chan & Misra, 1990; Cho et al., 2012). This public differentiation gives the positive impression that the individual is unique in their identity and individuality (Chan & Misra, 1990). Opinion leaders who can stand out and differentiate themselves from others would be able to successfully disseminate information about the brand to others, thus, increase market penetration (Baines, 2019; Chan & Misra, 1990). Secondly, an opinion leader must be very knowledgeable and familiar with the product they are selling, because the level of knowledge and information possessed will impact the quality of information that is disseminated to the target audience (Chan & Misra, 1990). Empirical studies show opinion leadership affects consumers' intention to follow the influencer's advice (Casalo, Flavian & Ibanez-Sanchez, 2020; Jiménez-Castillo & Sánchez-Fernández, 2019).

Studies have found that social media influence led to positive consumer behavioural outcomes (Ki & Kim, 2019; Lim et al., 2017; Silva et al., 2020) like trust and brand engagement (Delbaere et al., 2020), and influence perception of information credibility and decision-making (Cooley & Parks-Yancy, 2019). Despite the positive implications of social media marketing through the use of influencers, there exists a dark side of social media influencing that could affect the consumption of fashion brands in Nigeria (Baccarela et al., 2018; Scheinbaum, 2017). According to the theory of persuasion knowledge, the use of social media influencers has also been posed to have "inference of manipulative intent", which has negative effects on the perception of trustworthiness and corporate reputation (Doney & Cannon, 1997; Guo & Main, 2012; Walsh et al., 2009; Xie & Peng, 2009). Empirical studies show that customers may be deceptively exposed to purchasing from a fashion brand because of the influencer and observing a discrepancy between what was promoted via social media influencers and what was bought (Mavlanova et al., 2008; Mukonza et al., 2021). Social media influencers may also be perceived as not acting in the best interest of their consumers since they have been paid endorsement fees (Liljander et al., 2015; Gökerik et al. (2018)), and thus, we experience a lack of authenticity (Audrezet et al., 2018).

Conclusion

This chapter contributes to research on ethnicity and consumer purchasing behaviour by examining how Nigerian fashion brands influence the psychological choices of their target audience. A limitation of this study is its lack of scientific rigour which makes it impossible to generalize this study to a wider population. Issues of generalizability occur because of the focus on a single unit. However, this focus on a single unit enables a rich description and knowledge of the phenomena and advances the knowledge base of the area (Nguyen & Mogaji, 2022a; Reis, 2009; Stake, 2005).

Another limitation of the case study research includes issues of validity and reliability. Due to the subjectivity and role of the researcher's interpretations of the case, the problem of bias could occur. Hamil (1993, p. 23) states that case study research "lacks rigor in the collection, construction, and analysis of empirical materials that give rise to the study". This argument has been countered by other scholars who argue based on the strength of case study research and the difference in the "ideology, epistemology and methodology" it presents (Reis, 2009).

Another limitation of this research is its reliance on qualitative data sources from verbal reports like personal interviews with fashion designers. The use of other data sources like quantitative data would have enabled the means of 'perceptual triangulation' and provided a much fuller picture of the case at study.

The implication of the issues raised in this study is manifold. Firstly, government institutions in Nigeria have to make a significant investment in the fashion industry to reduce the cost of production for fashion designers in Nigeria. As much as this chapter has examined the role of fashion brands and their influence on consumer purchasing behaviour by influencing the self-identity of consumers through the use of African designs, more has to be done to ensure that the consumer can purchase Nigerian fashion brands by investing financially into the sector. Secondly, macroeconomic factors like an increase in the exchange rate, price inflation, level of disposable income, and government policies have affected consumer purchase behaviour.

To further advance research on fashion marketing in developing countries like Nigeria, we recommend studies that measure the extent to which African designs influence the self-identity of Nigerian women (Nguyen & Mogaji, 2021b). Also, future research should be undertaken on consumer behaviour across different ethnic groups in Nigeria. Due to the heterogeneity and highly fragmented market, understanding the diverse behaviours across multi-ethnic groups will help advance understanding of consumer behaviour in a highly fragmented society. In addition, future studies should examine the dark side of influencer or digital marketing in developing countries with a lack of respect for rule of law and a low deficit of trust.

References

Adelaja, O., Salusso, C. J., & Black, C. (2016). Design and development of western-style Nigerian apparel. *International Journal of Fashion Design, Technology, and Education, 9*(3), 169–175.

Agbadudu, A. B., & Ogunrin, F. O. (2006). Aso-oke: A Nigerian classic style and fashion fabric. *Journal of Fashion Marketing and Management, 10*(1), 97–113.

Agu, A. G., & Onuoba, O. A. (2016). Psychological influences and fashion consumption behavior of consumers in Southeast Nigeria. *International Journal of Research, 38*, 1.

Akinsola, W. (2019). The state of the Nigerian Fashion Industry. Retrieved December 2, 2020, from https://www.stearsng.com/article/the-state-of-nigerias-fashion-industry#:~:text=The%20global%20fashion%20industry%20isof%20that%20(%244.7%20billion).

Akutu, G. (2019). Awaiting gains of Nigeria's Multi-billion Naira Fashion Industry. Retrieved December 2, 2020, from https://guardian.ng/sunday-magazine/awaiting-gains-of-nigerias-multi-billion-naira-fashion-industry/.

Armstrong, G., Kotler, P., & Opresnik, M. O. (2020). *Marketing: An introduction*. Pearson. Hallow England.

Audrezet, A., De Kerviler, G., & Moulard, J. G. (2018). Authenticity under threat: When social media influencers need to go beyond self-presentation. *Journal of Business Research, 117*, 557–569.

Bagozzi, R. P., Gopinath, M., & Nyer, P. U. (1999). The role of emotions in marketing. *Journal of the Academy of Marketing Science, 27*(2), 184–206.
Briliana, V., & Mursito, N. (2017). Exploring antecedents and consequences of Indonesian Muslim youths' attitude towards halal cosmetic products: A case study in Jakarta. *Asia Pacific Management Review, 22*(4), 176–184.
Brooksworth, F., Mogaji, E., & Bosah, G. (2022a). Fashion Marketing in Emerging Economies: An introduction. In F. Brooksworth, E. Mogaji, & G. Bosah (Eds.), *Fashion Marketing in Emerging Economies (volume 1) – Brand, consumer and sustainability perspectives*. Springer.
Brooksworth, F., Mogaji, E., & Bosah, G. (2022b). Fashion Marketing in Emerging Economies: Conclusion and research agenda. In F. Brooksworth, E. Mogaji, & G. Bosah (Eds.), *Fashion Marketing in Emerging Economies (volume 1) – Brand, consumer and sustainability perspectives*. Springer.
Cai, S., & Xu, Y. (2006). Effects of outcome, process, and shopping enjoyment on online consumer behavior. *Electronic Commerce Research and Applications, 5*(4), 272–281.
Cakanlar, A., & Nguyen, T. (2019). The influence of culture on impulse buying. *Journal of Consumer Marketing, 36*(1), 12–23.
Chan, K. K., & Misra, S. (1990). Characteristics of the opinion leader: A new dimension. *Journal of Advertising, 19*(3), 53–60.
Chang, H. H., & Chen, S. W. (2008). The impact of online store environment cues on purchase intention. *Online Information Review, 32*(6), 818–841.
Chattaraman, V., & Lennon, S. J. (2008). Ethnic identity, consumption of cultural apparel, and self-perceptions of ethnic consumers. *Journal of Fashion Marketing, 12*(4), 518–531.
Chege, K. (2019). Africa Fashionomics: Making sense of the $31 Billion industry. Retrieved December 2, 2020, from https://theexchange.africa/africa/africa-fashionomics-making-sense-of-the-31-billion-industry/
Cho, Y., Hwang, J., & Lee, D. (2012). Identification of effective opinion leaders in the diffusion of technological innovation: A social network approach. *Technological Forecasting and Social Change, 79*(1), 97–106.
Choi, T. M., Lo, C. K., Wong, C. W., Yee, R. W., Shen, B., Wang, Y., & Shum, M. (2012). The impact of ethical fashion on consumer purchase behavior. *Journal of Fashion Marketing and Management: An International Journal, 16*(2), 234–245.
Christopher, M., Lowson, R., & Peck, H. (2004). Creating agile supply chains in the fashion industry. *International Journal of Retail & Distribution Management, 32*(8), 367–376.

Chung, E., & Fischer, E. (1999). It's who you know: Intracultural differences in ethnic product consumption. *Journal of Consumer Marketing, 16*(5), 482–501.
Cohen, J. B., Pham, M. T., & Andrade, B. E. (2006). *The nature and role of effect in consumer behaviour, to appear in handbook of consumer psychology*. Curtis P. Haugtvedt, Paul Herr, and Frank Kardes.
Cooley, D., & Parks-Yancy, R. (2019). The effect of social media on perceived information credibility and decision making. *Journal of Internet Commerce, 18*(3), 249–269.
Delbaere, M., Michael, B., & Phillips, B. J. (2020). Social media influencers: A route to brand engagement for their followers. *Psychology & Marketing*, 1–12.
Deshpande, R., Hoyer, W. D., & Donthu, N. (1986). The intensity of ethnic affiliation: A study of the sociology of Hispanic consumption. *Journal of Consumer Research, 13*(2), 214–220.
Dias, L. P. (2003). Generational buying motivations for fashion. *Journal of Fashion Marketing and Management, 7*(1), 78–86.
Doney, P. M., & Cannon, J. P. (1997). An examination of the nature of trust in buyer–seller relationships. *Journal of Marketing, 61*(2), 35–51.
Donthu, N., & Cherian, J. (1994). Impact of strength of ethnic identification on Hispanic shopping behavior. *Journal of Retailing, 70*(4), 383–393.
Eisenhardt, K. M. (1989). Building theories from case study research. *Academy of Management Review, 14*(4), 532–550.
Elsner, W., & Schwardt, H. (2015). From emergent cooperation to contextual trust, and to general trust: Overlapping meso-sized interaction arenas and cooperation platforms as a foundation of pro-social behaviour. *Forum for Social Economics, 44*(1), 69–86.
Erevelles, S. (1998). The role of affect in marketing. *Journal of Business Research, 42*(3), 199–215.
Escalas, J. E., & Stern, B. B. (2003). Sympathy and empathy: Emotional responses to advertising dramas. *Journal of Consumer Research, 29*(4), 566–578.
Farrag, D. A., & Hassan, M. (2015). The influence of religiosity on Egyptian Muslim youths' attitude towards fashion. *Journal of Islamic Marketing, 6*(1), 95–108.
Fasinu, D. T. (2020). Collaborative Entrepreneurship and Building Small Business Communities in the Nigerian Fashion Design Industry.
FBNQUEST. (2019). Retrieved December 2, 2020, from https://fbnquest.com/capital/insights/good-morning-nigeria/pins-and-needles-before-the-necessary-boost/.

Forney, J. C., & Rabolt, N. (1985–1986). Ethnic identity: Its relationship to ethnic and contemporary dress. *Clothing and Textiles Research Journal, 4*(2), 1–8.

Foxall, G. R. (1993). A behaviourist perspective on purchase and consumption. *European Journal of Marketing, 27*(8), 7–16.

Foxall, G. (2004). *Consumer psychology in behavioural perspective*. Beard Books.

Foxall, G. (2009). *Interpreting consumer choice: The behavioural perspective model* (Vol. 10). Routledge.

FT. (2017). My Fashion Nationalism, by Chimamanda Ngozi Adichie. Retrieved March 14, 2020, from https://www.ft.com/content/03c63f66-af6b-11e7-8076-0a4bdda92ca2.

Gabriel, O; Anaeto, E; Nwabughiogu, L; Elebeke, E., & Onuorji, S. (2016). Economic Recession worse than expected- National Bureau of Statistics. Retrieved March 17, 2020, from https://www.vanguardngr.com/2016/09/economic-recession-worse-expected-national-bureau-statistics/.

Gbadamosi, A. (2015). Brand personification and symbolic consumption among ethnic minority teenage consumers: An empirical study. *Journal of Brand Management, 22*(9), 737–754.

Gökerik, M., Gürbüz, A., Erkan, I., Mogaji, E., & Sap, S. (2018). Surprise me with your ads! The impacts of guerrilla marketing in social media on brand image. *Asia Pacific Journal of Marketing and Logistics, 30*(5), 1222–1238. https://doi.org/10.1108/APJML-10-2017-0257

Grant, I. J., & Stephen, G. R. (2005). Buying behaviour of "tweenage" girls and key societal communicating factors influencing their purchasing of fashion clothing. *Journal of Fashion Marketing and Management, 9*(4), 450–467.

Grine, F., & Saeed, M. (2017). Is hijab a fashion statement? A study of Malaysian Muslim women. *Journal of Islamic Marketing, 8*(3), 430–443.

Guba, E. G., & Lincoln, Y. S. (1994). Competing paradigms in qualitative research. *Handbook of Qualitative Research, 2*(163–194), 105.

Guo, W., & Main, K. J. (2012). The vulnerability of defensiveness: The impact of persuasion attempts and processing motivations on trust. *Marketing Letters, 23*(4), 959–971.

Hamel, J. (1993). *Case study methods. Qualitative research methods. Vol. 32*. Sage.

Harrison, T., Waite, K., & White, P. (2006). Analysis by paralysis: The pension purchase decision process. *International Journal of Bank Marketing, 24*(1), 5–23.

He, J., & Wang, C. L. (2015). Cultural identity and consumer ethnocentrism impact on preference and purchase of domestic versus import brands: An empirical study in China. *Journal of Business Research, 68*(6), 1225–1233.

Hogg, M. A. (2016). Social identity theory. In *Understanding peace and conflict through social identity theory* (pp. 3–17). Springer.

Huang, Y., Oppewal, H., & Mavondo, F. (2013). The influence of ethnic attributes on ethnic consumer choice of service outlet. *European Journal of Marketing, 47*(5/6), 877–898.

Jiménez-Castillo, D., & Sánchez-Fernández, R. (2019). The role of digital influencers in brand recommendation: Examining their impact on engagement, expected value and purchase intention. *International Journal of Information Management, 49*, 366–376.

Joshi, Y., & Rahman, Z. (2015). Factors affecting green purchase behaviour and future research directions. *International Strategic Management Review, 3*(1–2), 128–143.

Joy, A., Sherry, J. F. J., Venkatesh, A., Wang, J., & Chan, R. (2012). Fast fashion, sustainability, and the ethical appeal of luxury brands. *Fashion Theory, 16*(3), 273–295.

Kacen, J. J., & Lee, J. A. (2002). The influence of culture on consumer impulsive buying behaviour. *Journal of Consumer Psychology, 12*(2), 163–176.

Kaur, J., Mogaji, E., Wadera, D., & Gupta, S. (2022). "Sustainable consumption practices in Indian households: A saga of environment management linked to Indian ethos and generational differences", Society and Business Review, Vol. ahead-of-print No. ahead-of-print. https://doi.org/10.1108/SBR-08-2021-0132.

Khare, A. (2015). Antecedents to green buying behaviour: A study on consumers in an emerging economy. *Marketing Intelligence & Planning, 33*(3), 309–329.

Ki, C. W. C., & Kim, Y. K. (2019). The mechanism by which social media influencers persuade consumers: The role of consumers' desire to mimic. *Psychology & Marketing, 36*(10), 905–922.

Kim, S., & Arthur, L. B. (2003). Asian-American consumers in Hawai'i: The effects of ethnic identification on attitudes toward and ownership of ethnic apparel, importance of product and store-display attributes, and purchase intention. *Clothing and Textiles Research Journal, 21*(1), 8–18.

Kim, Y. K., & Kang, J. (2001). The effects of ethnicity and product on purchase decision making. *Journal of Advertising Research, 41*(2), 39–48.

Kim, J. O., Forsythe, S., Gu, Q., & Moon, S. J. (2002). Cross-cultural consumer values need and purchase behavior. *Journal of Consumer Marketing, 19*(6), 481–502.

Koslow, S., Shamdasani, P. N., & Touchstone, E. E. (1994). Exploring language effects in ethnic advertising: A sociolinguistic perspective. *Journal of Consumer Research, 20*(4), 575–585.

Kreglex. (2016). A Brief History of Nigerian Fashion. Retrieved December 2, 2020, from https://greyvelvetstores.com/2016/11/05/a-brief-history-of-nigerian-fashion/.

Laros, F. J., & Steenkamp, J. B. E. (2005). Emotions in consumer behaviour: A hierarchical approach. *Journal of Business Research, 58*(10), 1437–1445.

Liljander, V., Gummerus, J., & Söderlund, M. (2015). Young consumers' responses to suspected covert and overt blog marketing. *Internet Research, 25*(4), 610–632.

Lim, X. J., Radzol, A. M., Cheah, J., & Wong, M. W. (2017). The impact of social media influencers on purchase intention and the mediation effect of customer attitude. *Asian Journal of Business Research, 7*(2), 19–36.

Lindridge, A. (2005). Religiosity and the construction of a cultural-consumption identity. *Journal of Consumer Marketing, 22*(3), 142–151.

Loken, B. (2006). Consumer psychology: Categorization, inferences, affect, and persuasion. *Annual Review of Psychology, 57*, 453–485.

Martin, D., O'neill, M., Hubbard, S., & Palmer, A. (2008). The role of emotion in explaining consumer satisfaction and future behavioural intention. *Journal of Services Marketing, 22*(3), 224–236.

Mavlanova, T., Benbunan-Fich, R., & Kumar, N. (2008). Deception tactics and counterfeit deception in online environments. ICIS 2008 Proceedings, 105.

McCort, D. J., & Malhotra, N. K. (1993). Culture and consumer behaviour: Toward an understanding of cross-cultural consumer behaviour in international marketing. *Journal of International Consumer Marketing, 6*(2), 91–127.

Miao, M., Jalees, T., Qabool, S., & Zaman, S. I. (2019). The effects of personality, culture and store stimuli on impulsive buying behaviour. *Asia Pacific Journal of Marketing and Logistics, 32*(1), 188–204.

Miller-Spillman, K. A., Lee, M. Y., Graham, M. A., & Cho, B. (2016). Consumer groups for Ghanaian fabric products, based on aesthetics and socially responsible shopping behavior. *Journal of Global Fashion Marketing, 7*(2), 120–131.

Morgan, L. R., & Birtwistle, G. (2009). An investigation of young fashion consumers' disposal habits. *International Journal of Consumer Studies, 33*(2), 190–198.

Mukonza, C., Hinson, R. E., Adeola, O., Adisa, I., Mogaji, E., & Kirgiz, A. C. (2021). Green marketing: An introduction. In C. Mukonza, R. E. Hinson, O. Adeola, I. Adisa, E. Mogaji, & A. C. Kirgiz (Eds.), *Green Marketing in Emerging Markets. Palgrave studies of Marketing in Emerging Economies* (pp. 3–14). Palgrave Macmillan. https://doi.org/10.1007/978-3-030-74065-8_1

Nash, J. (2019). Exploring how social media platforms influence fashion consumer decisions in the UK retail sector. *Journal of Fashion Marketing and Management, 23*(1), 82–103.

Nguyen, P., & Mogaji, E. (2021a). Brand development through sustainability certifications in emerging markets: Adoption of B corporation certification in Vietnam. In O. Adeola, R. Hinson, & A. Sakkthivel (Eds.), *Marketing communications and brand development in emerging markets* (pp. 34–45). Palgrave.

Nguyen, N. P., & Mogaji, E. (2021b). Financial inclusion for women in the informal economy: An SDG agenda post pandemic. In O. Adeola (Ed.), *Gendered perspectives on Covid-19 recovery in Africa*. Palgrave Macmillan. https://doi.org/10.1007/978-3-030-88152-8_12

Nguyen, P. N., & Mogaji, E. (2022a). Emerging economies in fashion global value chain: Brand positioning and managerial implications. In F. Brooksworth, E. Mogaji, & G. Bosah (Eds.), *Fashion Marketing in Emerging Economies – Strategies, tools and insights for fashion brands* (pp. 234–345). Springer.

Nguyen N.P., Mogaji E. (2022b) A theoretical framework for the influence of green marketing communication on consumer behaviour in emerging economies. In: Mogaji E., Adeola O., Adisa I., Hinson R.E., Mukonza C., Kirgiz A.C. (eds) Green Marketing in Emerging Economies. Palgrave studies of Marketing in Emerging Economies. Palgrave Macmillan, . pp. 253–274. https://doi.org/https://doi.org/10.1007/978-3-030-82572-0_11

Niinimäki, K. (2010). Eco-clothing, consumer identity and ideology. *Sustainable Development, 18*(3), 150–162.

Noble, G., & Ang, I. (2018). Ethnicity and cultural consumption in Australia. *Continuum, 32*(3), 296–307.

Ogden, D. T., Ogden, J. R., & Schau, H. J. (2004). Exploring the impact of culture and acculturation on consumer purchase decisions: Toward a microcultural perspective. *Academy of Marketing Science Review, 3*(1), 1–22.

Ogunrin, F. O., & Inegbenebor, A. U. (2015). Distribution channels and internationalization in a developing-country clothing industry. *Journal of Research in Marketing and Entrepreneurship, 17*(2), 130–148.

Ojong, N., & Simba, A. (2020). Trust-building mechanisms in group-based microfinance: a Cameroonian perspective. In Forum for Social Economics (Vol. 49, No. 2, pp. 180–201). Routledge.
Orlikowski, W. J., & Baroudi, J. J. (1991). Studying information technology in organizations: Research approaches and assumptions. *Information Systems Research, 2*(1), 1–28.
Parker, J. R., Lehmann, D. R., & Xie, Y. (2016). Decision comfort. *Journal of Consumer Research, 43*(1), 113–133.
Peck, J., & Wiggins, J. (2006). It just feels good: Customers' affective response to touch and its influence on persuasion. *Journal of Marketing, 70*(4), 56–69.
Perry, P., & Kyriakaki, M. (2014). The decision-making process of luxury fashion retail buyers in Greece. *Journal of Fashion Marketing and Management, 18*(1), 85–106.
Pham, M. T. (2013). The seven sins of consumer psychology.
II Reed, A., Forehand, M. R., Puntoni, S., & Warlop, L. (2012). Identity-based consumer behavior. *International Journal of Research in Marketing, 29*(4), 310–321.
Reis, R. (2009). Strengths and limitations of case studies. Retrieved from. https://tomprof.stanford.edu/posting/1013
Saeed, M., Grine, F., & Shafique, I. (2020). Integrating factors influencing hijab purchase intention among Muslim women. *Journal of Islamic Marketing.*
Satz, D., & Ferejohn, J. (1994). Rational choice and social theory. *The Journal of Philosophy, 91*(2), 71–87.
Scheinbaum, A. C. (Ed.). (2017). *The dark side of social media: A consumer psychology perspective*. Routledge.
Schmitt, B. (2012). The consumer psychology of brands. *Journal of Consumer Psychology, 22*(1), 7–17.
Sethi, I., & Chawla, A. S. (2014). Influence of cultural, social and marketing factors on the buying behaviour of telecom users: A comparative study of rural, semi-urban and urban areas in and around Chandigarh. *Journal of Marketing Management, 2*(1), 97–110.
Shaw, C., & Ivens, J. (2002). *Building great customer experiences* (Vol. 241). Palgrave.
Sherman, E., Mathur, A., & Smith, R. B. (1997). Store environment and consumer purchase behaviour: Mediating role of consumer emotions. *Psychology & Marketing, 14*(4), 361–378.
Shin, J., Sudhir, K., & Yoon, D. H. (2012). When to "fire" customers: Customer cost-based pricing. *Management Science, 58*(5), 932–947.

Silva, M. J. D. B., Farias, S. A. D., Grigg, M. K., & Barbosa, M. D. L. D. A. (2020). Online engagement and the role of digital influencers in product endorsement on Instagram. *Journal of Relationship Marketing, 19*(2), 133–163.

Smallbone, D., Welter, F., & Ateljevic, J. (2014). Entrepreneurship in emerging market economies: Contemporary issues and perspectives. *International Small Business Journal, 32*(2), 113–116.

Smith, S., & Wheeler, J. (2002). *Managing the customer experience: Turning customers into advocates*. Pearson Education.

Stake, R. E. (2005). Qualitative case studies. In N. K. Denzin & Y. S. Lincoln (Eds.), *The sage handbook of qualitative research* (3rd ed., pp. 443–466). Sage.

Stayman, D. M., & Deshpande, R. (1989). Situational ethnicity and consumer behavior. *Journal of Consumer Research, 16*(3), 361–371.

Stets, J. E., & Burke, P. J. (2000). Identity theory and social identity theory. *Social Psychology Quarterly, 1*, 224–237.

Swarbrooke, J., & Horner, S. (2007). *Consumer behaviour in tourism*. Routledge.

Thaler, R. (1980). Toward a positive theory of consumer choice. *Journal of Economic Behaviour & Organization, 1*(1), 39–60.

Toure, K. D. (2019). African designers shine under Hollywood spotlight. Retrived December 14, 2021, from https://www.theafricareport.com/12408/african-designers-shine-under-hollywood-spotlight/

Tversky, A., & Kahneman, D. (1980). The framing of decisions and the rationality of choice (No. TR-2). STANFORD UNIV CA DEPT OF PSYCHOLOGY.

Ünal, S., Deniz, E., & Akin, N. (2019). Determining the factors that influence the intention to purchase luxury fashion Brands of Young Consumers. *Ege Academic Review, 19*(2), 1.

Uzo, U., Opati, T. Z., & Shittu, O. (2018). Characteristics of the African Buyer's purchase behaviour. In *Indigenous management practices in Africa*. Emerald Publishing Limited.

Valaei, N., & Nikhashemi, S. R. (2017). Generation Y consumers' buying behaviour in fashion apparel industry: A moderation analysis. *Journal of Fashion Marketing and Management, 21*(4), 523–543.

Walsh, G., Mitchell, V. W., Jackson, P. R., & Beatty, S. E. (2009). Examining the antecedents and consequences of corporate reputation: A customer perspective. *British Journal of Management, 20*(2), 187–203.

Watson, L., & Spence, M. T. (2007). Causes and consequences of emotions on consumer behaviour. *European Journal of Marketing, 41*(5/6), 487–511.

Welter, F. (2012). All you need is trust? A critical review of the trust and entrepreneurship literature. *International Small Business Journal, 30*(3), 193–212.
Xie, Y., & Peng, S. (2009). How to repair customer trust after negative publicity: The roles of competence, integrity, benevolence, and forgiveness. *Psychology & Marketing, 26*(7), 572–589.
Yalch, R. F., & Spangenberg, E. R. (2000). The effects of music in a retail setting on real and perceived shopping times. *Journal of Business Research, 49*(2), 139–147.
Zhong, Y., & Mitra, S. (2020). The role of fashion retail buyers in China and the buyer decision-making process. *Journal of Fashion Marketing and Management, 24*(4), 631–649.

7

South Africa: A Snapshot of Contemporary Fashion Retail

Ken Kweku Nimo

Introduction

The multi-faceted economy of South Africa, characterized by diverse racial, socio-cultural, economic and demographic units, offers a fascinating context for the study of fashion marketing in emerging economies. Fashion retail in South Africa dates to the propitious years of the Dutch Indies Company, which established the Cape of Good Hope as a stopover to replenish trade vessels along the Netherland-Java trade route (Thompson, 2000). This trading outpost quickly evolved into a complex and racially stratified colony that enjoyed a windfall of Western and Oriental goods (Thompson, 2000). Historically, the development of South Africa's fashion retail industry—comprising of a local manufacturing and a primarily import-oriented retail sector—can be segmented into three phases (Vlok, 2006). These phases include fashion retail in the

K. K. Nimo (✉)
University of Johannesburg, Johannesburg, South Africa

F. Brooksworth et al. (eds.), *Fashion Marketing in Emerging Economies Volume II*,
Palgrave Studies of Marketing in Emerging Economies,
https://doi.org/10.1007/978-3-031-07078-5_7

protectionist era of apartheid, followed by the liberal market regime post-apartheid and the era immediately after the 2008 global financial crisis.

Under Apartheid, South Africa weathered international trade sanctions and embargoes that transformed its sub-sectors into import-substituting industries (Morris & Barnes, 2014). The protectionist policies characterized by import quotas and high product-specific import tariffs spurred local production capacities and facilitated the rise of a vibrant local manufacturing and retail industry (Vlok, 2006). However, the emergence of democratic rule and neo-liberal trade policies marked the beginning of a disruptive import-oriented economy to the detriment of local industries (Vlok, 2006; Wolfhard, 2013; Morris & Barnes, 2014). In the context of a fragile local industry, South Africa's retail economy suffered further loss in the aftermath of the 2008 global financial crisis, which heralded the turbulent contemporary retail economy (Rena & Msoni, 2014).

Nevertheless, South Africa's economy has expanded under the impetus of a steadily rising middle class (Morris & Barnes, 2014). In luxury retail, the demand for imported luxury goods grew by 53.8% between 2013 and 2018 (Euromonitor, 2019). In 2017, South Africa accounted for 35% of the 6.5 billion USD worth of luxury goods consumed in Africa (AfriAsia, 2018). Consequently, South Africa has the biggest footprint of luxury retail with an expanding retinue of luxury brands such as Gucci, Louis Vuitton, Ralph Lauren, Dior, Givenchy, Burberry, Cartier, Coach, and Hermes and fast fashion brands such as Zara, Topshop, CottonOn, Forever21, H&M and Mango (Jacobs, 2013). South Africa remains the leading destination for fashion retail in Africa, outshining the contending economies of Morocco, Egypt and Nigeria.

Methodology

This chapter adopted a qualitative approach through a combination of document analysis and case studies (Bowen, 2009; Mogaji et al., 2021). While limiting, this methodology proved adequate due to the constraint on time and the impracticability of other methods during the intensive periods of the coronavirus pandemic. Furthermore, data collection through online surveys was undermined by delayed responses. Document analysis is a systemic procedure of reviewing or evaluating documents in both electronic and printed formats (Bowen, 2009). Document analysis emphasizes a thorough examination and evaluation and a balanced interpretation of available documents to derive meaning, gain understanding and establish empirical knowledge (Corbin & Strauss, 2008). The analytic procedure entails identifying, selecting, appraising and synthesizing data that is relevant to the phenomenon under study (Bowen, 2009). Consequently, this chapter utilized a variety of organizational and institutional reports, online publications and available academic literature on South Africa's emerging fashion retail economy. Document analysis was complemented by case studies, which examined the operation of a handful of local designers and the designer collective known as *Africa Rise.*

Literature Review

South Africa's fashion retail economy has evolved into a liberal market economy. Despite the extensive media coverage of the burgeoning industry, only a handful of academic publications have explored this terrain (Stiehler, 2017). In a report on the textile industry in Sub-Saharan Africa, Vlok (2006) investigates the historical antecedent to South Africa's clothing and textile industry, dissecting the factors militating against a once prosperous industry. Morris and Barnes (2014) explored the challenges to avert the decline of South Africa's apparel sector, while Mbatha and Mastamet-Mason (2015) distilled the challenges and opportunities of the clothing industry through Porter's Diamond Model. They proposed reforms to upskill industry workforce, improve supply chain infrastructure and modernize production technology. Studies on fashion marketing are mostly consumer-centric and include an exploration of the peculiar shopping styles of millennials (Mandhlazi et al., 2013). Meanwhile, Steinfield (2015) explored the tensions within social class and race in South Africa's luxury market, while Goldberg (2011) interrogated the relationship between status and conspicuous consumption. Stiehler (2017) has also examined the consumer typology of luxury brands in South Africa, while de Villiers et al. (2018) investigated the role of retail atmospherics in enhancing consumer experience and purchase intention, with brand attitude and brand experience as mediators.

Globalization is the lifeline of a dynamic dress culture, providing access to a wider variety of imported goods through new production and supply chain models, as well as disruptive social media (Hines, 2007; Ramdass & Kruger, 2011; Nguyen & Mogaji, 2022a). The overbearing impact of globalization and delocalization has fueled competition, prompting South African retailers to adopt agile supply chain strategies to mitigate abrupt shifts in trends and market volatilities (Muhwati & Salisbury, 2017). Despite the imminent threat, South Africa's fashion retail economy continues to thrive, with a bevy of large, medium scale and small independent brands found in retail hotspots across the country. The proliferating fashion manufacturing and retail industry embody the challenges and opportunities of emerging economies.

Contemporary Fashion Retail Outlook

The fashion retail sector in South Africa is vibrant and diverse, consisting of numerous international and local establishments. South Africa's retail industry is well structured and adequately insulated against external forces through robust import policies and exacting investment regulations (Spinks, 2014). In the context of volatile and peculiar local markets, many international brands have entered South Africa through partnerships with local establishments (Flanders, 2016). In luxury retail, the Surtee Group is a pioneering luxury retail establishment with a portfolio of over 20 reputable luxury brands, which include mono-brand stores Giorgio Armani, Versace, Michael Kors, Burberry, Jimmy Choo and Coach. The Group recently acquired Luminance, a multi-brand concept store with a portfolio of local and international brands. The Apsley Group is yet another contending force in luxury retail, with exclusive licensing of foremost brands such as Hermes, Tom Ford, Ralph Lauren, Balmain, Saint Laurent and Valentino (Lodestar Marketing Research, 2015). Richemont, founded by South African business magnate Johan Rupert wields substantial market equity through a ubiquitous network of the group's masons such as Cartier, Montblanc, Chloe and AZ Factory

(Euromonitor, 2019). Louis Vuitton operates outside the licensing model with two directly operated stores in Johannesburg and Cape Town.

The mid-range and mass-market segments are just as competitive with a handful of dominant brands, which possess an expansive footprint. In 2011, Zara debuted at the Sandton City retail mall, followed by Australian competitor CottonOn. Other major brands with thriving retail concerns in South Africa include Topshop, Forever21 and H&M. Leading indigenous retail groups include the Foschini Group, Truworths, Mr. Price Group, Woolworths and Pepkor. The retail chain is intermediated by specialist agencies that procure and import an extensive variety of garments on behalf of local retailers. The major retail intermediaries include Charl Roos, Walt Import and Export, G&T Fashion and Karina M (Flanders, 2016). Smaller boutique agencies also procure and distribute, often providing integrated PR and marketing services to smaller independent brands in the premium and luxury segments (Brooksworth et al., 2022a, 2022b). An excellent example is The Fashion Agent, a Johannesburg-based agency that represents a growing roster of reputable African brands such as Rich Mnisi, Thebe Magugu, Clive Rundle and Lukhanyo Mdingi. The Fashion Agent serves local brands in the critical capacity as professional buyers and distributors while facilitating a growing network of wholesalers, retailers, independent boutiques and concept stores across Africa. Online retail is yet another growing niche that has seen the emergence of online-first retailers such as Superbalist, Zando and Net-a-porter.

The South African fashion retail terrain also comprises small and independent brands that operate at the peripherals of the formal retail economy. Many of these distinguished independent brands are entering the sphere of formal retail under the patronage of budding concept stores such as the SpaceSA and the luxury retail concept store House of Nala. South Africa's retail hotspots include Hyde Park Corner, Sandton City Mall, Melrose Arch and the V&A Waterfront Mall for luxury retail. The Mall of Africa is the largest retail center in South Africa; other popular centers include Cresta Mall and the Four Ways Shopping Mall.

A Blistering Storm

According to the 2016 Global Retail Development Index (GRDI), South Africa's retail economy has become stagnant (Kearney, 2016). The 2016 ranking reflects a legacy of sluggish consumer spending and uncertainties in the shadows of a recessionary economy (OECD, 2020b). The compounding ills of the retail sector, exacerbated by intense competition, have forced many new entrants to withdraw or consolidate their retail footprint (Broll, 2017). Recent casualties include legacy establishments such as South Africa's oldest high-end department store—Stuttaford's, which closed in 2018 after years of unsuccessful rescue attempts. Local retail giant, the Edcon Group, announced the closure of 24 stores, hinting at further downsizing in the foreseeable future. Several leading international brands such as Mango, Nine West and River Island have either withdrawn from the South African market or significantly reduced their retail footprint (Broll, 2017).

The COVID-19 pandemic follows up to a legacy of retail woes that has spurred a gloomy retail outlook and a decline in global apparel retail (Amed et al., 2021). The pandemic's year-long impact has dampened the optimism of a rapid economic rebound and concomitant revival of the apparel retail industry. Indeed, the complexities of fashion marketing resulting from this pandemic are deepening in emerging economies where the ramifications of a recessionary global economy may persist into the next decade (McKinsey & Co, 2020). This seems to be the plight of South Africa's already belligerent retail economy, with major retailers on the brink of bankruptcy. Amid widespread job losses, diminishing spending power and general lackluster consumer confidence, uncertainty in the fashion retail economy abounds as fashion marketing enters a tempestuous terrain. In the context of a steadily contracting market and intense competition among local and international brands, the stage is set for overwhelming complexities in South Africa's fashion retail industry.

Addressing the Fundamentals

The coronavirus pandemic constitutes the most vicious threat to the sustenance of local and international brands in emerging economies such as South Africa. However, the unprecedented shortfalls in imports, and disruptions to the global supply chain, offer emerging economies an opportunity to recalibrate. South Africa's clothing and textile sector contributed 1.7% to GDP and employed almost 2% of the total workforce in 2016 (DTIC, 2020). In a country where the local market accounts for nearly 70% of locally manufactured apparel, the current retail figures of an estimated 15 billion USD underscore immeasurable potential for the economy (Statista, 2019). In the wake of a spiraling unemployment rate (estimated at 50% in Q4 of 2020), resuscitating the clothing manufacturing and retail industry is crucial to post-COVID economic recovery efforts. Fortunately, the pandemic's existential threat and concurrent opportunity coincide with the Government's ambitious plan to revive South Africa's garment manufacturing and retail sector. The South Africa Garment Industry Master Plan, unveiled in late 2019, seeks to grow the local industry and its interrelated sectors to boost employment by more than 50% of its current levels, expand and modernize manufacturing infrastructure to animate the commitment of retailers seeking to source locally (DTIC, 2020; Jenvey, 2020). An essential element of this strategy is the renewed 'Buy Local' campaign to propel locally manufactured garment and textile products. Beyond the local market, the strategic direction also benchmarks the potential of export markets to the UK post-Brexit and the African continent under the recently enacted African Continental Free Trade Agreement (AfCFTA) (DTIC, 2020).

Embracing Digital

Despite the proliferation of smart and internet-enabled digital devices, the digital retail landscape in South Africa has exhibited lackluster performance in the past few decades. The slowly evolving digital retail landscape is hinged primarily on South Africa's entrenched mall culture and the multiplicity of challenges associated with the fledgling digital retail economy (PWC, 2012). In the face of an unwavering proclivity for brick-and-mortar retail, online sales accounted for a mere 1.4% of total retail purchases in 2019 (Davis, 2019), explicating retailer apathy for e-commerce. The challenges to online retail include inadequate distribution and delivery infrastructure, the threat of cyber fraud and a grossly underwhelming online shopping experience (Watling et al., 2019). Furthermore, a significant segment of the local market is underserved, due to limited access to banking services and the high cost of internet data (Watling et al., 2019). Notwithstanding, the prevailing low penetration rate, the expanding millennial market is driving growth in online retail, with e-commerce offering renewed opportunities at unlocking higher-order supply chain value in South Africa's stagnant retail market (Watling et al., 2019).

Once again, the coronavirus pandemic emerges as a pivotal phenomenon in animating the once lethargic digital retail market. Within a relatively short period, the mandatory lockdown regulations thrust online retail volumes up by 40% (Watling et al., 2019). Experts believe this uptick in digital retail activity will persist into the coming decade as multiple factors such as new work-life schedules, convenience and paranoia of public retail spaces emerge in the post-COVID era (Sibahle, 2020). Nevertheless, in South Africa's emerging economy, the brick-and-mortar store remains central to a holistic omnichannel experience, resulting in a hybrid system of traditional and cutting-edge retail futures (McCormick et al., 2014). In addition to a spiraling growth in digital retailing, some local brands expanded their retail footprint. Premised perhaps on much favorable lease terms, local brands have embraced the unprecedented opportunity to locate in high-end retail hotspots. A few of the most recent retail expansions include:

- Maxhosa's flagships in the Mall of Africa and the V&A waterfront mall
- Kat Van Duinen's flagship in the V&A Waterfront
- Africa Rise collective retail stores in Sandton City, Newtown and Merlyn Pretoria
- David Tlale's uber-luxury stores in Merlyn Pretoria, Melrose Arch and the V&A Waterfront Mall in Cape Town
- The House of Nala concept store in The Leonardo, Sandton City

Collaboration over Competition

The collapse of major third-party retailer Stuttaford's and the sale of Luminance Pty is a significant setback to local brands that relied on large retail establishments to access markets in high-end retail centers like Sandton City, Hyde Park Corner and the V&A Waterfront Mall (Appiah-Nimo, 2019). However, from the ashes of collapsing big retail boxes, a new concept store of collaborative brands is rising. The aptly named Africa Rise concept store is an innovative solution to the diminishing retail footprint of local brands in South Africa's most strategic retail hotspots. The store features a collective of emerging and established premium African brands providing a variety of distinctive garments, leathercraft, jewelry, accessories and art. The Africa Rise concept store, while novel to South Africa's local luxury retail ecosystem, follows in step with pioneering collective—The Space SA—and is underpinned by the twentieth-century concept of co-opetition (Brandenburger & Nalebuff, 1996). Despite its popularity among some of the largest firms in the integrated technology industry (Adner et al., 2013), co-opetition marks a radical departure from the convention of vicious competition among players in South Africa's fashion industry.

Barely a year into its inception, Africa Rise is present in three vibrant retail hotspots: Sandton City Mall, Menlyn Mall in Pretoria and Marshalltown in Johannesburg's central business district. The bargaining power of Africa Rise served as a shield to protect the collective of otherwise vulnerable brands against the tide of store closures amid the devastation of COVID-19. Africa Rise, while not novel, is a reference for ingenuity, community and collaboration embodied in the ancient African ideal of Ubuntu (Martin-Leke & Ellis, 2014), offering new pathways of collaboration in an industry that is riddled with vicious competition. Co-opetition is beneficial to brands and consumers alike, offering consumers a wider selection of complementary products while providing participating brands access to wider markets and cost-sharing advantages (Rusko, 2012). Beyond the potential of cooperating to access local markets, Africa Rise is pioneering new pathways of collaboration that harnesses the synergies of skills and resources across the challenging manufacturing and supply chain terrain (Appiah-Nimo, 2019).

Less New, More Thrift

According to Shahbandeh (2021), the global second-hand clothing industry, estimated at 33 billion USD will double to 64 billion USD by 2024. Africa consumes 40% of the world's cast-away clothes. Given its devastating impact on local textile and apparel industries, the second-hand clothing industry evokes much ambivalence among many African economies (Thomas, 2003; Norris, 2012). However, recent concerns over the scourge of fast fashion and its concomitant cast-away culture have thrust the re-use economy into favorable light (Park & Armstrong, 2020). Today, the market for second-hand clothing transcends the poor, with the introduction of veritable quality clothing from premium brands, expanding patronage across the stratum of society (Laitala & Klepp, 2018; Jordan, 2020). Furthermore, the stigmatization associated with second-hand clothing has waned under a watershed of alternative vocabulary, with terms such as vintage, thrifting, upcycling and re-commerce dominating the contemporary discourse.

The second-hand economy has been boosted further through technology and the sharing economy (Hristova, 2019; Kaur et al., 2022). The convergence of these unlikely phenomena has birthed a cohort of pioneering online clothing resale (OCR) platforms that apparently guarantee the longevity of garments (Armstrong & Park, 2017). Trailblazers in the global e-commerce industry such as ThreadUp, Rent the Runway, The RealReal, Poshmark and Vestiaire Collective have attracted unprecedented media attention in recent years (Toma, 2019). In South Africa, digital platforms such as BidorBuy, Facebook marketplace, Gumtree and OLX dominate the digital second-hand economy, intermediating millions of Rands in B2B, B2C and C2C transactions (Davis, 2019). In a relatively short time, luxury e-commerce platforms Luxity and The Changing Room, which operate a hybrid e-tail and brick-and-mortar model, have gained market leadership and account for the largest resale of international luxury brands in South Africa (Jordan, 2020). Luxity and The Changing Room are reputable for rigorous product authentication, offering value for authentic pre-owned luxury goods. Akin to global trends, Luxity and The Changing room are reorienting consumer attitudes toward second-hand clothing from stigmatization to guilt-free preloved fashion, through innovative retail strategies. South Africa's re-commerce economy is thriving, indicative in the double-digit year-on-year growth of luxury. According to Luxity's State of the Luxury Market Africa report (2020), Louis Vuitton maintained its position as the most sought-after brand, with onsite search interest in pre-owned Louis Vuitton growing almost 200% from 2019. Meanwhile, the Chanel flap bag's value trumped the inflation rate in South Africa to record a 17.7% appreciation in value (Luxity, 2020).

For decades, the second-hand clothing industry has been steeped in controversy. In the light of deepening concerns over climate change, waste and the destructive forces of hyper-consumption, the re-use economy could offer some respite. Despite advancing new forms of consumption, critics fear that the re-use economy could become a culprit of greenwashing and deindustrialization, perpetuating inequalities and stunting industrial growth in emerging economies (Norris, 2012). For emerging economies aspiring toward a vibrant textile and apparel industry, navigating the threats associated with the invasion of second-hand clothing and fast fashion goods could constitute the most daunting challenge.

South Africa Fashion Retail Futures

The disruptive impact of the global coronavirus pandemic on the growth trajectory of the apparel manufacturing and retail sectors is widely explored. The impact of the pandemic on developed and emerging economies will prevail into the foreseeable future, displacing entrenched consumption patterns and introducing new complexities to the retail economy (McKinsey & Co, 2020). Like many emerging economies worldwide, South Africa entered a technical recession leading to further contraction in consumer markets and lackluster consumer confidence. Despite the uncertainties confronting the retail economy, some present and imminent trends will persist into the future under the prevailing catalysts of globalization, shifts in consumer demography and technology. Some of these trends, specific to South Africa's retail economy, are explored to provide a crystal ball view into fashion retail's future in Africa's largest retail economy.

The Social Window

The tight lockdown restrictions in South Africa, amid the ravaging COVID-19, occasioned a meteoric rise in the use of the newly introduced social media app TikTok (Goldstuck & Patricios, 2020). Millions of TikTok users, glued to their mobile devices, watched hilarious 60-second videos from people of all races, gender and social status. TikTok has grown exponentially to become the second most downloaded app on the Android Play store in 2020 (Goldstuck & Patricios, 2020). While TikTok may be the prodigy of the moment, its efficacy as a marketing tool is contested. Nevertheless, Facebook remains the social platform of choice for marketing in South Africa, with 89% of respondents from the SocialSA survey ascribing to its use. The platform also accounted for the highest advertising spending according to 59.4% of respondents. While not indicative of their effectiveness, the survey also observed that 77% of respondents engaged actively on Twitter, 75% on LinkedIn and 68% on Instagram (Goldstuck & Patricios, 2020).

The inevitable rise of social media as critical marketing tool is premised on the sizeable mobile device subscription base, an expanding access to improved internet services and the declining cost of internet data (Shapshak, 2019). Most importantly, millennials and Gen Z consumers' proclivity to social media is a significant impetus for growth as this demography accounts for approximately 40% of global consumption (Deloitte, 2020). Furthermore, the financial and human resource cost necessary for brands to pivot online is driving growth on the social media landscape. In the absence of a functional e-commerce website, the transactional extension to social media, known as social commerce (s-commerce), enables in-app conversions and sales, thereby leveraging the prolonged hours consumers on social media. Hence, the likely dominance of s-commerce in the immediate future, as brands big and small, reorients their social media platforms into social shopfronts.

Green Leap

The calamitous events of 2020 have deepened the cracks in the economic and social structures that underpin various industries across the globe. The impact of the pandemic is bittersweet, deepening inequality and yet accelerating trends for sustainable futures (BoF and McKinsey & Co, 2021). For example, Brydges and Hanlon (2020) observed the asymmetry in worker solidarity as brands moved to alleviate the pandemic's impact on its 'visible' workforce, comprising primarily of front-end retail staff, while ignoring the plight of the 'invincible' supply chain workers upstream. Most profoundly, the fashion industry reckoned with its legacy of waste and ecologically destructive practices, as leading designers, top executives and retailers from around the world engaged introspectively on the status quo (Wong, 2020).

South Africa's over-reliance on Chinese imports adversely impacted the local retail economy in the wake of COVID-19-related travel and external trade disruptions. Woolworths, a top fashion retailer, announced significant shortfalls in products, while Mr. Price, a fast fashion brand that thrives on the rapid just-in-time model, suffered significant losses. The inherent disadvantages of delocalized, albeit cost-effective, supply chains are evident, often characterized by high risks and vulnerabilities to disruptions such as the recent COVID-19 pandemic (Plambeck, 2012; Soyka, 2012). On the contrary, localized supply chain guarantees greater agility, transparency and sustainable ecological footprint that foster a favorable brand image (McCormick et al., 2014). South African brands, operating under a truncated global supply chain, quickly adapted to localized production by procuring stock and critical personal protective gear from local manufacturers. The pandemic has also renewed the commitment to the 'buy local' campaign with local retailers pledging to contribute up to 440 million USD to activate the apparel industry master plan (DTIC, 2020).

South Africa's clothing manufacturing and apparel retail industry has also witnessed increased activism in recent times. The response of the industry in the collective fight against COVID-19 underscores the growing sense of responsibility. Other societal ills that have attracted the industry's attention include the infamous gender-based violence and killings meted out against South African women; the Black Lives Matter movement and the most recent End SARS campaign, in which brands employed multiple media channels to solidarize with victims around the world. The empathy for consumers and the support of social causes will persist into the future, birthing even more significant commitment to ideals of equity, compassion and community among consumers and industry stakeholders. New models of retail and manufacturing will increasingly prioritize people over profit in the context of shifting demography and ideals toward eco and socially conscious Millennials and Generation Z consumers. Other vectors of sustainability that will be supercharged in the coming decades include the newfound proclivity toward thrifting, re-commerce and an upsurge in circular production models.

Immersive Omnichannel Retail

South Africa is known for its prolific mall culture, with brick-and-mortar retail accounting for a little over 60% of retail (Flanders, 2016). However, analysts have predicted a significant shortfall in foot traffic in brick-and-mortar outlets as e-commerce breaks through the resistance (Watling et al., 2019). While the upsurge of e-commerce impacts the operations of brick-and-mortar stores, the current rate of e-commerce assimilation does not imply the apocalypse of brick-and-mortar retail. On the contrary, the various channels of e-commerce, s-commerce, and brick and mortar are converging into a seamless and immersive omnichannel experience (Caro et al., 2020). The strained retail environment, characterized by economic uncertainties, dampened consumer confidence, low disposable incomes and intensifying competition, warrants brands to innovate or perish. In this regard, a cohesive omnichannel strategy becomes a competitive edge.

In omnichannel retailing, a retailer aligns the various channels of consumer engagement into a singular seamless experience (Blázquez, 2014). A pleasant omnichannel experience is devoid of discord or channel conflicts, ushering the consumer from one channel to the other seamlessly for an optimized experience of the product or service offering. Contrary to the perception of a diminishing role, the brick-and-mortar retail front remains the central hub of marketing for most brands and retailers, a cathedral for captivating the imagination of consumers through a multisensory stimulating environment. de Villiers et al. (2018), in a study on fashion retail atmospherics in South Africa, observed that the store environment positively influenced brand attitude and brand experience and purchase intentions. Pioneering efforts in omnichannel retail include the digital-first platforms developed by South Africa's major retailers Mr. Price, Woolworths and Takealot that offer e-commerce to doorstep services or e-commerce to priority self-service pickups in-store. Omnichannel retail is also valuable to brands and retailers as each touchpoint provides data and insight on consumer preferences and imminent trends necessary for improving efficiency and consumer experience (Juaneda-Ayensa et al., 2016).

The Rise of Independent Brands

South Africa's fashion ecosystem is dominated by independent brands and retailers. Despite the vulnerabilities of independent brands to the unprecedented shocks of 2020, the relatively smaller brands proved the most resilient amid the collapse of big retail boxes. Their survival was due to the existence of small loyal and community-based patronage, and the reflex and agility in responding to external threats. In the context of diminished consumer confidence and disposable incomes, the South African retail landscape has polarized brands, starkly contrasting major retailers from uniquely placed small independent brands. With increasing concerns about safety in public spaces and large shopping centers, consumers are likely to drift toward smaller independent brands for convenience, value for money and personalized products and services. Furthermore, independent brands may expand their footprint in major retail centers as large vacant spaces are repurposed to accommodate smaller brands under sufficiently flexible lease terms (Broll, 2017). This phenomenon could foster greater collaboration among local brands as retail models like Africa Rise proliferate in major retail centers.

Retail Technology

The advanced technologies of Industry 4.0 hold immeasurable potential for the global fashion industry. The imagined future of fashion manufacturing and retail often entails an orchestra of advanced systems and processes devoid of substantive human participation. In a model proposed by CB Insights (2020), consumers can access in real-time fully customized items, which are produced through advanced technologies such as CAD systems, 3D additive manufacturing, facilitated by Robotic cutters and sewers. In retail, the convergence of Augmented Reality (AR) and the algorithms of Big Data and Artificial Intelligence hold the most imminent prospect (Dwivedi et al., 2021). The once futuristic phenomenon is rapidly becoming a reality in some advanced economies around the world (McCormick et al., 2014).

The imminent deployment of cutting-edge manufacturing and retail technology is propelled by the inherent competitive advantage. For example, Virtual Reality (VR) has the capability to extend the showroom experience beyond the limitations of a physical retail store, thereby mitigating access to meaningful shopping experiences for consumers in remote locations. Augmented Reality and virtual commerce (v-commerce) can expand the potential of fashion retail where consumers can purchase products and services while still in the AR mode (McCormick et al., 2014). Through AR, products on the retail shelf are animated with additional details such as product specifications, their supply chain journey and mockup of the products in use. The hyper-realistic environments created through VR and AR can deepen and transform a mundane shopping activity into a thrilling out of the world experience (Mogaji, 2021).

While the deployment of cutting-edge manufacturing and retail technology is likely to lag in emerging economies such as South Africa (McCormick et al., 2014; OECD, 2020a), the country is making remarkable strides through proactive strategies. In 2019, South Africa hosted Africa's first FashionTech conference to explore indigenous applications of cutting-edge technology in retail. This conference challenged young creative minds through a 24-hour Hackathon to foster innovation utilizing breakthroughs in AR, AI, wearable tech and the internet of things (IoT). The future of fashion retail in the context of cutting-edge technology is exciting; however, it remains to be seen how fast these novel technologies will proliferate South Africa's fashion retail economy.

Summary

The fashion manufacturing and retail industry in South Africa have weathered many turbulent years and in the past decades, causing it to shrink from the largest employer to one of South Africa's least contributors to GDP and job creation. The global coronavirus pandemic is the latest blow, shattering any hope of recovery and introducing new complexities to South Africa's already battered economy. Until the recent disruption in the global supply chain and its impact on the volume of garment and textile imports from Asia, low-priced imports have persisted as the most devastating of all challenges (Mukonza et al., 2021). Emerging Trends in the post-COVID world point to unprecedented shifts in consumer behavior and marketing paradigms across disparate sectors of South Africa's economy. Nevertheless, substantial opportunities avail to marketers as the interplay of historic inefficiencies, and market failures warm up to new realities and incalculable futures.

New frontiers in technology hold significant potential for deepening brands' reach in existing markets while creating supplemental higher-order value (Nguyen & Mogaji, 2022b). As the South African economy slowly recovers from the clutches of a technical recession, new opportunities are rife amid aggressive government interventions and expanding markets under the continent-wide AfCFTA. The challenges and inherent opportunities underscore the need for remedial policy framework in which localized production and supply chain infrastructure is revamped. Such efforts are already underway in the form of a renewed industrial policy action plan, which seeks to onshore 65% of the total garment volume in retail. The government's commitment to investing across the industry's value chain and establishing a conducive investment climate through various incentives is the surest way to revive the economy. More importantly, the global catastrophe offers the global fashion industry a rare opportunity to reset, with emerging economies such as South Africa pioneering a more inclusive and sustainable future.

References

Adner, R., Oxley, J. E., & Silverman, B. S. (2013). Collaboration and competition in business ecosystems. In R. Adner, J. E. Oxley, & B. S. Silverman (Eds.), *Collaboration and competition in business ecosystems—Advances in strategic management* (Vol. 30). Emerald Group Publishing.

AfriAsia. (2018). *The AfrAsia Bank Africa Wealth Report 2018*. Johannesburg: AfriAsia Bank.

Amed, I., Berg, A., Balchandani, A., Hedrich, S., Rolkens, F., Young, R., Jensen, J. E., & Pent. (2021). *The state of fashion 2021*. New York: BoF and McKinsey & Co.

Appiah-Nimo, K. (2019). Analyzing the impact of operational challenges on value perceptions of South African luxury fashion brands. *Journal of Design, Business and Society, 5*(2), 169–192. https://doi.org/10.1386/dbs.5.2.169

Armstrong, J. C. M., & Park, H. (2017). Sustainability and collaborative apparel consumption: Putting the digital 'sharing' economy under the microscope. *International Journal of Fashion Design, Technology and Education, 10*(3), 276–286. https://doi.org/10.1080/17543266.2017.1346714

Blázquez, M. (2014). Fashion shopping in multichannel retail: The role of technology in enhancing the customer experience. *International Journal of Electronic Commerce, 18*(4), 97–116. https://doi.org/10.2753/JEC1086-4415180404

BoF and McKinsey & Co. (2021). *The state of fashion 2021*. New York: BoF and McKinsey & Co.

Bowen, G. A. (2009). Document analysis as qualitative research method. *Qualitative Research Journal, 9*(2), 27–40.

Brandenburger, A. M., & Nalebuff, B. J. (1996). *Co-opetition*. Doubleday.

Broll. (2017). *Struggling retailers: Big boxes are closing down, what now?* Johannesburg: Broll.

Brooksworth, F., Mogaji, E., & Bosah, G. (2022a). Fashion marketing in emerging economies: An introduction. In F. Brooksworth, E. Mogaji, & G. Bosah (Eds.), *Fashion marketing in emerging economies (volume 1)—Brand, consumer and sustainability perspectives*. Springer.

Brooksworth, F., Mogaji, E., & Bosah, G. (2022b). Fashion marketing in emerging economies: Conclusion and research agenda. In F. Brooksworth, E. Mogaji, & G. Bosah (Eds.), *Fashion marketing in emerging economies (volume 1)—Brand, consumer and sustainability perspectives*. Springer.

Brydges, T., & Hanlon, M. (2020). Garment worker rights and the fashion industry's response to COVID-19. *Dialogues in Human Geography, 10*(2), 195–198. https://doi.org/10.1177/2043820620933851

Caro, F., Gürhan Kök, A., & Martínez-De Albéniz, V. (2020). The future of retail operations. *Manufacturing and Service Operations Management, 22*(1), 47–58. https://doi.org/10.1287/msom.2019.0824

CB Insights. (2020). *The future of fashion: From design to merchandising, how tech is reshaping the industry*. https://doi.org/10.4324/9781315160344-12

Corbin, J., & Strauss, A. (2008). *Basics of qualitative research: Techniques and procedures for developing grounded theory* (3rd ed.). Sage.

Davis, L. (2019). What does the current South African ecommerce landscape look like?—Flicker Leap. *flickerleap*. Retrieved December 15, 2020, from https://flickerleap.com/south-african-ecommerce-landscape/

de Villiers, M. V., Chinomona, R., & Chuchu, T. (2018). The influence of store environment on brand attitude, brand experience and purchase intention. *South African Journal of Business Management, 49*(1). https://doi.org/10.4102/sajbm.v49i1.186

Deloitte. (2020). *The Deloitte Global Millennial Survey 2020: Resilient generations hold the key to creating a "better normal"*. Deloitte Global.

DTIC. (2020). Briefing on the retail-clothing, textile, footwear & leather master plan to the select committee on trade and industry. South Africa, pp. 1–20.

Dwivedi, Y. K., Hughes, L., Ismagilova, E., Aarts, G., Coombs, C., Crick, T., & Williams, M. D. (2021). Artificial Intelligence (AI): Multidisciplinary perspectives on emerging challenges, opportunities, and agenda for research, practice and policy. *International Journal of Information Management, 57*(4), 101–194.

Euromonitor. (2019). *Luxury goods in South Africa*. Johannesburg. http://www.euromonitor.com/luxury-goods-in-south-africa/report

Flanders Investment & Trade. (2016). *South Africa retail fact sheet: Apparel*. Johannesburg.

Goldberg, R. H. (2011). *Determining consumer ethnocentrism and lifestyle among Black Diamonds in Sandton*. North-West University-Potchefstroom Campus.

Goldstuck, A., & Patricios, O. (2020). *The South African Social Media Landscape*. Johannesburg: World Wide Worx.

Hines, T. (2007). Globalization: Global markets and global supplies. In T. Hines & M. Bruce (Eds.), *Fashion marketing: Contemporary issues* (2nd ed., pp. 1–25). Elsevier.

Hristova, Y. (2019). The second-hand goods market: Trends and challenges. *Izvestia Journal of the Union of Scientists—Varna. Economic Sciences Series, 8*(3), 62–71. https://doi.org/10.36997/ijusv-ess/2019.8.3.62

Jacobs, S. (2013). Africa the new Mecca for luxury brands. *African Business Magazine*. Retrieved November 20, 2017, from http://africanbusinessmagazine.com/uncategorised/africa-the-new-mecca-for-luxury-brands/

Jenvey, N. (2020). South Africa clothing sector master plan key to revival, just-style. *www.just-style.com*. Retrieved November 19, 2020, from https://www.just-style.com/analysis/south-africa-clothing-sector-master-plan-key-to-revival_id139513.aspx

Jordan, E. (2020). Luxury for less: Two South African stores embrace the second-hand luxury market. *wantedonline*. Retrieved December 31, 2020, from https://www.wantedonline.co.za/style/fashion/2019-05-22-luxury-for-less-two-south-african-stores-embrace-the-second-hand-luxury-market/

Juaneda-Ayensa, E., Mosquera, A., & Murillo, Y. S. (2016). Omnichannel customer behavior: Key drivers of technology acceptance and use and their effects on purchase intention. *Frontiers in Psychology, 7*(2), 1–11. https://doi.org/10.3389/fpsyg.2016.01117

Kaur, J., Mogaji, E., Wadera, D., & Gupta, S. (2022). Sustainable consumption practices in Indian households: A saga of environment management linked to Indian ethos and generational differences. *Society and Business Review, ahead-of-print*(ahead-of-print). https://doi.org/10.1108/SBR-08-2021-0132

Kearney, A. (2016). *The 2016 Global Retail Development Index: Global Retail Expansion at a Crossroads*. https://www.atkearney.com/documents/10192/8226719/Global+Retail+Expansion+at+a+Crossroads–2016+GRDI.pdf/dc845ffc-fe28-4623-bdd4-b36f3a443787

Laitala, K., & Klepp, I. G. (2018). Motivations for and against second-hand clothing acquisition. *Clothing Cultures, 5*(2). https://doi.org/10.1386/cc.5.2.247_1

Lodestar Marketing Research. (2015). *The luxury fashion industry in South Africa: Industry report*. Switzerland Global Enterprise.

Luxity. (2020). *Luxity's state of the luxury market Africa 2020*. Retrieved December 18, 2020, from https://luxity.co.za/state-luxury-market-africa-2020/

Mandhlazi, L., Dhurup, M., & Mafini, C. (2013). Generation Y consumer shopping styles: Evidence from South Africa. *Mediterranean Journal of Social Sciences, 4*(14), 153.

Martin-leke, S., & Ellis, E. (2014). African luxury: Luxe Ubuntu. In G. Atwal & D. Bryson (Eds.), *Luxury brands in emerging markets* (pp. 177–178). Palgrave Macmillan. https://doi.org/10.1057/9781137330536_17

Mbatha, S., & Mastamet-Mason, A. (2015). Competitive advantage challenges affecting the apparel manufacturing industry in South Africa (AMISA): Application of porter's five factor conditions. *International Journal of Social, Behavioral, Educational, Economic and Management Engineering, 9*(8), 2730–2736.

McCormick, H., Cartwright, J., Perry, P., Barnes, L., Lynch, S., & Ball, G. (2014). Fashion retailing—Past, present and future. *Textile Progress, 46*(3), 227–321. https://doi.org/10.1080/00405167.2014.973247

McKinsey & Co. (2020). *A perfect storm for fashion marketplaces*. McKinsey Apparel, Fashion and Luxury Group. McKinsey & Co.

Mogaji, E. (2021). *Brand management*. Palgrave Macmillan.

Mogaji, E., Adeola, O., Hinson, R. E., Nguyen, N. P., Nwoba, A. C., & Soetan, T. O. (2021). Marketing bank services to financially vulnerable customers: Evidence from an emerging economy. *International Journal of Bank Marketing, 39*(3), 402–428. https://doi.org/10.1108/IJBM-07-2020-0379

Morris, M., & Barnes, J. (2014). The challenges to reversing the decline of the apparel sector in South Africa. In *International Conference on Manufacturing-Led Growth for Employment and Equality in South Africa*, pp. 1–22.

Muhwati, C., & Salisbury, R. H. (2017). Agility in a South African fashion industry supply chain. *Journal of Contemporary Management, 14*(1), 864.

Mukonza, C., Hinson, R. E., Adeola, O., Adisa, I., Mogaji, E., & Kirgiz, A. C. (2021). Green marketing: An introduction. In C. Mukonza, R. E. Hinson, O. Adeola, I. Adisa, E. Mogaji, & A. C. Kirgiz (Eds.), *Green marketing in emerging markets* (Palgrave Studies of Marketing in Emerging Economies) (pp. 3–14). Palgrave Macmillan. https://doi.org/10.1007/978-3-030-74065-8_1

Nguyen, P. N., & Mogaji, E. (2022a). Emerging economies in fashion global value chain: Brand positioning and managerial implications. In F. Brooksworth, E. Mogaji, & G. Bosah (Eds.), *Fashion marketing in emerging economies—Strategies, tools and insights for fashion brands* (pp. 234–345). Springer.

Nguyen, N. P., & Mogaji, E. (2022b). A theoretical framework for the influence of green marketing communication on consumer behaviour in emerging economies. In E. Mogaji, O. Adeola, I. Adisa, R. E. Hinson, C. Mukonza, & A. C. Kirgiz (Eds.), *Green marketing in emerging economies* (Palgrave Studies of Marketing in Emerging Economies) (pp. 253–274). Palgrave Macmillan. https://doi.org/10.1007/978-3-030-82572-0_11

Norris, L. (2012). Trade and transformations of secondhand clothing: Introduction. *Textile: The Journal of Cloth and Culture, 10*(2), 128–143. https://doi.org/10.2752/175183512X13315695424473

OECD. (2020a). *Business Insights on Emerging Markets 2020*. Paris: OECD Emerging Markets Network, OECD Development Centre.

OECD. (2020b). *OECD Economic surveys: South Africa, Economic Outlook*. http://documents1.worldbank.org/curated/en/688761571934946384/pdf/Doing-Business-2020-Comparing-Business-Regulation-in-190-Economies.pdf

Park, H., & Armstrong, C. M. J. (2020). Secondhand clothing sales are booming—And may help solve the sustainability crisis in the fashion industry. *theconversation.com*. Retrieved January 2, 2021, from https://theconversation.com/secondhand-clothing-sales-are-booming-and-may-help-solve-the-sustainability-crisis-in-the-fashion-industry-148403

Plambeck, E. L. (2012). Reducing greenhouse gas emissions through operations and supply chain management. *Energy Economics, 34*, 64–74.

PWC. (2012). *South African retail and consumer products outlook 2012–2016*. http://www.pwc.co.za/assets/pdf/retail-and-consumer-products-outlook-2012-2016.pdf

Ramdass, K., & Kruger, D. (2011). An analysis into the impact of globalization on the clothing industry in conjunction with the clothing industry in South Africa. In *Technology Management in the Energy-Smart World (PICMET)*, Portland, OR, USA, pp. 2562–2571.

Rena, R., & Msoni, M. (2014). Global financial crises and its impact on the South African economy: A further update. *Journal of Economics, 5*(1), 17–25. https://doi.org/10.1080/09765239.2014.11884980

Rusko, R. (2012). Perspectives on value creation and coopetition. *Problems and Perspectives in Management, 10*(2), 60–72.

Shahbandeh, M. (2021). Secondhand apparel market value worldwide from 2012–2024. *Statista.com*. Retrieved January 22, 2021, from https://www.statista.com/statistics/826162/apparel-resale-market-value-worldwide/

Shapshak, T. (2019). Let it rain 5G: Pure-play operator rain launches Africa's first commercial 5G network. *forbes.com*. Retrieved January 8, 2021, from https://www.forbes.com/sites/tobyshapshak/2019/09/18/let-it-rain-5g-pure-play-operator-rain-launches-africas-first-commercial-5g-network/?sh=5eb2c64765e8

Sibahle, M. (2020). Coronavirus to drive permanent uptick in SA's online shopping. *itweb*. Retrieved January 7, 2021, from https://www.itweb.co.za/content/o1Jr5Mx96e2qKdWL

Soyka, P. A. (2012). *Creating a sustainable organization: Approaches for enhancing corporate value through sustainability*. Pearson Education.

Spinks, R. (2014). Can international fashion brands compete in South Africa? *theguardian.com*. Retrieved January 12, 2021, from https://www.theguardian.com/sustainable-business/sustainable-fashion-blog/international-fashion-brands-south-africa

Statista. (2019). Forecast: Industry revenue of "retail trade in textiles, clothing, footwear and leather goods" in South Africa 2011–2023. *Statista.com*. Retrieved January 10, 2021, from https://www.statista.com/forecasts/424593/retail-trade-in-textiles-clothing-footwear-and-leather-goods-revenue-in-south-africa

Steinfield, L. (2015). Consumer types versus stereotypes: exploring social tensions in the luxury market of South Africa. Saïd Business School RP 2015-9. University of Oxford, UK.

Stiehler, B. E. (2017). *Identification and assessment of luxury brand segments in the emerging markets: Case of South Africa*. KTH Royal Institute of Technology.

Thomas, V. M. (2003). Demand and dematerialization impacts of second-hand markets. Reuse or more use? *Journal of Industrial Ecology, 7*(2), 65–78.

Thompson, L. (2000). *The history of South Africa* (3rd ed.). Yale University Press.

Toma, G. (2019). The RealReal IPO: First startup from resale's new wave to go public sees shares soar. *Forbes.com*. Retrieved January 2, 2021, from https://www.forbes.com/sites/glendatoma/2019/06/28/the-realreal-ipo-luxury-reseller-latest-retailer-to-go-public/?sh=285b34ee6289

Vlok, E. (2006). The textile and clothing industry in South Africa. In H. Jauch & R. Traub-Merz (Eds.), *The future of the textile and clothing industry in Sub-Saharan Africa*. Friedrich-Ebert-Stiftung.

Watling, J., Mccabe, J., & Seedat, Y. (2019). *Rethinking the eCommerce opportunity in South Africa: How retailers can pivot to digital customers*. Johannesburg: Accenture.

Wolfhard, K. (2013). *Conspicuous consumption and race: Evidence from South Africa, papers on economics and evolution*. http://www.econbiz.de/archiv1/2010/107655_conspicious_consumption_race.pdf

Wong, Z. B. (2020). The fashion industry just outlined a vision for the future. Will rewiring fashion be good enough? *Forbes.com*. Retrieved January 4, 2021, from https://www.forbes.com/sites/zoewong1/2020/05/23/the-fashion-industry-just-outlined-a-vision-for-the-future-will-rewiringfashion-be-good-enough/?sh=4051e65b20db

8

The Rise of Female Empowerment in Egypt: The Fashion Psychology Behind Their Attire and Armour

Yasmina Nessim and Aurore Bardey

Introduction

> *Over the years I have learnt that what is important in a dress is the woman wearing it.*
> —Yves Saint Laurent

The fashion arena suffers from radical volatility and an overwhelming repertoire of garment and brand selection. All individuals and institutions associated with the fashion world—be them industry conglomerates, stylists, designers, or even devout shoppers—will preach their belief in the symbolic values of their clothing, inadvertently unveiling the effect

Y. Nessim (✉)
Pstyled, Cairo, Egypt
e-mail: yasmina@pstyled.com

A. Bardey
Burgundy School of Business, Dijon, France
e-mail: aurore.bardey@bsb-education.com

F. Brooksworth et al. (eds.), *Fashion Marketing in Emerging Economies Volume II*,
Palgrave Studies of Marketing in Emerging Economies,
https://doi.org/10.1007/978-3-031-07078-5_8

of selected garments on their cognitive processes and emotionality. Of most recent advancements, the fashion industry has embraced the relationship between clothing and human cognition—with particular emphasis on self-expression. It cannot be deemed as a pure coincidence that fashion runways are illuminated like "skittle packets of brights; from Fanta orange at Armani and scarlet at Maison Margeila; beauty and the beast yellow and candy floss pink at Giambattista Valli" (Bramley, 2017), while the world is ever more exposed to global pandemics, political chaos, and economic sufferings.

With specific regard to the Middle East and North Africa (MENA) region, clothing practices and purchases are now more acts of declaration than distraction (Mukonza et al., 2021). Abaza (2007) discusses the means by which ethnic attire has "transformed from being an austere market of resistance to Western and upper-class pretensions to a new form of 'embourgeoisement' with the aspirations for the social inclusion that this entails—[it] has become a new means to social elevation". There appears to be a general consensus that there is more to the realm of fashion and clothing than the fluorescent colours of store windows; instead, the use of fashion for expression, empowerment, and communication shines brighter.

Clothing is universally accepted and, under regulated circumstances, used as a mechanism of self-expression and means of conveying one's inner self: social aspiration, political affiliation, self-perception, and so on (Moody et al., 2010; Entwistle & Wilson, 2001). In addition, publications over the past decade have documented the means by which individuals reinforce these said beliefs and preferences through their consumption patterns (Kaur et al., 2022). This is predominantly carried out through brand loyalty, affiliation, and advocacy (Mogaji, 2021). Recent research preceding the present study has noticed a newfound trend towards local consumption; shoppers in the region are investing in both modest fashion and home-grown labels that mirror their culture (Assomull, 2019).

The research on fashion as a transformative and expressive tool in the MENA region is outdated and inconclusive and does not consider the fashion psychology behind both variables (Brooksworth et al., 2022a, 2022b). Studies' methodological approaches also disregarded the way in which expression through clothing practices can elicit a sense of empowerment. The current study aims to use fashion psychology in assessing how apparel is used to empower women in the MENA region, and how consumption patterns have changed as a consequence. The main objective of this qualitative study is, thus, to assess the rise of female empowerment in the MENA region through fashion. Ultimately, the research at hand aims to foster an honest and representative depiction of the relationship between clothing and the human psyche. The current study hopes to assess the ways in which the global fashion industry can understand and cater to their audience; personalising their offerings to the different cultural and personal characteristics. This, in turn, could revolutionise the art and science of fashion.

Literature Review

Power in the Definition of 'Empowerment'—Or Lack Thereof

Empowerment is a powerful and passionate term that is frequently used across disciplines and amongst a repertoire of different academics and policy makers. In addition, the past decade has witnessed the public 'trending' and mainstreaming of the phenomenon, categorising it as a global movement and a hashtag imprinting on all corners of the Twittersphere. However, policy practitioners and scholars have critiqued the normalisation of the "empowerment" revolution, concerned that it confines the power and purpose of the concept solely to fields of development and economic growth (Batliwala & Pittman, 2010). Ironically, however, there is no conclusive definition for 'empowerment', despite its ever-growing universal popularity. Debates persist over the true meaning of the term (Beteta, 2006; Drydyk, 2013), whilst many simultaneously consider the indefiniteness an opportunity for policy practitioners and scholars to "work it out" in both theory and practice (Batliwala, 1994).

Empowerment, in its versatile nature, demands a multitude of approaches to test its generalisability and efficiency across different cultural and social settings. The impact of the movement differs from country to country, but it's palpable in even the most conservative of nations. While some intellectuals focus on the "dichotomy of top-down versus grassroots and participatory approaches to the processes of empowerment, others tend to focus on the process from a developmental standpoint", with minimal regard for the mechanisms of empowerment on an introspective and individual level and its power on the concepts of "agency", "control", and "choice" (Shalaby & Moghadam, 2016; USAID, 2012). Feminist studies have also witnessed a change in dialogue when referencing empowerment; "power" has deviated from a focal notion that "simply conceptualises empowerment as the end goal, to a more nuanced approach that takes into consideration the context and barriers to women's *exercise* of power" (Shalaby & Moghadam, 2016; Rowlands, 1998). Empowerment is, therefore, conceptualised as a mechanism to achieve desirable outcomes and specific goals (Shalaby & Moghadam, 2016). Its true *power* lies in its unquestionable ability to impact societal relations.

Studies concentrating predominantly on the dimension of individual versus collective power have surfaced in light of this newfound narrative. Moser, for instance, defines empowerment as "the ability to determine the choices in life and to influence the direction of change, through the ability to gain control over crucial material and non-material resources" (Moser, 1993). Similarly, Kabeer's theoretical framework represents empowerment as "a process of change during which those who have been denied the ability to make *choices* acquire such an ability" (Kabeer, 1999). Empowerment is, according to Kabeer, a process that thrives from one's capacity to make choices, irrespective of the context or nature of the choices. Three key elements are necessary for the exercise of choice: resources, agency, and achievements (Kabeer, 1999; Nguyen & Mogaji, 2021). *Resources* are external to the individual's control or capabilities, *agency* is the introspective process that depends on the individual's ability to uncover his/her own objectives and desires, and *achievement* is the final outcome of this process of change. It is as a result of this framework that empowerment is regarded as both a process and an outcome (Papart et al., 2002).

Concentrating on the MENA region, Haghighat defines empowerment from a sociocultural perspective and suggests that "women's empowerment cannot simply be defined in terms of being able to perform specific activities or benefiting from propitious outcomes. It is a result from a process whereby women can freely analyse, develop, and voice their needs and interests without being predefined or unwillingly imposed by religion, government, or social norms and where their influence and control extends beyond familial and kinship circles" (Haghighat, 2013). Such a premise demands that women today act as moderators of change (Shalaby, 2014) who willingly take part in the transformative process currently changing the region and its societies.

Empowerment: A Redefined 'E' in MENA

There has been a global and substantial interest in gender issues, with female empowerment gaining a momentum and traction of its own. Since the late 1990s, there has been a general consensus that the empowerment of women has a significant and direct impact on the processes of national growth and development (UNIDO, 2003). More specifically, the UN decade for women (1975–1985), the 1995 Beijing Fourth World Conference on Women, and the resulting Platform for Action (United Nations, 1995) place great emphasis on women's empowerment breathing life into equality, development, and peace (Shalaby & Moghadam, 2016) and consequently paving the way to a new realm of feminist scholarship.

Decades of research and advocacy by women's rights activists in academia, NGOs, and policy making agencies have demonstrated—with particular regard to the Middle East and North Africa (MENA) region—the extent to which the *femme fatale*'s role is fundamental for societal and economic progress (Bahramitash & Esfahani, 2016). Roudi-Fahimi and Moghadam (2006) discuss the efforts of female activists—generally from the more educated societal segments—challenging the status quo: demanding equality, and calling for women's economic, political, and social empowerment. In response, neoliberalism has led to gender-related economic policies concentrating on raising employment for women, derived from the premise that increased employment contributes directly to women's economic empowerment. Consequently, for instance, the role of female entrepreneurs—especially in small and medium enterprises

(SMEs)—has blossomed as a matter of interest. Egypt and Lebanon having relatively high rates of female ownership among SMEs (Bahramitash & Esfahani, 2016) is a good case in point. Women across the region are not only thrusting their way into the public arena, but also simultaneously busting the "long-standing cultural stereotypes about their roles in society—not only in Egypt, Tunisia, and Libya but also in Bahrain, Syria, and Yemen" (Shalaby & Moghadam, 2016).

Fashion in the Middle East and North Africa: What Does It MENA?

As women continue to enter the professional workforce in the MENA region, the contemporary and ethnic ready-to-wear aisles are growing. Consumers in the region have developed a taste for local and humble labels that mirror their cultural heritage and that aid in spreading global awareness of the region's traditions and cultures (Assomull, 2019) versus the traditional big-name designer brands. Contrary to the region's infamous selection of couture, ready-for-the-red-carpet designs, off-the-rack designers are increasingly seeing more appeal and demand. Industry officials predict that home-grown fashion—currently at approximately 5%—will account for over 30% of ready-to-wear fashion retail in the foreseeable future. This is a direct result of more regional designers dedicating collections to all things cultural, casual, and contemporary.

According to the Dubai Design and Fashion Council, the MENA fashion industry is growing at an annual compound rate of 6% (estimated worth at the end of 2019: $55 billion). Motives to increase tourism in Saudi Arabia, the rise in women's spending power and the evolution of consumer preferences are examples of the key factors that have helped stimulate the market. In addition, Ghizlan—founder of *The Modest*, a fashion e-commerce platform that provides a curated edit of modest dressing—has conducted research that predicts the modest fashion market's worth at $484 billion by the end of 2020. Finally, with consumer attitudes changing, the fashion industry in the region is gaining more traction in the global fashion narrative. The MENA region "is starting to shift from being a historian importer of fashion trends to a nascent exporter" (Iftahy et al., 2019). With such a profound transformation in trade comes an increase in global connection—with Internet penetration in the UAE and Saudi Arabia at 99 and 89%, respectively, compared to just 57% in China (Iftahy et al., 2019).

'Walk Like an Egyptian', But Make It Fashion

Egyptian fashion today is fostered by the coexistence of Islamic, Western, and ethnic chic. The movement towards ethnic attire began under the rule of Sadat, who supported its adoption amongst the growing population of university students in the 1970s. It was advertised as a practical and comfortable solution to poverty for many students of rural origin. The outfits were both subdued in their design and ability to escape the acute class differences on campus (Abaza, 2007). Decades have passed and the symbolism of ethnic dress has evolved significantly. The fashion industry in Egypt is blossoming by virtue of new authentic and ethnic collections, and the local production of Western designs. Egyptian brands are popularising Egyptian linen and cotton in their products, selling at competitive prices, with quality finishing, giving the younger generation an alternative to the imported clothing options. Abaza (2007) refers to the developments as "the democratisation of taste in the Egyptian fashion scene", consequently proving a more subtle distinction between classes than 20 some years ago.

Suzanne Kuempel, a German designer, organised a fashion show in 2004 at The Goethe Institute in Cairo in hope of showcasing an avant-garde ethnic-inspired collection of apparel. Kuempel—herself an "ethno-designer"—was captivated by the traditions of the Bedouins of South Sinai and travelled to the Eastern desert to learn about their patterns and embroidery. The result of her endeavours was both contemporary and fashionable "ethnic"-inspired design (Abaza, 2007). In a similar pursuit, Shahira Mehrez, a specialist in Islamic art and architecture, helped render the *galabeyya*—a traditional Egyptian garment native to the Nile Valley—as chic and fashionable among the well-to-do classes. The lack of a characterised national dress and the devaluation of traditional local apparel have encouraged esteemed cultural figures like Mehrez to try to sponsor and revive a proud Egyptian lifestyle and aesthetic.

Fashion and Psychology: Torn at the Seams

The intricacy of the relationship between fashion and the human psychology is one that has gone misconstrued. Recent studies in social psychology have devoted a very finite amount of their research and efforts to the investigation and elaboration on the "phenomenology of dress", with fashion being either "overtly marginalised, devalued, trivialised, or entirely neglected in scholarly discourse" (Brydon & Niessen, 1998; Entwistle & Wilson, 2001; Kawamura, 2005; Tseëlon, 2001a). Albeit there being a substantial growth in interest in the fashion-sphere from both integrative scholarly and industrial perspectives, clothing practices have altogether been given the "cold shoulder" from psychology (Masuch & Hefferon, 2014). However, provided the assumption that fashion style and clothing functions are somewhat psychologically stimulated, the relationship is one that demands revision and further analyses.

Most recently, fashion and clothing practices are empirically confined to the bounds of social psychology and "person perception" (Masuch & Hefferon, 2014; Frith & Gleeson, 2004; Tseëlon, 2001b) with particular disregard to the impact on body-image and well-being. The limited research in this realm of research has been dedicated to the manifestation of fashion's negative implications on body-image: concentrating predominantly on the interrelation between clothing and eating disorders (Trautmann-Attmann & Widner Johnson, 2007), depression (Dubler & Gurel, 1984), schizophrenia (Andreasen, 1982; Arnold et al., 1993), and it being a "potential signifier and consequence of profound individual identity crises and loss of reality" (Masuch & Hefferon, 2014; Campo et al., 2007). In addition, contemporary research in the vein of consumer psychology argues that the prospects of engaging in excessive and compulsive buying behaviours are heightened when one is absorbed in the fashion field (Park & Burns, 2005; Trautmann-Attmann & Widner Johnson, 2007). The instances mentioned function as mere fragments of how fashion and clothing functions are negatively portrayed in contemporary psychology.

Masuch and Hefferon's (2014) grounded theory analysis proposes an introductory exploratory topic of fashion from a positive psychological perspective through the unveiling of previous writings which remained fairly unheeded. Earlier research highlights the importance of material possessions, with specific regard to clothing, as extensions of our innate and extrinsic selves (James, 1980). James (1980) elaborates further and discusses the importance of appearing soignée to humankind in contrast to naked beauty and allure, dictating that "individuals would by all means prefer to be physiologically unattractive dressed in the finest gowns to being natural beauties clothed in rags" (Masuch & Hefferon, 2014; James, 1980). In contrast to the arguments posed by modern-day psychologists, earlier findings illustrate how fashion can foster positivity through the quotidian act of dressing (Hall, 2003; Lotze, 2003). The ritual in itself is argued to involve "positive feelings of sensual and psychological comfort, satisfaction and happiness which culminate in self-enhancement" (Masuch & Hefferon, 2014; Hall, 2003; Lotze, 2003). In addition, Horn's (1968) theory on the relationship between clothing practices and positive emotionality demonstrates the means by which clothing functions allow for more positive self-perceptions and a more profound degree of self-worth. However, the research supporting the interrelationship between clothing and positive psychological repercussions is mere theories and hypotheses, and although they may aid in the dispute against the evident negativity bias in contemporary psychological speculations, they demand further practical and empirical research.

Negotiating Selfhood: Expressing Aspects of the Self

Analyses have indicated that the projects and elements that influence happiness are based on their beneficial impact and ability to facilitate self-expression, manifest social significance, and exude confidence (Christiansen, 2000). Of all dimensions meditated and assessed, self-expression correlated significantly and positively with the measure of happiness—surfacing as the most "powerful predictor of well-being in the regression analysis of all subjects in the sample" (Christiansen, 2000). Lynn and Snyder (2002) additionally highlight the societal benefits of individual uniqueness-seeking behaviours and the primal social diversification they ignite. Moreover, in reference to verbalisation of the self and the arts, Blomdahl et al. (2013) discusses the means by which art therapy promotes expression by encouraging the use of colours and symbols. Intimate thoughts and emotive experiences are communicated through an array of pigmentation and motif and subsequently provide an opportunity to narrate and understand oneself and one's story in the present life situation (Blomdahl et al., 2013).

The identity-establishing powers of fashion have been an invariable topic of debate within sociological theorising (Barnard, 1996; Davis, 1992). Masuch and Hefferon's (2014) study discusses the means by which clothing choices play a pivotal role in identity formation and identity management processes. Fashion was utilised as a vehicle of revelation, expression, and communication to various aspects of the private self, ultimately titled by Masuch and Hefferon (2014) as Expressing Aspects of the Self through one of two aspects of Negotiating Selfhood. Personality traits determine personal values and attitudes (Olver & Mooradian, 2003): foretell cognitive, emotive and mood affect, and behavioural patterns (Pervin, 1996). Fashion and clothing selection mirror, express, and regulate these factors and are thus a direct extension of personality. Humphrey et al. (1971) and Worrell (1977, cited in Dubler and Gurel, 184) dictate how clothing can be a means of expressing positive emotions or as a coping mechanism to overpower negative self-concepts. Hartley's (2019) qualitative analysis revealed the increasing likelihood of outfit selection as an expression of mood, control, or mask emotions. Similarly, Moody et al. (2010)—consistent with Feinberg et al. (1992)—displayed the repertoire of affectional levels an outfit can trigger and the power of clothing on individual emotions. The results additionally examined personality expression and management through clothing choice and the almost inevitable significance that the reflected/managed trait/mood will have on behaviour and potential social interaction.

Creating Sameness

The second attribute of the Negotiating Selfhood duo is the ability to 'Create Sameness'. Simmel (1957) argued that "clothing choices reconcile two coexisting yet contradictory psychological motivations: differentiation and imitation". The paradoxical juxtaposition between self-expression and the creation of sameness is also reminiscent of the uniqueness-seeking theory introduced by Snyder and Fromkin (1977) which suggests that individuals in association with Western contemporary industrialised societies demand a uniqueness defined as a "positive striving for differentness to other people". However, the items that are employed to project such uniqueness are one and the same as those that breed social belonging. The innate need to conform to social groupings is believed to be a fundamental human drive reflected in the universal need to belong (Masuch & Hefferon, 2014; Baumeister & Leary, 1995). Gerber and Wheeler's (2009) meta-analyses assess mood responses following exclusion and have reported that social exclusion prompted a direct link to a worsening mood and was associated with emotional distress. Contrastingly, inclusion-related occurrences triggered a reduction in negative affect, anger, depression (Zoller et al., 2010), and upturn in positive affect.

Masuch and Hefferon's (2014) accounts report using fashion to harmonically convey private and social selves. Clothing choices have been found to aid with social interaction and recognition of inner emotive states (Raunio, 1982). The expressive features of selected items help actualise a sense of togetherness with surrounding and compatible individuals whilst simultaneously presenting a prominent and sincere forefront (Raunio, 1982). And thus, the drive for uniqueness and definitive expression must be proportional to the antagonised need for similarity.

Aims and Objectives

Based on the literature cited, the aim of this study is to further understand and assess the portending nature of fashion on expression and empowerment, with particular regard to women in Egypt. The fundamental differences in aim between the current research and previous scholarly literature are (1) the fashion psychology rhetoric and (2) researching the phenomenon of empowerment amongst both consumers and designers alike within the same study. In particular, the research objectives are to explore the positive and predictive potential of fashion design and clothing practices. This study hopes to breathe new life into the relationship between well-being and empowerment, and how fashion can play a part in elevating both sensations.

Methods

Participants

Participants were selected using convenience and snowball sampling. In line with the chosen data analysis method, that is, Interpretative Phenomenological Analysis (IPA), the homogeneous sample consisted of five female fashion consumers and four female fashion designers. All participants were women aged between 18- and 24-year-olds, living and working in Egypt. Each participant identified as being interested in fashion. Participants were selected based on their demographics, age and gender, and interest in fashion. The sample fits the generic sample size recommendation made by previous researchers. Pseudonyms have been used to ensure participant anonymity.

Materials

One-to-one interviews were carried out with fashion consumers and fashion designers. Fashion consumers were asked five to six open-ended questions about their relationship with fashion as well as their experiences and thoughts on Egyptian female fashion consumer habits. Fashion designers were asked five to six open-ended questions about their relationship with fashion, their experiences, and opinions on the Egyptian fashion industry and Egyptian fashion consumers as well as their fashion design processes. To be able to explore these topics in-depth, the questions were slightly adapted according to each participant's answers during the interview.

Procedure and Data Analysis

In order to provide a comfortable and familiar environment for the participant, each interview took place in a location that was both quiet and lacked significance. Participants were made aware of the topics of the questions before starting the interview. An information sheet and consent form were signed by all participants before the interview. The open-ended interview method was used. On completion of the interview, participants were verbally debriefed.

Interpretive Phenomenological Analysis (IPA) was chosen due to the analytical focus and search for the meaning of the complex rather than to quantify the occurrence of patterns. Our data analysis followed the analysis processes of past researchers in the field. All interviews were transcribed. Each transcript was first read a few times, highlighting descriptive words and phrases. Then, the second stage was a more systematic and critical reading of the transcript to identify developing themes in the text. The third stage was grouping together these themes into clusters. The fourth stage consisted of summarising participant's themes, keywords, and quotations. The fifth and final step was consolidating themes across all transcripts to identify shared themes. Transcripts of consumers and designers were analysed separately.

The first author carried out all the interviews and the second author transcribed all the interviews. Both authors carried out the data analysis. The first author being Egyptian, and the second author being French; this dual data analysis provided an insider and outsider's point of view in the analysis.

Results

Two key themes were extracted from our data analyses: 'Self-Expression' and 'Change in Consumption Patterns'. Both themes were addressed and discussed from the perspective of the consumer and the designer.

Self-Expression

From Impress to Express: How Consumers Are Expressing Themselves Through Fashion

All participants indicated that fashion is a pillar of their lives and a means of their ability to express themselves. They all describe fashion as a reflection of their inner selves, their values, and their emotions. C1 describes fashion as a "reflection of yourself". C2 and C3 define fashion as a means to "feel like yourself" and "to feel comfortable", respectively. C5 eloquently echoes the thoughts of all other participants by stating:

> Fashion is like a mirror. It's a reflection of your inner self. You can use it to express yourself, your values, your beliefs, your innermost passions, and your emotions. It communicates who I am and what I stand for. (C5)

Our participants—as women who are intrigued and invested in the fashion industry—are impassioned by the importance of using dress as a means of self-declaration rather than dry distraction. When asked if there was any one piece of advice they would leave for young women in the region today, the commitment to expression was heartfelt:

> Dress the way you feel like dressing […] Learn your roots and what makes you feel good about yourself […] Wear something that is authentic to who you are. (C3)

> Express yourself. Wear what makes you comfortable; be you, do you. That's the most important thing to do. Be confident, be happy. (C4)

C2 and C4 elaborate further on the 'inner-self' phenomenon and how they manage to utilise fashion practice and the ritual of getting dressed to ameliorate their mood. Both participants highlighted the reciprocal relationship between fashion and mood, that is, mood will determine their dress, and yet fashion practices have the power to enhance mood and confidence.

> I see fashion as a means of expression but more so as a means to enhance what you're feeling or doing. It's more like if I feel good, I will dress well. But I think it can elevate [mood], and it can change mood. (C2)

> Fashion is an expression; it's how you feel. When you're having a bad day, it's something that will make you feel better; you can wear something that you're just so comfortable in, to enhance your confidence. (C4)

Designers have caught on to the shift in consumer behaviour and demand. As designers, they too understand that apparel can be a significant tool to communicate and reflect one's persona and consequently design to make their own "fashion a means of self-expression" (D1). When asked to elaborate on the impact of fashion as a mechanism for self-expression, participant D2 talks of her own experiences witnessing the "power of transformation":

> You can see a woman transform when she dresses comfortably, in a way that speaks to her, when she feels attractive [...] Whatever is going on in her life, whatever vision she has, whatever she wants; you can see how [fashion] can transform her. I see this with mothers, running after their kids. You see it at weddings and galas, the way women flourish. This is all fashion. It's the power of transformation. (D2)

From Express to Empower: A Message from Designers to Their Consumers

There appeared to be a general consensus between designers—an unspoken agreement—that their role as creators and providers is to aid in empowering their female consumers. Designers understand that "[fashion] is extremely empowering" (D3) and are committed to exercising their resources, designs, and businesses to deliver one key message to their female audiences:

> Focus more on what you want to wear rather than what other people expect you to wear. At the end of the day, what I always say is: 'if you're wearing

something that you love, your confidence will outshine anything and everything else'. (D3)

Don't be afraid. Don't be afraid to do whatever you want to do, really. We're all the same, we just want to be a part of something. We all have the same goal, so: speak up, live life, and be happy. And have a good time. (D4)

Change in Consumption Patterns

Bye Mainstream, Buy Local

All participants—consumers and designers—discussed the noticeable changes in consumption patterns over the last decade in the local fashion industry—be them changes in demand, in designs, or in the trade itself:

In Egypt, we were restricted [...] local brands have really stepped up. I think it's an incredible change from where we were three years ago. Now I can go into Cairo and buy a bag, maybe some shoes, it's great! Three years ago, there was hardly anything available—now the majority of my outfits are local. (C1)

[When I first started] Six years ago, the mentality was more close-minded. Back then, I never thought that my dresses would sell because they were a little out-of-the-box. People are [now] more open-minded towards what's accepted, in terms of openness, and showing more skin. The more revealing the dress, to more confident they are. It has changed, the culture has changed. (D3)

The local trends have evolved a lot, particularly in the past four years. There are a lot more people willing to go off the mainstream [...] there is an alternative movement. (D2)

The movement and shift in consumption are rooted in consumers' newfound appreciation for culture and "authenticity" (C3), and how it resonates and reflects the consumers' persona and heritage:

> With local designers, I am looking for something that expresses and shows our culture and heritage. I like to see design or colours that signify Egypt […] something that is really representative of Egypt; think lotus flower, for example. (C3)

> I like stories. We are more attracted to the story and to the fact that it comes from something that is related to us. (C1)

According to our consumer pool, designers have already started responding to the bright and patriotic mindset. Participants C4 and C5 touch on originality of the designs and produce:

> I'm happy that a lot of [new local designers] aren't copycats. I'm really happy that people are taking the time to put in the effort and the twist; it's very exciting to see. It's nice to see oriental designs and that designers are being creative. (C4)

> Local designers and designs are expressing what we're feeling. A lot more empowering prints and patterns, or cuts that are a little more risqué. I love seeing local designers really voice our own identities. (C5)

In addition, consumer interviewees discuss how designers are not only responding to consumer needs through their collections and designs, but also through their accessibility and availability. Participants state that they have "been buying more local" now that their preferences have steered away from the "more mass-produced products". C4 feels "that the local designers have stepped up their game and are more publicised" and that "[shoppers] have more platforms that help us explore them on".

We Hear You: Designers to the Egyptian Women

"In the MENA region, there is definitely a younger generation coming out and looking for inspiration here rather than from the West. They are embracing their ethnicity and culture and want to wear it" (D2). Designers have come to learn and respond to a more "educated" and "resourceful" audience (D2). The same designer shares:

> There is a definite shift in consumerism. [Shoppers] are not afraid of higher prices, as long as they know the value of the piece and that it resonates with them and their personalities [...] they are dressing according to their lifestyle, within a community, it's more authentic. (D2)

Designers have come to understand the importance of being "culturally relevant" (D4). They disclose their secret to being successful in the midst of this volatile environment:

> The most successful designers are the ones who are taking correct events into account. It's about stories, narratives, and what they stand for. (D4)

Discussion

Given the data, fashion choices appear to have a profound impact on consumers' self-expression and, consequently, their sense of empowerment. The research demonstrated that the changes in consumer demand in Egypt have a significant impact on the designs and number of designers in the region. Consequently, the response from designers—be it via collections, designs, or points of sale and contact—has further encouraged the community of proud and unapologetically *Egyptian* women; a community that has a clear preference to shop local. The analyses here show interesting implications for further psychological research, specific to the realm of fashion psychology, and suggest possibilities for potential applications in consumer behaviour and marketing.

Self-Expression and Empowerment

The data demonstrates that there is an undeniable sense of empowerment and passion that surfaces from both consumers and designers when discussing self-expression in relation to the art of dressing and fashion choices. In previous scholarly research, there appear to be an estimated 30 different definitions for empowerment (Alkire & Ibrahim, 2007). As a result, the nature of this research did not directly impose any one definition on the pool of interviewees. However, should we consider Kabeer's (1999) framework that empowerment is both a process *and* an outcome, the definition is clearly illustrated in the data. Where the *resource* is the selection of fashion choices available to Egyptian women: designed, manufactured, and sold by local designers who support the cultural female movement, and the *agency* is the newfound sense of pride, confidence, and desire to express the Egyptian woman's truest self. The resulting *achievement* is, therefore, an empowered community of women.

In addition, from a fashion psychology standpoint, research dictates that self-expression and social significance—coined the Negotiating Selfhood duo by Masuch and Hefferon (2014)—are crucial in order to influence happiness and well-being. The data and themes discussed in the study clearly demonstrate the use of fashion for self-expression, from both consumers and designers alike. However, the second attribute of Masuch and Hefferon's (2014) Negotiating Selfhood duo, 'Creating Sameness', is camouflaged in the conversation. Masuch and Hefferon's (2014) research talks of the importance of both showcasing private and social selves through clothing choices. Selected fashion details (i.e., colours, patterns, fabric, etc.) help realise a sense of togetherness amongst compatible individuals. C1 and C5 surface sub-themes of manifesting community and camaraderie during the discourse:

> Get whatever your message is out there and appreciate someone who will advocate for it. (C1)

> Be yourself. Express yourself. Embrace your story and your body and your style [...] I'm here and if you're like me, you are not alone. (C5)

Scholars view well-being—particularly psychological well-being—as a vehicle to empowerment (Browne, 2015). By that logic, we can assume that the two-part phenomenon of Negotiating Selfhood, evident here, elicits well-being, and well-being consequently elicits empowerment.

Change in Consumption Patterns

The themes and findings demonstrate how clothing can be used to express and empower Egyptian women and indicate the significance of the said relationship. Furthermore, it appears as though the relationship is amplified when the women are able to shop and dress locally. The findings support the literary findings and theorisations of preceding research; Abaza (2007), for instance, suggested that Egyptians are adopting ethnic stylings to reinvent and showcase their identities that were overpowered by the modernisation of the 1960s. Consumers and designers both feed into the new consumption pattern in Egypt; consumers are demanding designs that share their narrative, their heritage, and lifestyle; and designers are catering to the demand with more collections, contemporary takes on traditional designs and items, and accessibility.

Bourdieu's (1980) narrative on the competition between ethnic and mainstream fashion choices allows us to consider "ethnic-chic" as the agents of change. Western imports, as supported by the data, are a much longer and well-established tradition in Egypt, making local designs a more recent and refined taste and thus setting new standards in the market for "locally inspired tastes" (Abaza, 2007). Although one could view this change in demand as a direct consequence of globalisation and global interaction, it has nonetheless succeeded in fostering local designs and in helping to establish new preferences amongst the Egyptian people.

Implication of the Research and Future Work

The swift change in consumption patterns and personalities has surprisingly stimulated little attention from researchers and practitioners. Despite the obvious limitations, the recognition of gender equality and female empowerment as a critical prerequisite for national development continues to transform research and practice in other academic arenas. Nonetheless, the present study aims to fuel the discourse in relation to fashion marketing and psychology. However, it was not without its limitations: most research conducted prior to and including this study cannot proceed under the simplistic impression that the MENA region is one homogenous area where Arab women's experiences are identical (Shalaby & Moghadam, 2016). As maintained by Sabbagh (1996), the experiences of women and the challenges they face vary widely across the Arab world. Future research could consider contributions across different segments of Arab societies (i.e., United Arab Emirates, Kuwait, Lebanon, Morocco, etc.). In addition, although participants were selected from different backgrounds, age groups, and reside in geographic locations, a larger sample size would aid in the generalisation of the results to the wider population.

The research in this study aids in the understanding of how consumers in Egypt view the local fashion industry and how they apply its produce to express and empower themselves, whilst simultaneously gaining insight into the reactions and responses of regional designers. This information is aimed at designers and businesses—local and international—in hope that they too can apply this insight to better understand the mindset and behaviour of consumers in the region. This, in turn, can help transform their marketing practices and strategies. Literature preceding this study clearly suggests that Western *haute couture* will always have its place on the rails of the Egyptian woman's closet; however, our study unveiled a significant shift in preferences, in which consumers favour local designers more so than they did a decade ago due to their ability to mirror the individuality of the Egyptian woman. Nevertheless, all parties can benefit from collaborations, sharing resources and cultural insights in the future: consumers from a new set of choices, local designers by expanding their audience to the West, and high-street designers through an innovative and culturally relevant set of designs and apprehensions.

Marketers and managers of different fashion houses, agencies, and institutions—both in the MENA region and abroad—could benefit from the insight and information regarding the use of fashion and dress as a means of cultural and self-expression. Should they wish to further adapt their practices to this shift in consumer mindset and utilisation of their produce, they could dedicate more of their resources to hyper-personalising their messages, product designs, and even points of sale to women in search of aligning their fashion purchases with their innermost-selves. Consider, for instance, pop-up events and stores that not only cater to selling designs that represent women's heritage, but also offer different experiences, delicacies, and entertainment that transport them to their ancestral homelands, empower them through the wonderful sense of authenticity, and inspire them with the warmth of community (Mogaji et al., 2022).

The research has introduced a preliminary shift in consumption patterns from mainstream to local designers, from quantity to quality, and most importantly, from being trendy to being authentic. When this research was being conducted, data and resources were—and still are—scarce, perhaps this serves as a viable starting point for researchers, trend forecasters, and theorists to further enhance and understand the importance and reasoning behind the use of fashion as armour. Not solely in the regions discussed here, but in a multitude of different countries and cultures around the globe. In addition, it is imperative that research is conducted on the reasoning behind why women resort to local, ancestral, and even nostalgic dresses for strength and expression. Over past decades, political, societal, socio-economic, and even 'personal' distresses have become more and more accessible and industries varying from food and beverage, to music and fashion, have witnessed a shift in demand to all things familiar (Gökerik et al., 2018). Consumers gravitate towards items and objects that represent simpler, happier, and safer times. Researchers and industry officials should perhaps assess whether there should be more permanent and accessible collection within the fashion world that serves as a safety blanket, a time machine, a coat of armour, that protects, calms, and even excites today's consumer.

Conclusion

In India, Gandhi protested against European apparel, and clothing became a symbol of national importance. His preference for a modest 'loincloth' over the modern attires of the West was intended to create solidarity with the poor, and expose colonial exploitation. As a result of his preaching and promoting the simple cloth, he invented a national dress that became a powerful metaphor and mechanism for national liberation. Decades later, the importance of cultural symbolism in dress resonates here today. The present study demonstrated how women in Egypt—and perhaps in the neighbouring regions—have come to utilise the art of fashion to, like Gandhi, express their innermost beliefs and values.

The results of this study definitively challenge the aforementioned literature where clothing practices, and the fashion industry in its entirety, are demurred. In truth, the findings extend and reinforce the literary accounts of a former period from the psychology arena, supporting the more positive psychological theorisation and presenting the more pleasure-inducing powers of fashion (Nguyen & Mogaji, 2022a, 2022b). The literature that roots this study demonstrates the ways in which clothing can increase empowerment through the negotiation of the self, and the creation of sameness. The synergy of one or both of these variables—with the assistance of external resources—was found to constitute the well-being and empowerment of Egyptian women.

As the fashion market, in its entirety, continues to fragment, a deeper understanding of human psychology profiling and impression would assist in the development of more targeted and segmented strategies. Training in fashion psychology and culture can be used to educate fashion designers, stylists, and consumers on the importance of patterns, fit, camouflage, and texture. This can potentially develop an association during the embryonic stages of the designer-consumer relationship, especially in an environment where preferences are still relatively new. In doing so, consumers can deepen their emotional rapport with the garments, the brands, and the shopping experience, ultimately filling their closets with layers of happiness; resulting in the real-life materialisation of the 'look good, feel good' phenomenon.

References

Abaza, M. (2007). Shifting landscapes of fashion in contemporary Egypt. *Fashion Theory, 11*(2–3), 281–297.

Alkire, S., & Ibrahim, S. (2007). Agency and empowerment: A proposal for internationally comparable indicators. *Oxford Development Studies, 35*(4), 380–403.

Andreasen, N. C. (1982). Negative symptoms in schizophrenia: Definition and reliability. *Archives of General Psychiatry, 39*(1), 784–788.

Arnold, V. K., Rosenthal, T. L., Dupont, R. T., & Hilliard, D. (1993). Redundant clothing: A readily observable marker for schizophrenia in the psychiatric emergency room population. *Journal of Behavior Therapy and Experimental Psychiatry, 24*(1), 45–47.

Assomull, S. (2019). The Middle East embraces ready-to-wear. [online] Vogue Business. Retrieved September 10, 2020, from https://www.voguebusiness.com/fashion/middle-east-ready-to-wear-arab-fashion-kage-mrs-keepa

Bahramitash, R., & Esfahani, H. (2016). *Political and socio-economic change in the Middle East and North Africa* (1st ed., pp. 155–165). Palgrave Macmillan.

Barnard, M. (1996). *Fashion as communication*. Routledge.

Batliwala, S. (1994). *Women's Empowerment in South Asia: Concepts and Practices*. New Delhi: Food and agricultural Organization/Asia South Pacific Bureau of Adult Education.

Batliwala, S., & Pittman, A. (2010). Capturing Change in Women's Realities: A Critical Overview of Current Monitoring and Evaluation Frameworks and Approaches. Toronto: AWID. http://www.awid.org/About-AWID/AWID-News/Capturing-Changein-Women-s-Realities. Accessed 2 November 2020.

Baumeister, R. F., & Leary, M. R. (1995). The need to belong: Desire for interpersonal attachments as a fundamental human motivation. *Psychological Bulletin, 117*(39), 497–529.

Beteta, H. C. (2006). What is missing in measures of women's empowerment? *Journal of Human Development, 7*(2), 221–241.

Blomdahl, C., Gunnarsson, A., Guregård, S., & Björklund, A. (2013). A realist review of art therapy for clients with depression. *The Arts in Psychotherapy, 40*(3), 322–330. https://doi.org/10.1016/j.aip.2013.05.009

Bourdieu, P. (1980). *Questions de Sociologie*. Les Editions de Minuit.

Bramley, E. (2017). Dopamine dressing—Can you dress yourself happy? [online] *The Guardian*. Retrieved September 15, 2020, from https://www.theguardian.com/fashion/2017/feb/03/dopamine-dressing-can-you-dress-yourself-happy

Brooksworth, F., Mogaji, E., & Bosah, G. (2022a). Fashion marketing in emerging economies: An introduction. In F. Brooksworth, E. Mogaji, & G. Bosah (Eds.), *Fashion marketing in emerging economies (volume 1)—Brand, consumer and sustainability perspectives*. Springer.

Brooksworth, F., Mogaji, E., & Bosah, G. (2022b). Fashion marketing in emerging economies: Conclusion and research agenda. In F. Brooksworth, E. Mogaji, & G. Bosah (Eds.), *Fashion marketing in emerging economies (volume 1)—Brand, consumer and sustainability perspectives*. Springer.

Browne, E. (2015). Wellbeing through empowerment, improved enabling environment, and assets (GSDRC Helpdesk Research Report 1211). Birmingham, UK: GSDRC, University of Birmingham.

Brydon, A., & Niessen, S. A. (1998). *Consuming fashion: Adorning the transnational body*. Berg.

Campo, J., Hardy, S., Merckelbach, H., Nijman, H., & Zwets, A. (2007). The urge to change appearance in different psychopathological categories. *Acta Neuropsychiatrica, 19*(2), 104–108.

Christiansen, C. (2000). Identity, personal projects and happiness: Self construction in everyday action. *Journal of Occupational Science, 7*(3), 98–107. https://doi.org/10.1080/14427591.2000.9686472

Davis, F. (1992). *Fashion, culture, and identity*. University of Chicago Press.

Drydyk, J. (2013). Empowerment, agency and power. *Journal of Global Ethics, 9*(3), 249–262.

Dubler, M. L. J., & Gurel, L. M. (1984). Depression: Relationships to clothing and appearance self-concept. *Home Economics Research Journal, 13*(1), 21–26.

Entwistle, J., & Wilson, E. (2001). Introduction: Body dressing. In J. Entwistle & E. Wilson (Eds.), *Body dressing* (pp. 1–8). Oxford: Berg.

Feinberg, R. A., Mataro, L., & Burroughs, W. J. (1992). Clothing and social identity. *Clothing and Textiles Research Journal, 11*(1), 18–23.

Frith, H., & Gleeson, K. (2004). Clothing and embodiment: Men managing body image and appearance. *Psychology of Men and Masculinity, 5*(1), 40–48.

Gerber, J., & Wheeler, L. (2009). On being rejected: A meta-analysis of experimental research on rejection. *Perspectives on Psychological Science, 4*(5), 468–488. https://doi.org/10.1111/j.1745-6924.2009.01158.x

Gökerik, M., Gürbüz, A., Erkan, I., Mogaji, E., & Sap, S. (2018). Surprise me with your ads! The impacts of guerrilla marketing in social media on brand image. *Asia Pacific Journal of Marketing and Logistics, 30*(5), 1222–1238. https://doi.org/10.1108/APJML-10-2017-0257

Haghighat, E. (2013). Social status and change: The question of access to resources and women's empowerment in the Middle East and North Africa. *Journal of International Women's Studies, 14*(1), 273–299.

Hall, G. S. ([1898] 2003). Some aspects of the early sense of self. In K. K. P. Johnson, S. J. Torntore, & J. B. Eicher (Eds.), *Fashion foundations: Early writings on fashion and dress* (pp. 43–49). Berg.

Hartley, J. (2019). Fashion and mood: How clothes affect your emotions. https://www.smh.com.au/lifestyle/fashion-and-mood-how-clothes-affect-your-emotions-20150717-giei1f.html

Horn, M. J. (1968). *The second skin: An interdisciplinary study of clothing.* Houghton Mifflin.
Humphrey, C., Klaasen, M., & Creekmore, A. M. (1971). Clothing and self-concept of adolescents. *Journal of Home Economics, 63*(4), 246–250.
Iftahy, A., Mellens, M., Walia, N., & Youssef, A. (2019). A closer look at the fashion industry in Gulf Cooperation Council markets. [online] McKinsey & Company. Retrieved September 10, 2020, from https://www.mckinsey.com/industries/retail/our-insights/a-closer-look-at-the-fashion-industry-in-gulf-cooperation-council-markets
James, W. (1980). *The principles of psychology* (Vol. 1). Henry Holt & Co.
Kabeer, N. (1999). Resources, agency, and achievements: Reflections on the measurement of women's empowerment. *Development and Change, 30*, 435–464.
Kaur, J., Mogaji, E., Wadera, D., & Gupta, S. (2022). Sustainable consumption practices in Indian households: A saga of environment management linked to Indian ethos and generational differences. *Society and Business Review, ahead-of-print*(ahead-of-print). https://doi.org/10.1108/SBR-08-2021-0132
Kawamura, Y. (2005). *Fashionology: An Introduction to Fashion Studies.* Oxford: Berg.
Lotze, H. ([1887] 2003). Microcosmus: An essay concerning man and his relation to the world. In K. K. P. Johnson, S. J. Torntore, & J. B. Eicher (Eds.), *Fashion foundations: Early writings on fashion and dress* (pp. 40–43). Berg.
Lynn, M., & Snyder, C. R. (2002). Uniqueness seeking. In C. R. Snyder & S. J. Lopez (Eds.), *Handbook of positive psychology* (pp. 395–419). Oxford University Press.
Masuch, C.-S., & Hefferon, K. (2014). Understanding the links between positive psychology and fashion: A grounded theory analysis. *International Journal of Fashion Studies*, 1. https://doi.org/10.1386/infs.1.2.227_1
Mogaji, E. (2021). *Brand management.* Palgrave Macmillan.
Mogaji, E., Adeola, O., Adisa, I., Hinson, R. E., Mukonza, C., & Kirgiz, A. C. (2022). Green marketing in emerging economies: Communication and brand perspective: An introduction. In E. Mogaji, O. Adeola, I. Adisa, R. E. Hinson, C. Mukonza, & A. C. Kirgiz (Eds.), *Green marketing in emerging economies* (Palgrave Studies of Marketing in Emerging Economies) (pp. 1–16). Palgrave Macmillan. https://doi.org/10.1007/978-3-030-82572-0_1
Moody, W., Kinderman, P., & Sinha, P. (2010). An exploratory study: Relationships between trying on clothing, mood, emotion, personality and clothing preference. *Journal Of Fashion Marketing And Management: An International Journal, 14*(1), 161–179. https://doi.org/10.1108/13612021011025483

Moser, C. (1993). *Gender planning and development: Theory, practice and training*. Routledge.
Mukonza, C., Hinson, R. E., Adeola, O., Adisa, I., Mogaji, E., & Kirgiz, A. C. (2021). Green marketing: An introduction. In C. Mukonza, R. E. Hinson, O. Adeola, I. Adisa, E. Mogaji, & A. C. Kirgiz (Eds.), *Green marketing in emerging markets* (Palgrave Studies of Marketing in Emerging Economies) (pp. 3–14). Palgrave Macmillan. https://doi.org/10.1007/978-3-030-74065-8_1
Nguyen, N. P., & Mogaji, E. (2021). Financial inclusion for women in the informal economy: An SDG agenda post pandemic. In O. Adeola (Ed.), *Gendered perspectives on Covid-19 recovery in Africa*. Palgrave Macmillan. https://doi.org/10.1007/978-3-030-88152-8_12
Nguyen, P. N., & Mogaji, E. (2022a). Emerging economies in fashion global value chain: Brand positioning and managerial implications. In F. Brooksworth, E. Mogaji, & G. Bosah (Eds.), *Fashion marketing in emerging economies—Strategies, tools and insights for fashion brands* (pp. 234–345). Springer.
Nguyen, N. P., & Mogaji, E. (2022b). A theoretical framework for the influence of green marketing communication on consumer behaviour in emerging economies. In E. Mogaji, O. Adeola, I. Adisa, R. E. Hinson, C. Mukonza, & A. C. Kirgiz (Eds.), *Green marketing in emerging economies* (Palgrave Studies of Marketing in Emerging Economies) (pp. 253–274). Palgrave Macmillan. https://doi.org/10.1007/978-3-030-82572-0_11
Olver, J. M., & Mooradian, T. A. (2003). Personality traits and personal values: A conceptual and empirical integration. *Personality and Individual Differences, 35*(1), 109–125.
Papart, J., Rai, S., & Staudt, K. (Eds.). (2002). *Rethinking empowerment: Gender and development in a global/local world*. Routledge.
Park, H.-J., & Burns, L. D. (2005). Fashion orientation, credit card use, and compulsive buying. *Journal of Consumer Marketing, 22*(3), 135–141.
Pervin, L. A. (1996). *The science of personality*. John Wiley.
Raunio, A-M. (1982). Favorite clothes—A look at individuals' experience of clothing. In U. Suojanen (Ed.), *Clothing and its social, psychological, cultural and environmental aspects* (Research Report No. 161). Department of Teacher Education, University of Helsinki, pp. 179–194.
Roudi-Fahimi, F., & Moghadam, V. (2006). Empowering women, developing society: Female education in the Middle East and North Africa. *Al-Raida Journal, 23–24*(114–115), 4–11.
Rowlands, J. (1998). A word of the times, but what does it mean? Empowerment in the discourse and practice of development. In H. Ashfar (Ed.), *Women and empowerment* (pp. 1–11). St. Martin's Press.

Sabbagh, S. (1996). *Arab women: Between defiance and restraint*. Olive Branch Press.
Shalaby, M. (2014). Trajectories of change: Challenge and transformation in the wake of the Arab Spring. James A. Baker III Institute for Public Policy.
Shalaby, M., & Moghadam, V. (2016). *Empowering women after the Arab Spring* (pp. 1–9). Nature America Inc..
Simmel, G. ([1905] 1957). Fashion. *The American Journal of Sociology, 62*(6), 541–558.
Snyder, C. R., & Fromkin, H. L. (1977). Abnormality as a positive characteristic: The development and validation of a scale measuring need for uniqueness. *Journal of Abnormal Psychology, 86*(5), 518–527.
Trautmann-Attmann, J., & Widner Johnson, T. (2007). Compulsive consumption behaviours: Investigating relationships among binge eating, compulsive clothing buying and fashion orientation. *International Journal of Consumer Studies, 33*(3), 267–273.
Tseëlon, E. (2001a). Ontological, epistemological and methodological clarifications in fashion research: From critique to empirical suggestions. In A. Guy, M. Banim, & E. Green (Eds.), *Through the wardrobe: Women's relationships with their clothes* (pp. 237–254). Berg.
Tseëlon, E. (2001b). Fashion research and its discontents. *Fashion Theory, 5*(4), 435–451.
UNIDO (United Nations Industrial Development Organization). (2003). A path out of poverty: Developing rural and women entrepreneurship. New York: UNIDO.
United Nations, Platform of Action, Fourth World Conference on Women, Beijing, China, 4–15 September 1995 (New York: UN, 1996): para. 69; and United Nations, The Beijing Declaration (New York: UN, 1996): paras. 13, 14, and 17.
USAID. (2012). Gender equality and female empowerment policy. http://www.usaid.gov/sites/default/files/documents/1870/GenderEqualityPolicy.pdf
Zoller, C., Maroof, P., Weik, U., & Deinzer, R. (2010). No effect of social exclusion on salivary cortisol secretion in women in a randomized controlled study. *Psychoneuroendocrinology, 35*, 1294–1298.

9

Fashion Analytics in Africa and Middle East: Strategies, Tools, and Insights for Fashion Brands

Coy Griffin

Introduction

This chapter aims to introduce and highlight the data-driven marketing practices and structures of fashion brands within the Middle East and African (MEA) region. The methodology is to identify **fashion analytics** in MEA through the analyses of the effectiveness of advanced data-driven marketing practices and capturing the top data measurements to analyse fashion consumers in emerging fashion markets in MEA. **Fashion analytics** can help designers manage inventory, profitability, and consumer targeting efficiently.

Data-driven practices are essential because fashion houses in emerging markets typically rely on physical, creative, or traditional marketing practices in fashion to build fashion houses, not analytical ones. According to

C. Griffin (✉)
YOC LLC, New York, NY, USA
e-mail: coy@theyoc.com

F. Brooksworth et al. (eds.), *Fashion Marketing in Emerging Economies Volume II*,
Palgrave Studies of Marketing in Emerging Economies,
https://doi.org/10.1007/978-3-031-07078-5_9

Heuritch, there are three main types of data analytics typically used in the fashion industry (Mollard, 2020).

- Descriptive analytics: involves summarising data to explain what has already happened. This can be anything from past sales data, stock, or consumer habits.
- Predictive analytics: predicts what is likely (or not) to happen in the future. This method uses historical data to identify future patterns using statistics and algorithms, from predicting consumer behaviour to demand.
- Prescriptive analytics: advises on possible future outcomes. In other words, this approach attempts to guide decisions on the future.

As local consumers and brands become more connected to and leverage the internet to shop and gain traction (Iftahy, 2019, p. 2), we can expect the local digital marketing landscape and fashion practices to grow correspondingly. According to McKinsey & Company, "Middle Eastern consumers are also becoming increasingly connected. Internet penetration in the UAE and Saudi Arabia is at 99 and 89 percent respectively, compared to just 57 percent in China" (Iftahy, 2019, p. 2).

The first section addresses the cultural decisions which are important to consider within the current and future state of the MEA fashion industry. We will provide insights into fashion brands within the following countries of the **MEA region: Nigeria, South Africa, the UAE, and Saudi Arabia, among others**. As the digital landscape increases, fashion brands are adopting new data-driven technologies to track user interactions.

Therefore, the second section inspects the analytical frameworks that drive decisions within the arising landscapes by examining the data-driven marketing case studies, literature reviews, and frameworks. This section features how MEA brands readjusted or adopted e-commerce and digital behaviour tactics due to COVID-19.

The third section highlights the qualitative and quantitative Key Performance Indicators (KPIs) used to measure successful MEA fashion brands' SEO and Social Media. Currently, fashion analytical tools in

MEA regions are used to improve sales/product performance, understand consumer data points, and develop efficient designs (Oh, 2020, p. 1).

The final section examines the progression of the MEA's latest trends in artificial intelligence, voice technology, and machine learning. Fashion brands are using data analytics, machine learning, and artificial intelligence (Oh, 2020, p. 1) to develop and produce fashion styles that resonate with their respective markets. These new tools help brands make business decisions by using consumer and marketing insights.

Section 1: Cultural Decisions Needed to Consider Within the MEA Region

According to Dr Keunyoung Oh, analytics is used by "fashion professionals to improve sales and margins because fashion brands and retailers need to develop, manufacture, and sell styles that resonate with consumers." In the top fashion cities like New York or France, internal teams collaborate with technical teams to create analytical solutions to understand consumers, increasing the demand for data analysts within the fashion industry. Fashion analysts use internal and predictive data to predict consumer behaviour, trends, and profits. According to Fashion United, brands should hire analysts who collect and define data to uncover meaningful insights. Brands that aren't leveraging data are missing essential information to grow their business.

In Africa, consumer growth in the overall market is expected to remain steady due to relevant cultural and financial references (Brooksworth et al., 2022a, 2022b). As Nigeria grows constantly within the expanding middle class, we can expect the fashion sector to follow (Business of Fashion | McKinsey & Company, 2019). But as emerging fashion markets grow so does the importance of digitally relevant analytical tools to make impactful fashion marketing decisions. In the current landscape, according to Fashionomics Africa, "there is insufficient data on the African fashion sector, and the systems to fill this data gap are lacking."

In order for African brands to capture data within the future landscape, there needs to be improvement within the current one. There are three levels of data that are needed: continental, national, and consumer. On the continental level there is currently little public data available about the Intra-African trade and other impacts from countries that have developed domestic fashion economies. The national data typically lumps all creative and cultural industries together, which does not provide enough information to make informed decisions within the fashion sector. When data is available it's usually focused on exported textiles, manufacturing, or other sectors. The unaggregated and lack of data does not give policy makers and practitioners an actual depiction of the fashion industry within the continent. Nationally, this can prevent policy makers from creating policies to protect their fashion industries or reallocate funds to them. For business owners, the lack of global data may make it difficult to seek investments or financial assistance.

Although there is a lack of global data currently in the fashion industry, there are examples of emerging brands using logistical and internal predictive analytics to grow their business outside the continent. South African brand KISUA serves a global customer base. In order to maintain the international customer base, the brand has implemented logistics and distribution centres across major international hubs like Africa, the United States, and Europe (Fashionomics Africa, 2020b). Implementing various distribution centres in popular hubs grants KISUA an advantage to reach international consumers faster than other African retailers without distribution centres.

Nisha Kanabar, founder and chief executive of Industrie Africa, initially launched a database of designers on the continent. Using her knowledge and access to the database, she pivoted to e-commerce using 20 designers from various African countries, and only keeping small amounts of inventory on hand, proving that utilising a database can help ignite fashion companies on the continent (Okwuosa, 2020).

In the future, African fashion brands should use data-based software as an additional resource to explore growth opportunities. Fashionomics Africa states, "South African shoppers surveyed in February 2020 spent an average of $109 on online purchases. While this figure is the highest in Africa, it is $400 lower than the global average. In fact, the six African countries featured are still ranked in the global bottom 10" (Fashionomics Africa, 2020a). Although e-commerce in Africa is still maturing, leading fashion brands can leverage developed analytical aspects to continue growth in their sector. Unfortunately, in African countries, there is minimal public fashion data available.

To combat these issues and create additional opportunities for rising brands, governments and data agencies should publish data that reflects the bespoke fashion sectors and leverage the African Union to re-evaluate the impact of economic tools for trading. Smaller fashion companies with limited data resources can leverage social media tools and analytics to align their KPIs. We will expand on these KPIs in section 3.

In the Middle East, rising brands leverage the digital e-commerce landscape as an additional resource to explore growth opportunities. In the UAE and Saudi Arabia, e-commerce continues to show growth at approximately 40 per cent per year for the next five years. Consumers are adapting to popular international retail sites like Amazon, Farfetch, Jollychic, and Yoox Net-a-Porter while local players from the region Ounass, the Modist, and Namshi are following a similar model to increase consumer traction (Iftahy, 2019). Each of these e-commerce websites collected consumer data, which provide fashion brands with prescriptive and descriptive analytics about their customers. These insights may have not been easy to capture within a store.

In conclusion, as the middle class grows in Africa, we can expect brands to invest in data systems that align with their consumer growth. In the Middle East, e-commerce growth in the UAE and Saudi Arabia region provides brands.

Section 2: Data Frameworks

This subsection evaluates case studies and identifies the common data-collection frameworks in the MEA region and provides actionable and analytical resources. A data framework refers to the process of building a model for managing internal and external data. The framework or system sets the guidelines and rules of the interaction and manipulation of the data to track business key performance indicators. The first segment applies to responses to economic market crises, and the last two segments should unlock customer insights, respectively (in order of the frameworks). The frameworks were created to replace the one-size-fits-all approach to e-commerce, but instead categorise frameworks based on the level and probable trajectory of customer demand and factors such as supply-chain capacity and flexibility (McKinsey & Company, 2020).

The first framework unlocks common archetypes and actionable data-driven tools to overcome crises within the MEA digital landscape. The second framework can be used to unlock various dimensions of customer data. The final framework guides fashion brands through modern segmentation using data-driven aspects. *This section captures Learning Objective 2*: identify and apply analytical frameworks to make data-driven decisions within the arising MEA landscape post-COVID.

Section 2.1: Data Framework Pre-COVID-19

Before the 2020 global pandemic, MEA retailers were not adopting e-commerce as much as their internationally developed counterparts. COVID-19 forced retailers to adjust to e-commerce and digital behaviours (McKinsey & Company, 2020).

Framework 1

During the 2020 COVID-19 pandemic, countries within the MEA region searched for digital solutions and frameworks to ensure customer relations were maintained via e-commerce channels (McKinsey & Company, 2020). The strategies were bucketed into three sections (archetypes) to minimise the impact of the crisis and sustain their business. The MEA fashion brands crisis archetypes ranged from below. Once an MEA business identifies its corresponding archetype, it must focus on recouping sales using data-driven e-commerce strategies.

The first archetype uncovers MEA retailers with an online presence and a growing demand during a crisis and according to McKinsey & Company, "players with an online presence seeing a rapid increase in demand (for example, those associated with grocery and essential products) should sustain their activities through steps such as optimising baskets and rationalising product ranges to enable consistent delivery."

While in the process of sustaining their business, fashion brands should leverage data-driven tools which track KPIs with real-time dashboards and with up-to-date measurements. Fashion brands in MEA regions should partner with third-party sites to scale internal processes. Decisions should be made based on consumer analytics systems, product availability data points, and simple internal processes. Investing in such tools will provide the insights needed to identify where to invest marketing efforts (McKinsey & Company, 2020).

Section 2.2: Data Framework Post-COVID

The second archetype shows key data strategies for MEA retailers with an online presence and rapid decline in demand. During the COVID-19 pandemic, luxury retailers with this archetype could adapt specified data-driven digital marketing efforts (McKinsey & Company, 2020) to expand their e-commerce business. Retailers with lower website traffic can improve their websites by experimenting with innovative, data-driven activities on their website and app. They should use website-related KPIs to remove low-performing website elements and enhance high-performing activities. MEA brands could review the marketing analysis of search engine traffic and social media activity to identify where they can reduce cost and cost-per-click (CPC). Once costs have been decreased, brands can reallocate budgets to focus on customer engagement. Leveraging social media chat features, online sales representatives can virtually provide assistance to targeted customers (McKinsey & Company, 2020).

The third archetype consists of MEA brands building an online presence and embracing social media. According to McKinsey & Company, "players lacking an online presence must make no-regret moves, such as embracing social-media marketing. They should also find ways to sell online, through either third-party platforms or their own bespoke offerings."

MEA brands without an online presence can use social media data points to quickly identify visual images and items that resonate with their users and possibly identify their top-selling items. MEA brands that lack a consumer presence can leverage existing e-commerce platforms to reach their audience. E-commerce websites typically charge 25–30 per cent commission, but the commission prices may be outweighed by the potential consumer reach (McKinsey & Company, 2020). New York-based e-commerce website *Folklore* only features emerging designer brands from Africa, giving them an opportunity to reach an international audience (2018). Lastly, MEA brands can build their own e-commerce website. During a crisis, marketing initiatives will be important to keep consumers engaged. Using marketing initiatives like special offerings—tailored messaging, personalisation enablers to manage mobile/web user interactives and off-the-shelf marketing solutions like Mailchimp—can help MEA brands quickly build a digital solution and to build an online presence (McKinsey & Company, 2020).

An example of a fashion retailer using personalisation to reach their customers is e-retailer *very.co.uk*. According to Google & Bain, this website created an "estimated 3.5 versions of its website to shoppers based on their first and third party data." First-party data is the information collected directly from the audience. Third-party data is purchased from outside sources who aren't the original collectors of the data. During personalisation from the study, customers may see a different version of the websites based on the analytics and data collected per user (Think with Google, 2019). Personalising aspects of the website based on specific user preferences, location, and so on can help developing countries target specific customers with an added experience. Exhibit A demonstrates the implications below:

Exhibit A: (McKinsey & Company, 2020). *Illustrative examples of ecommerce implications* [Diagrams]. Available from https://www.mckinsey.com/middle-east/our-insights/how-middle-east-and-africa-retailers-can-accelerate-e-commerce-imperatives-for-now-and-the-next-normal [Accessed 11/1]

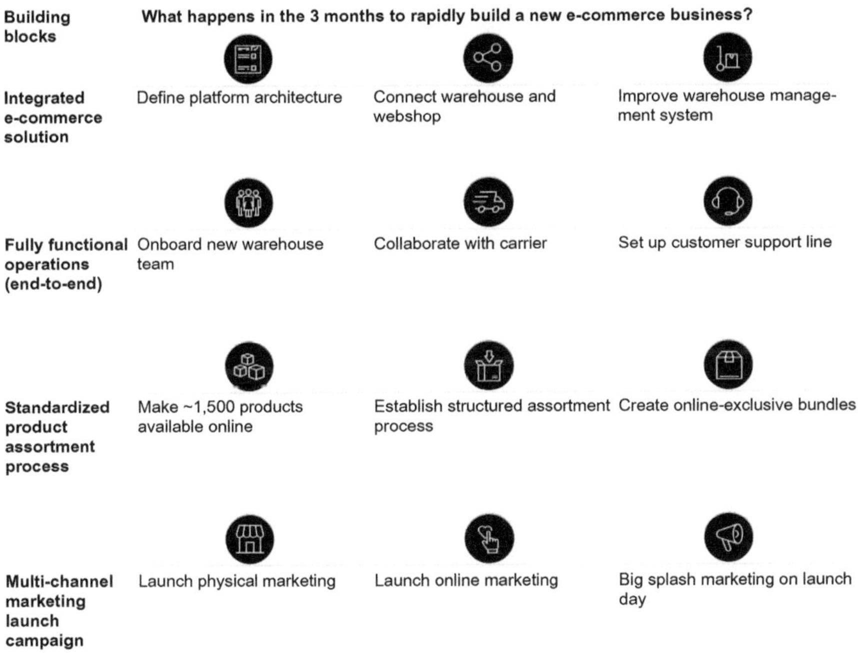

Successful MEA retailers used digital tools to quickly respond to business needs during the pandemic. MEA brands could re-evaluate their current placement in the digital landscape and leverage data-driven partnerships to combat challenges (McKinsey & Company, 2020).

Framework 2

The second framework should be used to identify the four dimensions of consumer data. As emerging fashion brands build their audiences, it is essential to identify high-value customers and associated key attributes. Consumer attributes can consist of gender, loyalty level, age group, and propensity to buy. Brands can unlock key attributes by analysing online and offline behaviours, product affinities, and demographics (How to Harness the Four Dimensions of Customer Data, 2019). Once the attributes are identified, brands can send marketing initiatives to consumers with the same attributes to initiate conversions.

Fashion analysts and marketers can use their first-party data (the insights collected directly from the brands audience) to identify demographics, behavioural data, contextual data, and predictive analytics. Gruzbarg supports this idea and states that "fashion analysts and marketers should be able to use their customer data, or first-party data." To identify these four dimensions, analysts should answer, "Who is the customer?" (to determine the demographics); "What are their past buying behaviours?" (to obtain behavioural data); "What is the customer currently doing or buying?" (to understand current contextual marketing data); and "How will the customer respond in the future?" (to predict future analyses). Please see Exhibit B for a reference to Gruzbarg's dimensions:

Exhibit B: Example of Definitions (Amended from WWD, How to Harness the Four Dimensions of Customer Data. WWD) (Gruzbarg, 2019)

1. **Demographics:** More or less stable traits like gender, age, or income. For example, an older customer is overall more likely to be interested in certain fashion accessories than a younger customer.
2. **Historic/Behavioural Data:** Past behaviours—purchase transactions, carts abandoned, and so forth—can be a good predictor for future actions. For example, a customer who has purchased a pair of shoes at the beginning of the season at full price is more likely to do so again in the future.
3. **Streaming/Contextual Data:** A customer's current digital behaviours—web pages they are viewing, e-mails they open, ads they are clicking on—indicate she is interested in certain products at the moment and currently in shopping mode.
4. **Predictive Analytics:** By finding insights locked away in data from the three dimensions above, AIs and predictive analytics detect invisible patterns even the savviest marketer may miss. For example, the woman browsing that high-ticket clothing item may share key attributes with customers who purchase gourmet cookware, making for a strong cross-sell opportunity.

Framework 3

Once brands identify the corresponding four dimensions of their consumer, they can implement Framework 3, Modern segmentation. Exhibit C suggests that modern segmentation highlights "the customer's holistic interactions with the brand over time (i.e. spending patterns, engagement signals, etc.) in order to identify profiles and preferences."

Exhibit C: Example of Use Modern Segmentation Framework (Amended from How to Harness the Four Dimensions of Customer Data, WWD.) (Gruzbarg, 2019)

1. Start with a specific-use case. Instead of mining all the data to identify an ideal customer, begin with a simple, practical goal you want to achieve. Then partner with data and analytics teams to discover as much as possible about customers who already engage with the brand in the ways you desire. Do you want to launch a retention campaign? Start with segments based on days since last purchase and reach out to them with relevant offers. Loyalty acquisition programme? Use lifetime value to understand who has the potential to increase spend velocity. Cross-sell a new category? Estimate the likelihood to purchase within it.
2. Test, measure, iterate. Build testing into the earliest efforts at modern segmentation. This helps refine future iterations of the strategy and helps demonstrate the business value of this new approach to key decision-makers, which is critical in winning their buy-in to scale modern segmentation across all the activities. [Gruzbarg] worked with one brand that established a cross-functional team that ensures every segmentation strategy has a specific KPI goal, every test is set-up appropriately, and all results are transparent to key stakeholders. This helped turn an academic exercise into a powerful tool to drive the business.
3. Scale with smart hub technology. In building out a test case, one may run up the limits of the brand's IT, data, and analytics resources. How could one ever scale modern segmentation given their current resources? One option is to adopt what Gartner calls smart hubs (Bloom, 2018). These solutions are designed to speed and automate critical steps in modern, data-driven segmentation, including:

- unification of data (historic/behavioural and contextual) from across disconnected marketing systems;
- self-service access to that data for marketers;
- predictive insights that grow out of all that data; and
- coordinated execution across all channels.

The pandemic significantly affected online African brands. The Business of Fashion states, "Prior to the pandemic, revenues from the overall African the e-commerce market were projected to reach $19.8 billion this year and achieve a compound annual growth rate (CAGR) of 17.1 percent over the next four years, according to data from Statista."

With this exponential growth, we can expect to see a rise in digital payment options. Successful fashion brands use data and technology to build an e-commerce company. According to Forrester, 60–73 per cent of all data within an enterprise goes unused for analytics, which creates a lost opportunity for fashion brands to leverage analytics to grow their business (Think with Google, 2019). Emerging brands can use the frameworks to ensure they are capturing the right analytics for their business (Mogaji et al., 2021).

In conclusion, countries within the MEA region were forced to pivot their business using data-driven strategies to align with the e-commerce channels their customers were using. The archetypes could be used as a guide to help MEA brands minimise negative business impacts during future global crises and sustain their business during uncertain times.

Section 3: How to Collect Qualitative and Quantitative SEO and Social Media Data in MEA Regions?

This section introduces data-collection methodologies and cites examples of successful consumer analytics tools to generate insights. This portion explores the top key performance indicators and evaluates advanced marketing schemas per emerging market. This section also highlights successful MEA fashion brands.

The subsection includes case studies with MEA fashion brands employing and investing in analytical methods and technologies to reach key consumers. Additionally, this portion features factors such as search engine data, the digital social media landscape, and the emergence of customer retention. These factors are considered and interpreted to forecast the negative or positive effects of the data landscape per region.

Section 3.1: Search Engine Data

MEA consumers rely on search engines and digital technologies to find the right item. MEA fashion brands with a search engine optimisation (SEO) strategy will continue to see growth within the market. SEO is a digital marketing strategy used to increase the quality of traffic to the website using organic search engine results. In order for consumers to see the websites appear on a search engine, website content should leverage SEO keywords. There are two types of keywords: branded versus non-branded. Branded terms include a trademark name or variation (i.e. Nike or Nike Group). Non-branded terms do not include the logo name (i.e. Sporting Brand or Sporting Shirt). Analyses of non-branded and branded keywords can help business owners determine which terms are leading customers to their website.

As text searches mature, we can expect Google's visual searches, which use images to assist consumers with product identification to do so as well. Google Shopping in Middle Eastern countries allows users to quickly compare fashion prices and create a seamless shopping experience.

There will be more reliance on search engine optimisation to reach and help customers make decisions. In Exhibit 4, please see a few key insights related to search engine optimisation below:

Exhibit 4: (Source amended from Think with Google (2019) Bullet 2: *The 4 focus areas of MENA's rising fashion e-commerce scene*. [Data Points]. In: *The 4 focus areas of MENA's rising fashion e-commerce scene*. [online]. [Accessed: 11 November 2020].) Available from https://www.thinkwithgoogle.com/intl/en-145/marketing-strategies/data-and-measurement/4-focus-areas-menas-rising-fashion-e-commerce-scene/

The Google and Bain study conducted consumer research with over 6000 people in KSA, the UAE, and Egypt and found that 56 per cent of consumers start their shopping journey by using search engines.

- According to Consumer Barometer, 69 per cent of fashion shoppers in KSA and 61 per cent in the UAE were inspired and made initial discoveries online versus 36 per cent and 26 per cent in the UK and the US, respectively.
- When it comes to fashion in the Middle East and North Africa (MENA), 66 per cent of Google search queries are generic (indicating "open to choice") compared to 32 per cent in the UK.
- "When it comes to non-brand and brand-specific queries by category in the UAE and KSA, in the fashion category, 66 per cent of queries were non-branded and 34 per cent were branded. This means that consumers are open to choice."

MENA consumers continue to rely on search engine data to begin their shopping journey. Therefore, fashion brands should consider optimising their non-branded items to appear in searches pertaining to their ideal customers. Leveraging Google tools such as Google Ads to test and bid for various non-branded versus branded terms will help customers discover the brand, and figure out which keywords consumers are using to search for the brand. Once a brand develops an SEO strategy, it's important to use analytical based metrics to see what is driving visitors to the e-commerce site.

MEA countries can use a variety of analytics tools to capture these metrics. Leveraging tools like Google Analytics, Google Ads, SEMrush, and Google's PageSpeed can help emerging fashion brands collect related metrics. Google Analytics is a web tool that tracks audience and website traffic, and additional key insights based on the website and associated applications. Google Ads is an online advertising platform where advertisers can bid various advertisements on display to users. The platform also places ads within the search engine results, and non-search websites, apps, and videos (Google Ads, n.d.). SEMrush offers analytical solutions for SEO, social media, competitive research, and more (SEMrush, n.d.).

Google's PageSpeed allows brands to enter their website URL and receive site speed insights (Google's Page Speed, n.d.).

The following is a list of SEO metrics to consider:

Organic Traffic: When a user visits a website solely from an organic search. This is helpful to measure SEO strategy and its impact on customers.

Click-Through Rate (CTR): The percentage of users who click on the page in the search result to visit the website. This metric shows which search pages are grabbing users' attention.

Bounce Rate: The percentage of users who land on a page and then leave without visiting another page. A large percentage of users who leave a website after visiting a particular page may indicate that their landing page does not include relevant information. A website with a low bounce rate may indicate that the pages are relevant to the consumer. Please note that the preferred bounce rate will vary per website and the positive or negative effects should align with the brand's goals.

Keyword Rankings: This metric can be used to determine where a business ranks compared to competitors. To determine where a website page ranks, one can type in the associated keyword and locate where the website page sits compared to others. Tools like SEMrush can also be used to identify the search engine rankings.

Conversion Rate: This metric is the core of a brand's SEO strategy, as it's determined by overall website goals. It measures when a web page visitor converts into a customer based on the brand's rules. The conversion rate can be captured when a user makes an online purchase, submits a lead form, signs up for a newsletter or additional website actions that can be tracked.

Site Speed: Users expect a faster page load, especially as users continue to shift to mobile for their shopping experiences. Google states, "Fifty-four percent of people say that as the load time for a brand's mobile site increases, so does their frustration which affects the bottom line. In retail, we've seen that a one-second delay in mobile load times can impact conversion rates by up to 20 [per cent]" (Coe, 2019).

User experience is essential to a website ranking and may affect its conversion rate. Google's PageSpeed insights can be used to determine a website's performance, and receive advice on how to improve its speed.

When developing SEO strategies in Middle Eastern companies, it's essential to identify a businesses' goals prior to keyword research. If a fashion brand's goal is to gain more customers that speak Arabic and English, it should ensure that it is utilising keywords based on the commonly used terms from its country and audience. Once the keywords are confirmed, website content pages, titles, URLs, or other text areas should include the common keywords. The optimal number of keywords may vary based on the website and the search engine algorithms during the time. If consumers speak Arabic and English, ads using Arabic and English keywords to compare their CPC, bid price, and traffic should be run.

According to Hootsuite Global Digital Overview, African nations have the fastest-growing internet community, therefore, fashion brands utilising the search engine space may have an advantage over competitors who enter the market late. Additionally, brands who do not implement a search engine optimisation strategy in their analytics roadmap may miss opportunities to reach customers, and won't collect search engine data insights. Not collecting these insights can hinder businesses from using a variety of KPIs and goals that could optimise their future strategies.

Section 3.2: Social Media

This section explores the importance of using social media insights to reach customers and grow digital business in MEA regions.

According to Hootsuite Global Digital Overview, "African nations make up the remainder of the bottom 10 countries by social media penetration, and a number of countries across the region actually registered declines in social media use over the past 12 months" (Kemp, 2019).

Within the African continent, there are many barriers which may delay fashion companies in creating e-commerce channels due to low-internet accessibility. According to Business of Fashion, advisors at "Fitch

Solutions predict that there will be a longer-term uptake of online shopping and other services beyond the initial boost that was prompted by the pandemic" (Okwuosa, 2020). Because of this, Facebook and Google are planning to provide high-capacity undersea fibre-optic cables to improve internet connection.

As social media continues to grow in African countries, local fashion brands can leverage Facebook and Instagram's "Buy" feature to activate shopping (Fashionomics Africa, 2020b). Using social media tools in combination with efficient logistics operations can provide customers with high-quality merchandise (Gökerik et al., 2018).

Middle Eastern countries, specifically the UAE and Qatar, are within the top social media penetration compared to other countries. Although these countries rank high they exceeded the total population, therefore, the numbers may be inflated due to expat communities and high-tourist rates. Additionally, users in this region use a substantial share of Snapchat (Kemp, 2019). Emerging fashion brands could reference consumer data points to explore expat and local social media marketing opportunities to reach their target audience within their region.

Fashion brands should consider second- and third-party data-collection methods to activate consumer insights. Combining first- and second-party data can allow MEA brands to identify powerful information within Google Analytics and Google Trends. Marketing teams can build a 360° view of their audience and use these tools to gain a deeper understanding of their audience to create affinity groups. Affinity marketing gathers customers who share the same interests in groups. Once brands identify those groups, they can create personalised campaigns to optimise conversions for each. E-commerce retailer Johnson & Johnson used this method to identify key users and cultivate marketing creatives (Rateb & Ghorra, 2020). According to Think with Google, by reviewing their first-party data, Johnson & Johnson MENA recorded a "50 [per cent] year-on-year increase in males vs female website sessions, evolving from a 80-20 split of female vs male in 2018 and a 70-30 one in 2019, highlighting how quickly this audience was shifting" (Rateb & Ghorra, 2020).

Section 3.3: Successful Fashion Brands Leveraging Data

According to a recent report by Google and Bain, "fashion e-commerce in MENA is the second biggest category after electronics and is worth $1.6 billion in 2018." In 2019, the three largest markets in MEA were Saudi Arabia, Egypt, and the UAE.

Please exhibit six for more report details from Google and Bain:

- Saudi Arabia is the largest market for online fashion in the region, worth $715 million in 2018 and is expected to reach $3 billion by 2022.
- The UAE is the most advanced market for online fashion, is valued at $650 million, and is projected to reach $1.9 billion by 2022.
- Egypt is valued at $125 million and the rest of the GCC at $140 million and is projected to reach $300 million and $500 million by 2022, respectively.

Although there is a huge tourist expansion in the Middle Eastern countries, the ideology of supporting local brands is still prevalent. Pakistani fashion brand Khaadi specialises in traditional ready-to-wear and unstitched fabrics. What makes this retailer so special is its use of local specific fabric concepts within its larger-scale stores (Business of Fashion | McKinsey & Company, 2019). Khaadi created an international presence by servicing its customers in emerging and mature markets.

Section 3.3.1: Jumia Case Study

This case study explores the conflicts of creating a fashion brand leveraging Social media insights in Nigeria.

The Nigerian e-commerce brand, Jumia, has accomplished a "local and global reach." Jumia partnered with an international investment firm Rocket Internet, a German investment firm for additional funding to expand their business. Jumia's initial rival was another Nigerian brand called Konga (Okwuosa, 2020). Jumia thoroughly studies the market using predictive analytics before entering a market. According to Business of Fashion, "We start with a very deep knowledge of the market," said Poignonnec, who is also co-chief executive of Africa Internet Holdings (AIH), a partnership between Rocket Internet, MTN and Millicom which runs those group" (Thomasson, 2014).

Due to conflicting competitor interests in the beginning of the company's operation, Jumia was able to become a major player across the African continent, and Konga remained local (Africa's $20 Billion E-Commerce Opportunity). By April 2019, Jumia became the first African start-up to be listed on the New York Stock Exchange, but due to fraud allegations and lawsuits, the stock value plummeted within the same year. This resulted in Jumia closing down operations in three African countries, being unable to turn a profit. According to BBC, "the retailer received a surge of customers as online shopping accelerated, and before the rush, the African online retailer had ended last year with 6.1 million active consumers on its websites, up from 4 million previously."

When a retailer has an online e-commerce infrastructure platform already in place, during the time of a crisis, online sales can thrive. Even with a few hiccups, Jumia is often called "the Amazon of Africa" (Africa's $20 Billion E-Commerce Opportunity). Since both sites sell everything from computers to jeans and earrings. Although the retailer sells general items, Jumia hasn't been able to reach the luxury market yet, indicating there is still a lot of room for growth.

Section 4: Predicting Trends in the Data Landscape

The following subsection examines the progression of the innovative fashion market, investigates the current fashion systematic ecosystem, and predicts the latest trends. The statistical visualisations feature emerging regions that use non-traditional marketing structures to exceed their competitors. This section highlights ***Learning Objective 4:*** Describe how artificial intelligence, voice technology, and machine learning will affect the data landscape in MEA.

Section 4.1: Artificial Intelligence

According to Oh, artificial intelligence (AI) is a combination of technologies including natural language processing, computer visions, machine learning, deep-learning algorithms, and VR/AR/MR technologies. AI-based fashion applications can be used in analytics to support business KPIs. Fashion brands in developing regions use AI-powered companies such as Contentsquare, Dynamic Action, and SAP for Retail to make data-driven decisions. As artificial intelligence analytical tools mature in MEA, we can expect more innovations within this region.

Although advancements in AI can grant emerging brands the opportunity to make better decisions, the technology will only be as powerful as the data generated (Dwivedi et al., 2021). It is essential for fashion brands to collect meaningful data prior to AI implementation. Exhibit 6 references how artificial intelligence can be used to assist emerging companies.

Exhibit 6: (Source amended from Fashionomics Africa) *The future of work in textiles, clothing, leather and footwear* [online]. [Accessed: 11 November 2020].) Available from https://fashionomicsafrica.org/modules/fashioreports/public/storage/wcms_669355.pdf

Digital technologies have the potential to –	
Market intelligence	Help brands analyse and understand millions of data points about current market trends (AI)
	Enable brands to pick out micro trends in what is being purchased and where (AI)
	Allow a brand to analyse data from RFID tags and sensors sewn into garments to learn about actual consumer use and properties of the materials used (RFID, sensors, AI)
Design	Help designers forecast projected demand for new products (AI)
	Allow designers and consumers to see how designs will look in real-life situations (AVR)
	Help designers classify and better pick colours and avoid mistakes (new software)
	Assist producers in tailor-making designs to individual body sizes and shapes using software that detects contours and body shapes (new software)
Materials	Help manufacturers predict the mechanical properties of a garment (RFID, sensors)
	Assist in classifying and grading garments and in identifying and analysing faults (AVR, new software)
	Help manufacturers with future decisions on the best raw materials suppliers and fabrics to use (AI)
Suppliers & logistics	Assist brands and manufacturers in better supply chain management and just-in-time production (RFID, sensors, Internet of Things, AI, blockchains)
	Improve logistics management, reduce delays in production and overcapacity (RFID, sensors, Internet of Things, AI, blockchains)
	Help buyers and suppliers to make and account for payments (blockchains)
Production	Assist manufacturers in production planning and control and online monitoring (RFID, sensors, Internet of Things, AI, blockchains)
	Help manufacturers optimize spreading, cutting, bundling, sewing, pressing and packaging and other processes (RFID, sensors, Internet of Things, AI, blockchains)
	Assist brands and buyers in monitoring working conditions (e.g., hours and overtime), occupational safety and health (e.g., noise, dust, heat, air quality) and environmental performance (RFID, sensors, Internet of Things, AI, blockchains)
Marketing	Assist brands in better targeting specific consumer categories and groups (new software, AI)
	Allow brands to better use social media to engage and interact with customers (new software, AVR, AI)
	Allow brands and retailers to influence buying behaviours of consumers (new software, AI)
Retail	Help a brand understand how consumers shop, when, and through which channels (RFID, sensors, AI)
	Allow a brand to better understand how consumers interact with clothing in-store (RFID, sensors, AI, blockchains)
	Help retailers sell additional items through personalized offers based on items already purchased (AI, new software, blockchains)
Customer service	Respond to enquiries immediately using chatbots (AI)
	Improving the shopping experience through AI shopping assistants that offer conversation products and services (AI)
	Provide customers with suggestions according to their recorded need or their recent product searches (AI)

(Fashionomics Africa, 2020b)

Although artificial intelligence may have a large impact on the fashion industry, it will be a while until AI is completely implemented in MEA. Microsoft interviewed AI leaders in 112 companies, within 7 sectors and 5 countries in MEA. He indicated that AI is in the conversational stage at the C-suite level and is not commonly implemented in daily operations. Exhibit 7 displays the C-suite perspective of the future of AI.

> 80 [per cent] of the companies respond that AI is considered an important topic on the executive management level. This is significantly higher than on the nonmanagerial/ employee level where AI is only considered an important topic in 26 [per cent] of the companies. Interestingly, Board of Directors also came out lower with only 37 [per cent] of responders reporting that AI is important to their board. (Microsoft & Ey, 2019)

Exhibit 7: (Source amended from Microsoft & EY) *Artificial Intelligence in Middle East and Africa*. [online]. [Accessed: 11 November 2020].) Available from https://info.microsoft.com/rs/157-GQE-382/images/report-SRGCM1065.pdf

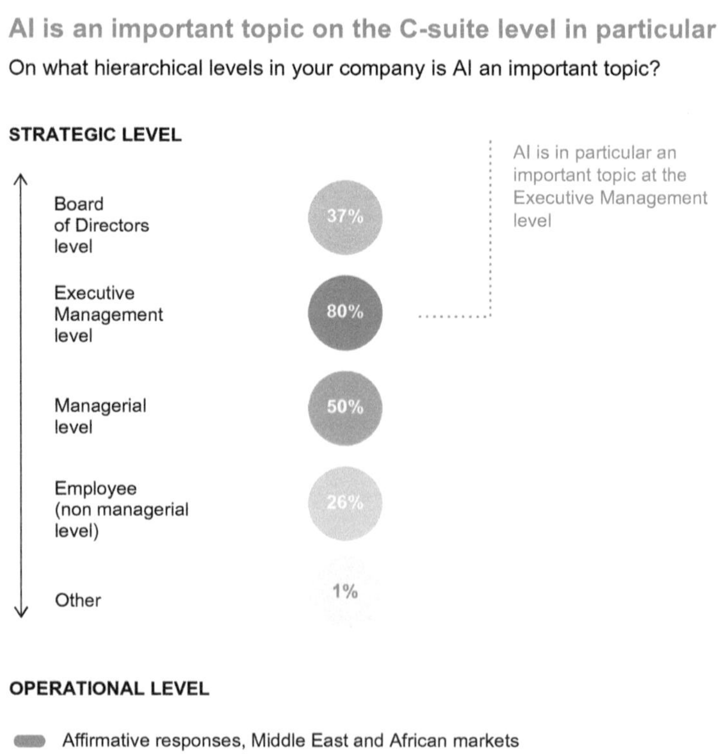

Section 4.2: Voice Recognition Technology

Voice Recognition technology leverages AI to support brands and retailers by providing a personalised experience for customers. This increases conversion, brand awareness, repeat purchases, and loyalty. Google Home and Amazon Echo are common voice command devices that use AI and speech recognition to meet user demands (Computer.org & Martinez, n.d.). According to the 2018 Google Report (Google, 2018; Google Analytics, n.d.), 27 per cent of the online global population is using voice search on mobile. The next phase of the digital landscape will incorporate voice control, and international brands like Google, Facebook, and Amazon will create tools to service voice users. As this continues to increase globally, the feature is more relevant in developed markets. UK's fast fashion retailer ASOS used Google Assistant to create Enki–ASOS voice search. Users can simply say "Hey Google, talk to ASOS" and Eniki will display the latest products and recommended items. This feature can be useful for brands with large product inventory. ASOS's senior product manager stated, "With 85,000 products on site at any one time, and on average 5,000 new items added each week, it's more important than ever to make it easy for our customers to stay on top of what's new on ASOS" (Digital Spy, 2018).

Countries with lower literacy rates may take longer to adapt to voice control initiatives (Kemp, 2019); therefore, MEA regions should ensure voice control features are tailored to their consumers. Additional challenges are integrating AI systems with e-commerce applications, identifying SEO opportunities, and accurately extracting voice-to-data analysis.

Section 4.3 Machine Learning

The machine-learning algorithm is a branch of "artificial intelligence to create executable solutions for how to ensure maximum sales by optimising product assortment, efficient allocation and a great customer experience" (Oh, 2020). We can expect fashion brands to use software with machine-learning capabilities to streamline the design process using various data imports. ML and AI company, YoonaTech, allows designers to import or select the number of designs, material types, colours, gender, and mood boards. Once all of the selections are made, Yoona uses ML and AI to develop multiple designs based on selections—essentially, using the brand's data to create fashion designs which streamline the process. Leveraging fashion analytics to develop a new collection may be the new wave of the future.

As emerging fashion brands in MEA recognise the importance of gathering data for their brands' growth, we will begin to see a surge in data analytics tools specifically within ML and AI to expand the fashion industry. We can expect a sector of fashion analytics to boom within the next few years.

Term Definitions

Artificial Intelligence:	A combination of technologies including natural language processing, computer visions, machine-learning, and deep-learning algorithms, VR/AR/MR technologies.
Bounce Rate:	The percentage of users who land on a webpage and then leave without visiting another page.
Branded Keywords:	A brand name or brand variation (i.e. Nike or Nike Group).
Click-Through-Rate (CTR):	The percentage of users who visit a website after seeing the page in the search results.
Consumer Attributes:	This represents customer characteristics such as gender, loyalty level, age group, and propensity to buy that offer data for businesses to analyse.
Conversion Rate:	The core of an SEO strategy, as determined by the business's overall website goals.
First-Party Data:	Represents the data and information collected directly from the audience.

Keyword Rankings:	A metric used to determine where a website ranks on search engines compared to competitors.
Machine Learning:	A branch of AI and the study of computer algorithms that improve automatically through experience and by the use of data
Non-branded Keywords:	Terms that do not include a brand name (i.e. Sporting Brand or Sporting Shirt).
Organic Traffic:	The tool that measures visits to a website solely from an organic search.
Search Engine Optimisation:	A digital marketing strategy used to increase the quality of traffic to the website using organic search engine results.
Site Speed:	Insights on speed to determine a website's performance and receive advice on how to improve.
Third-Party Data:	Represents the data purchased from outside sources who aren't the original collectors of the data.
Voice Recognition Technology:	A software programme or device that decodes the human voice.

References

BBC. (2020, April 28). *Jumia: The e-commerce start-up that fell from grace* [Online]. Retrieved May 17, 2021, from https://www.bbc.com/news/world-africa-52439546

Bloom, B. (2018, January 29). *Smart Hubs vs. Dumb spokes: CDPs and the undiscovered country* [Online]. Retrieved May 17, 2021, from https://blogs.gartner.com/benjamin-bloom/2018/01/29/smart-hubs-vs-dumb-spokes-cdps-and-the-undiscovered-country/

Brooksworth, F., Mogaji, E., & Bosah, G. (2022a). Fashion marketing in emerging economies: An introduction. In F. Brooksworth, E. Mogaji, & G. Bosah (Eds.), *Fashion marketing in emerging economies (volume 1)—Brand, consumer and sustainability perspectives*. Springer.

Brooksworth, F., Mogaji, E., & Bosah, G. (2022b). Fashion marketing in emerging economies: Conclusion and research agenda. In F. Brooksworth, E. Mogaji, & G. Bosah (Eds.), *Fashion marketing in emerging economies (volume 1)—Brand, consumer and sustainability perspectives*. Springer.

Business of Fashion | McKinsey & Company. (2019, November 20). *The State of Fashion 2020* [Online]. Retrieved May 17, 2021, from https://www.mckinsey.com/~/media/mckinsey/industries/retail/our%20insights/the%20state%20of%20fashion%202020%20navigating%20uncertainty/the-state-of-fashion-2020-final.pdf

Coe, M. E. (2019, February 1). Milliseconds earn millions: Why mobile speed can slow or grow your business. *Think With Google* [Online]. Retrieved May 17, 2021, from https://www.thinkwithgoogle.com/marketing-strategies/app-and-mobile/mobile-site-speed-importance/

Computer.org & Martinez, M. (n.d.). *Voice technology: As Google Duplex wows and scares, a post-screen world emerges with questions that the smart speakers cannot answer* [Online]. Retrieved May 17, 2021, from https://www.computer.org/publications/tech-news/trends/voice-assistants-technology-smart-speakers

Digital Spy. (2018, October 10). ASOS's Google Assistant lets you shop with your voice. *Digital Spy* [Online]. Retrieved May 17, 2021, from https://www.digitalspy.com/tech/apps/a868123/asos-google-assistant-lets-you-shop-with-your-voice/

Dwivedi, Y. K., Hughes, L., Ismagilova, E., Aarts, G., Coombs, C., Crick, T., & Williams, M. D. (2021). Artificial Intelligence (AI): Multidisciplinary perspectives on emerging challenges, opportunities, and agenda for research, practice and policy. *International Journal of Information Management, 57*(4), 101994–102014.

Fashionomics Africa. (2020a, February 2). The future of work in textiles, clothing, leather and footwear. *Fashionomics Africa* [Online]. Retrieved May 17, 2021, from https://fashionomicsafrica.org/modules/fashioreports/public/storage/wcms_669355.pdf

Fashionomics Africa. (2020b, August 26). Unlocking the potential of the creative and cultural industries in Africa. *Fashionomics Africa* [Online]. Retrieved May 17, 2021, from https://fashionomicsafrica.org/modules/fashioreports/public/storage/5f4793dadf3c2-20200827110706-The+Future+of+African+Fashion,+Film,+&+Music-compressed.pdf

Folklore. (2018, September 8). *Introducing the Folklore* [Online]. Retrieved May 17, 2021, from https://www.thefolklore.com/pages/about-us

Gökerik, M., Gürbüz, A., Erkan, I., Mogaji, E., & Sap, S. (2018). Surprise me with your ads! The impacts of guerrilla marketing in social media on brand image. *Asia Pacific Journal of Marketing and Logistics, 30*(5), 1222–1238. https://doi.org/10.1108/APJML-10-2017-0257

Google. (2018, N/A N/A). Voice search mobile. *Think With Google* [Online]. Retrieved May 17, 2021, from https://www.thinkwithgoogle.com/marketing-strategies/search/voice-search-mobile-use-statistics/

Google Ads. (n.d., N/A N/A). *Google Ads* [Online]. https://ads.google.com/home/

Google Analytics. (n.d., N/A N/A). *Google Analytics* [Online]. Retrieved May 17, 2021, from https://analytics.google.com/

Google's Page Speed. (n.d., N/A N/A). *Google's Page Speed* [Online]. Retrieved May 17, 2021, from https://developers.google.com/speed/pagespeed/insights/

Gruzbarg, T. (2019, September 5). How to Harness the Four Dimensions of Customer Data. *WWD* [Online]. Retrieved May 17, 2021, from https://wwd.com/business-news/business-features/retail-customer-data-segmentation-1203252192/

Iftahy, A. (2019, December 6). *A closer look at the fashion industry in Gulf Cooperation Council markets* [Online]. Retrieved May 17, 2021, from https://www.mckinsey.com/industries/retail/our-insights/a-closer-look-at-the-fashion-industry-in-gulf-cooperation-council-markets#

Kemp, S. (2019, January 31). *Digital 2019: Global Digital Overview. Hootsuite* [Online]. Retrieved May 17, 2021, from https://datareportal.com/reports/digital-2019-global-digital-overview?rq=Digital%202019%3A%20Global%20Digital%20Overview

McKinsey & Company. (2020, October 14). How Middle East and Africa retailers can accelerate e-commerce: Imperatives for now and the next normal. *McKinsey & Company* [Online]. Retrieved May 17, 2021, from https://www.mckinsey.com/middle-east/our-insights/how-middle-east-and-africa-retailers-can-accelerate-e-commerce-imperatives-for-now-and-the-next-normal

MICROSOFT & EY. (2019, October 1). *Artificial Intelligence in Middle East and Africa Microsoft* [Online]. Retrieved May 17, 2021, from https://info.microsoft.com/rs/157-GQE-382/images/report-SRGCM1065.pdf

Mogaji, E., Balakrishnan, J., Nwoba, A. C., & Nguyen, N. P. (2021). Emerging-market consumers' interactions with banking chatbots. *Telematics and Informatics, 65*(12), 101711–101721.

Mollard, M. (2020, March 5). *How to harness data analytics for fashion* [Online]. Retrieved May 17, 2021, from https://www.heuritech.com/blog/articles/data-analytics-for-fashion/

Oh, K. (2020, June 25). The roles of data analytics in the fashion industry. *Journal of Textile Engineering Fashion Technology, 6*(3) [Online]. Retrieved May 17, 2021, from https://medcraveonline.com/JTEFT/JTEFT-06-00237.pdf

Okwuosa, A. (2020, September 1). Africa's $20 billion E-Commerce opportunity. *Business of Fashion* [Online]. Retrieved May 17, 2021, from https://www.businessoffashion.com/articles/global-markets/africa-e-commerce-opportunity-industrie-africa-afrikrea-kisua-jumia-superbalist

Rateb, D., & Ghorra, J. (2020, November 1). Why, after 125 years, one MENA brand shifted away from traditional audiences with inclusive marketing. *Think with Google* [Online]. Retrieved May 17, 2021, from https://www.thinkwithgoogle.com/intl/en-145/consumer-insights/consumer-trends/why-after-125-years-one-mena-brand-shifted-away-traditional-audiences-inclusive-marketing/

SEMrush. (n.d., N/A N/A). *SEMrush* [Online]. SEMrush. Retrieved May 17, 2021, from https://www.semrush.com/

Think with Google. (2019, June 1). The 4 focus areas of MENA's rising fashion e-commerce scene. *Think With Google* [Online]. Retrieved May 17, 2021, from https://www.thinkwithgoogle.com/intl/en-145/marketing-strategies/data-and-measurement/4-focus-areas-menas-rising-fashion-e-commerce-scene/

Thomasson, E. (2014, July 28). Africa e-commerce firm expands to new markets. *Reuter* [Online]. Retrieved May 17, 2021, from https://www.reuters.com/article/us-africa-retail-internet/africa-e-commerce-firm-expands-to-new-markets-idUSKBN0FX0ZN20140728

Part IV

Conclusion

10

South American, Asian and African Perspectives in Fashion Marketing: Conclusion and Research Agenda

Frederica Brooksworth, Emmanuel Mogaji, and Genevieve Bosah

Introduction

The purpose of this volume was to highlight the potential for fashion marketing in emerging economies by highlighting the plethora of information present in regions such as South Asia, Africa, South America and the Middle East. Emerging economies are an area of interest on account of the projected growth of these markets, and the resultant investment

F. Brooksworth (✉)
Fashion Education Group, London, UK
e-mail: frederica@internationalfashioneducation.org

E. Mogaji
Greenwich Business School, University of Greenwich, London, UK
e-mail: e.o.mogaji@greenwich.ac.uk

G. Bosah
University of Hertfordshire, Hertfordshire, UK
e-mail: g.bosah@herts.ac.uk

F. Brooksworth et al. (eds.), *Fashion Marketing in Emerging Economies Volume II*,
Palgrave Studies of Marketing in Emerging Economies,
https://doi.org/10.1007/978-3-031-07078-5_10

opportunities they present to both global and local businesses; as well as the research data they offer to the growing global fashion research community. There is an evident need for greater study into the profitability in these markets by considering consumer behaviour, identity, sustainability, luxury fashion branding and marketing, and digital technology as areas of interest. Further research into the viability of investment in emerging economies is needed to highlight the challenges and opportunities present within these economies as well as provide insight into strategies that can be employed to overcome challenges and successfully penetrate the market. The works included in this volume explore different themes of research by region, with each chapter highlighting a specific area of the retail industry. This chapter will highlight the key points of each chapter, elucidate the key findings in the chapter, discuss the implications of each respective study, identify limitations present in each work and present potential avenues for future research on the themes being discussed. This is to highlight the importance of the work being included in this volume, as well as exemplify the reach that the content of this volume has within the global fashion industry.

Summary of Chapters

Bardey, Mehdiratta, and Turner (2022) explore the attitudes of Generation Z consumers regarding Western and Indian fashion brands in Chap. 2. India has been reported as having a growing consumer market, with high projected growth on account of its robust supply industry. For this reason, the study into the perception of Indian and Western brands is warranted; to better understand the needs of Indian fashion consumers. This is combined with the growing interest in Generation Z and their buying habits, which have been influenced by globalisation, rapid digital and technological advancement and socio-cultural components of fashion. The intention of this study was twofold: to explore attitudes to Indian and Western brands and to measure the brand equity of Indian and Western brands among Generation Z consumers. This was to better understand and communicate with their Indian consumers through gaining insight into their fashion sensibilities. This study indicated that culture, self-expression and identity were pertinent themes across the participants and had an influence on how brands were perceived. One key takeaway from this study was the need for Indian brands to better incorporate contemporary trends and styles into their product offering to better appeal to the Generation Z cohort. While Indian brands were regarded more positively for their durability, novelty and product quality; their ability to appeal to Generation Z fell short as contemporary trends and styles were being overlooked within Indian-brand product offerings (Bardey et al., 2022, p. 9). Future research could consider how to incorporate young Indian consumers' proclivity for traditional garments, as well as the presence of a strong brand story when considering entry into the Indian retail market. India as an emerging market presents several possibilities, particularly with the growth present within the retail industry and the globalised style sensibilities of younger consumers.

Sandes (2022) outlines the characteristics of the Brazilian menswear market in Chap. 3, to understand the dynamics of the market from the perspective of experts in the industry. The focus on the menswear market is to address the gap in the existing literature on Brazilian fashion, with womenswear being the focus of study in recent years. The menswear market makes for an interesting site of research on account of the recognised shift in culture that is paying more attention to men's relationship to fashion and dressing. The purpose of this study was to explore the cultural underpinnings of the menswear market in emerging markets and how men are using fashion within respective emerging markets, using Brazil as a case study. Brazil was chosen as the site for research on account of its growing retail industry as well as being one of the leading emerging markets in Latin America. The results of this study indicated that fashion choices and buying patterns among male consumers in Brazil were hindered by cultural perceptions of fashion as being feminine. These perceptions informed both buying and dressing behaviours of men in the Brazilian market, according to the Brazilian designers, product managers, journalists and brand managers that participated in this study. This study is useful in informing fashion brands intending to appeal to male consumers in Brazil, by highlighting potential challenges and opportunities within the Brazilian menswear market. While this study is insightful, future research into the Brazilian menswear market could benefit from seeking the perspectives of consumers, to gain first-hand information on fashion sensibilities and changing perceptions of masculinity as well as shopping habits. One of the recommendations of this study for businesses looking to invest in the Brazilian menswear market was the diversification of product offerings to invite more individuality and experimentation within men's dressing habits. This is on account of the changing perceptions of masculinity among Brazilian men (Sandes, 2022, p. 20). Brands and researchers alike can use these insights to inform marketing and communication studies for future considerations of the Brazilian menswear market.

Ala, Nair, and Rasul (2021) interrogate the power of neuromarketing in Southeast Asia in Chap. 4. This is to explore the efficacy of psychology-based marketing techniques in an emerging market. This chapter intended to analyse the use of emotional responses as a reliable measure for successful marketing strategies to identify and employ the best possible marketing techniques within the luxury sector. This study aimed to consider the variety of perspectives from the cultural diversity of Southeast Asian consumers and compare this to the current data covering neuromarketing, market research, product development and consumer behaviour. Offering a range of perspectives from this region adds to the existing literature while presenting an opportunity for further research into the needs of Southeast Asian consumers. This overview presents an opportunity for fashion marketers as neuromarketing techniques can interrogate the psychological need that fashion fulfils, as well as the emotional component of purchase intention (Ala et al., 2021). As this marketing strategy is fairly new and this overview is insightful to the possibilities of neuromarketing techniques, research in this area is hindered by ethical and legal considerations of consumer privacy, rights and well-being. Future research could benefit from exploring the effects of neuromarketing in a post-COVID scenario, as a means to understand how marketing techniques have changed as well as consumer attitudes, behaviours and expectations.

In Chap. 5, Kay and Young (2022) consider how branding activities have changed for artisanal brands in India, where the emerging market has impacted the brand story of local, traditional-based brands in the country. While artisanal fashion has a long history in India for its handmade embellishments and use of artisan textiles, the change of the market is worth exploring with consideration to how COVID-19 has made brands consider their positioning. Artisanal brands are also considered to be more vulnerable to the tumultuous nature of the market post-COVID. This study offers insight into the requirements needed for artisanal brands to be able to compete with both local and international competitors within an abnormal scenario, as well as investigates what qualities contemporary consumers are looking for in a brand. This adds to the existing literature on emerging marketing branding practices, while considering a fairly unique aspect of the Indian market. Within the investigation of branding practices, this study paid specific attention to the ability to craft a unique and relatable brand story. Similar to the work of Bardey et al. (2022) in Chap. 2, artisanal brands would need to improve their branding to compete for the attention of younger consumers from both international and local competitors. The results of this study indicated that considerations of traditional artisan craftsmanship were not enough to separate international and local brands from Indian artisanal brands within the consumer buyer journey. The brand story remained to be an imperative part of gaining and maintaining consumer attention, as a means to develop a competitive advantage. Future studies can benefit from investigating the incorporation of branding strategies into digital marketing initiatives, for artisanal brands to penetrate the global market and encourage investment in Indian artisanal fashion.

Chapter 6 contains the work of Joseph (2021) in the analysis of how Nigerian fashion brands influence consumer purchasing behaviour. A case study approach from the perspective of the brand is an innovative way to understand the emerging market and the players in it. This study considers the brand's role in consumer decisions: as a guide to understand and appeal to Nigerian consumers. As Nigeria is considered to be one of the more robust retail industries in Africa (Joseph, 2021), an exploration of marketing strategies from Nigerian brands adds insight into cultural and social perspectives of appealing to an emerging African market. This study indicated that the appeal of cultural identity used in tandem with marketing techniques were useful strategies for Nigerian brands. Future research could explore the role of ethnicity and cultural identity in marketing within emerging markets, as far as localising brand messaging to suit local consumers. The consideration of consumer perspectives is another avenue for future research, as the results from a study of this nature could be widely applicable and give more insightful information into the make-up of the Nigerian market. This can be considered alongside the comparison of marketing techniques from successful international brands within the Nigerian market. This can also assist in adding to the research being done on emerging markets in Africa specifically.

Appiah-Nimo (2021) analyses the contemporary retail landscape of South Africa in Chap. 7, to give insight into the current opportunities within South African retailing to potential entrants. The study presents the South African retail market as a case study for reviewing marketing initiatives in an emerging market, as a means to present South Africa as a viable option for retail. South Africa is considered to be a leading retail destination in Africa (Appiah-Nimo, 2021) on account of the high investment rate from international luxury and fast fashion brands. This overview provides details on the history of South African retail, as well as the potential for its development. This study found that the mixture of local and international brands is an attractive feature of the market, as it attracts consumers from different segments of the economy. This can be considered in addition to the growth of South African luxury brands both locally and internationally, ultimately driving investment back to the country through successful marketing and branding strategies. While there is a variety of international brands in the country, future research can examine strategies for the retention of international brands as a result of the stagnancy of the market in 2016 and the following years (Appiah-Nimo, 2021, p. 3). Investigating brand retention can be a useful avenue for research on account of import challenges South Africa has faced due to the COVID-19 pandemic and the tumultuous nature of the global supply chain. The results of this study also indicated that future research can make use of the discrepancy between international and local digital marketing capabilities with a focus on omnichannel retailing to better understand consumer behaviours.

Pstyled and Bardey (2022) in Chap. 8 analyse the psychological element of fashion by investigating how fashion fosters feelings of empowerment in women in Egypt. This study adds to the growing body of research of countries in the Middle East and Northern Africa (MENA) region and interrogates how fashion can act as a communicative agent. This study provided an insightful investigation into what it means to be empowered and fashion sensibilities among women in Egypt and ultimately aimed to understand consumer needs within the MENA region. This study highlights how individual beliefs can be reinforced through consumption habits such as brand loyalty and affiliation. These beliefs are supplemented by strong branding and marketing strategies employed by brands to fully connect with their consumers. The attention to empowerment is valuable in this study, as a means to understand how women, as consumers, support the national economy of Egypt; and how appealing to female consumers can assist in national economic growth (Pstyled & Bardey, 2022, p. 6). The main finding of this study elucidated that buying practices impacted individuals' positive self-regard. Fashion in this study is attributed to being an expressive object assisting in fostering feelings of empowerment among participants in this study. This is twofold as designers felt emboldened to utilise their cultural identity when crafting their product offering, as well as consumers feeling connected to local brands and their brand story (Pstyled & Bardey, 2022). While this study is useful in adding to the literature surrounding fashion psychology and positive self-regard, future research can explore empowerment through a more objective means, to craft workable strategies for potential entrants to the Egyptian retail market in line with the findings of a study of this nature. This can be done in tandem with greater consideration for the different ethnic groups and cultures present within the MENA region, as a means to diversify responses and get a greater understanding of cultural identity as a part of fashion in this region.

In Chap. 9, Griffin (2021) discusses the efficacy of data-driven marketing practices in Africa and the Middle East to highlight the opportunities and challenges within each emerging market. As the fashion industry is more and more globalised, the effects of the evolution of digital technologies are more apparent. The need to integrate data-driven marketing strategies is evident, with Griffin (2021) giving an overview of the current practices being used and how African and Middle Eastern retailers can make use of these strategies effectively. The results of this study prove useful in highlighting the digital capabilities present in each region as well as the importance of having an adaptable digital strategy to keep up with international competitors and the demands of the market. This overview also indicated the importance of data-driven marketing in Africa and the Middle East specifically as emerging markets, to be able to get the most out of their marketing efforts. Avenues such as data analytics, artificial intelligence, greater commitment to e-commerce and social media marketing were some of the noteworthy solutions for these markets to apply. Future research into marketing strategies in Africa and the Middle East can consider comparative studies to tailor marketing solutions to a specific region.

Agenda for Future Research

There are still many uncovered grounds with regard to fashion marketing. While this book has made significant contributions, there are still opportunities for further research to better understand the market and marketing strategies for fashion brands, recognising the inherent challenges and opportunities in these emerging markets. In addressing these research agendas, it is important to recognise that one cap does not fit all, though the focus is on emerging markets, different countries and regions will still have unique features that shape the marketing of fashion brands. Irrespective of this vast demography across these emerging markets and following on from the conversations in Volume 1 (Brooksworth et al., 2022a, 2022b), these seven strands of research are presented agenda for future research:

1. ***Fashion and Sustainability***: This is becoming a crucial topic in fashion marketing, and it is important to examine it further in the context of the emerging markets (Kaur et al., 2022) to understand fashion brands' effort towards sustainability, their challenges and how these challenges can be addressed. Perhaps building on the works of Adjabeng (2021) who provided an exploratory study of fashion designers' knowledge, practices and challenges in Ghana, to better understand the fashion designers' awareness about issues around sustainability and it can be addressed. Fashion contribution towards the Sustainable Development Goals is also important and worth exploring. Future research can explore fashion brands' effort towards getting

sustainability certifications. Camacho (2021) provided insight into sustainable fashion in Mexico by examining the BCorp certification while Nguyen and Mogaji (2021b) explored BCorps in Vietnam. It is important to understand the adoption of these certifications across the market and their impact on their brand.

2. ***Fashion and Technology***: It is important now for brands to have a deep understanding about their customers and therefore technology in fashion is important. To have a deep understanding, data science and analytics are important in making an informed business decision. Griffin (2021) presented strategies and tools for fashion analytics in Africa and Middle East, identifying the effectiveness of advanced data-driven marketing practices and fashion consumer analytics in emerging markets. The prospects, challenges and opportunities of these technologies can also be explored in different contexts. Social media cannot be ignored as well, as Kharuhayothin and Patarapongsant (2021) explored consumers' perceptions of fast fashion influencers on Instagram; the understanding of consumers' engagement with social media will remain of high importance for brands (Mogaji, 2021).
3. ***Fashion and Consumer Behaviour***: As earlier stated, there are different layers to a typical consumer of fashion in an emerging market. It is therefore important to have a better understanding of their behaviour as this will shape all the fashion business practices. Joseph (2021) presented a study on how Nigerian fashion brands influence customer purchasing behaviour; Bardey and Nessim (2021) explored fashion psychology behind the attire and armour of Egyptian women; Bardey et al. (2021) provided insights into Indian Generation Z consumers' attitudes towards Western and Indian Fashion; these studies highlight the unique features of the customers and how best to target them. In targeting these customers, brands need to also understand the existing perception and if to change it or build on it. Sestino (2021) presented a review of literature on the perception of fashion products in the emerging markets which suggests how intricate this can be. But beyond the basic understanding of their behaviour, neuromarketing can play a crucial role, and it will be important to extend the theoretical insight into the power of neuromarketing provided by Ala et al. (2021).

4. ***Fashion and Supply Chain Management***: Developing nations still face a dilemma about their production infrastructure, consumer consumption and international trades (Nayak et al., 2019). These have a considerable impact on fashion marketing. The cost of labour is significantly cheap. Factories can employ many people to make the apparels, but access to materials can be costly. Future research should endeavour to understand this intricate nature of the supply chain as it affects the emerging market and endeavours to provide both managerial and policy implications, perhaps extending the works of Nguyen and Mogaji (2021b) which focused on emerging economies' fashion brand positioning within the fashion global value chain. Brands in emerging markets need to know their strength within the supply chain and improve on their weaknesses. Transportation policies and infrastructure to support this supply chain need to be examined (Mogaji, 2020). Ethical manufacturing and sustainability in fashion is also an area worth exploring, especially in the context of the new strand of fashion market that has emerged from these studies (Nayak et al., 2019), to understand how fashion designers design, make and sell their clothes are integrating sustainability in their business practice.
5. ***Fashion and Public Relations, Advertising and Communications***: When all the products have been made, marketing communication becomes important—to communicate to stakeholders about the new design, either through fashion weeks as Jacob (2021) explored or even through social media (Gökerik et al., 2018; Kharuhayothin & Patarapongsant, 2021). Future research needs to understand how fashion brands in emerging markets communication is like and how they can improve their communication strategies, perhaps sharing some good practices that can be adopted across the market. Kay and Young (2021) identified the prospects of building the brand through storytelling, even in challenging times, which can be a start of future research, to understand storytelling as a communication strategy. Future studies can also explore green marketing strategies of fashion brands in emerging markets. Mackie and Campbell (2021) have started this strand of research by identifying the increasing prevalence of greenwashing and green marketing in emerging markets. Another notable contribution in this strand of research on green marketing is

the theoretical framework for the influence of green marketing communication on consumer behaviour in emerging economies by Nguyen and Mogaji (2021c). Communicating the good deeds of the brand is also important, and this serves as an extension of Adapa and Yarram's (2021) work on how the apparel industry in India is communicating their Corporate Social Responsibility (CSR) activities. This can further be expanded into other areas to understand the CSR activities of fashion brands and how they are being communicated.

6. ***Fashion and Strategic Business Planning***: Starting a business is not very easy, and it can be more challenging for a startup fashion brand in an emerging market (Brooksworth et al., 2022a). It is anticipated that future research will investigate the barriers and challenges of starting a business and provide ideas around strategic business planning. This may build around entrepreneur strands of research (Lang & Liu, 2019), but ultimately, the idea is to make starting a business easier based on empirical research and insight (Mukonza et al., 2021; Mogaji et al., 2022).
7. ***Fashion Events and Experiences***: The ambience and the experiences of fashion marketing are worth exploring further within the emerging market context, creating an understanding around brand experiences on brand resonance in multi-channel retailing (Huang et al., 2015). With Appiah-Nimo (2021) presenting a snapshot of contemporary retail in South Africa and Sandes (2022) discussing the characteristics of fashion's menswear market in Brazil, there are gaps in knowledge about how the experiences within the retail environment can be improved.

Conclusion

The present volume sought to draw attention to the possibilities for fashion marketing in emerging economies. Emerging markets have been acknowledged within fashion marketing as worthy sites for research on account of their projected growth. This growth, coupled with the lack of research into regions like South America, Asia, Africa and the Middle East, makes this volume a useful guide for dissecting the challenges and opportunities present within emerging markets in these regions. The ideas presented in this book elucidate the importance of expanding research data to include emerging markets. This is on account of the necessary information provided on areas such as consumer behaviour, identity, sustainability, luxury fashion branding and marketing, and digital technology. The themes covered in this book all can be applied to the respective markets being examined and require further study to fully understand the needs of each region.

This book represents a significant contribution to the growing body of work on fashion marketing, especially in emerging economies. We thank all the authors who submitted articles for consideration in this edited book. We appreciate their dedication, perseverance and willingness to go through the long review process. We are grateful to the reviewers who contributed their valuable time and talent to develop this edited book and ensured the quality of these chapters with their constructive comments and suggestions. We believe this book contains significant work that is profoundly meaningful for stakeholders interested in fashion marketing and management.

We acknowledge that we have not been able to provide a holistic view of fashion marketing and management in emerging economies, many of which have not been submitted to this edited book; however, we hope we have been able to capture some theoretical insights that are available at this point. We hope that readers will find these chapters in this book both enriching and thought-provoking and that the insights provided in the collection of research materials will enhance the understanding in this area, inspire further interest in fashion marketing, provide a basis for sound management decisions and stimulate new ideas for future research.

References

Adapa, S., & Yarram, S. R. (2021). Communication of CSR practices and apparel industry in India—Perspectives of companies and consumers. In F. Brooksworth, E. Mogaji, & G. Bosah (Eds.), *Fashion marketing in emerging economies—Strategies, tools and insights for fashion brands*. Springer.

Adjabeng, H. A. (2021). Sustainable fashion in Ghana: An exploratory study of fashion designers' knowledge, practices, and challenges. In F. Brooksworth, E. Mogaji, & G. Bosah (Eds.), *Fashion marketing in emerging economies—Strategies, tools and insights for fashion brands*. Springer.

Ala, M., Rasul, T., & Nair, S. (2021). The power of neuromarketing: Taking luxury fashion marketing in Southeast Asia markets to a whole new level. In F. Brooksworth, E. Mogaji, & G. Bosah (Eds.), *Fashion marketing in emerging economies—Strategies, tools and insights for fashion brands*. Springer.

Appiah-Nimo, K. (2021). South Africa: A snapshot of contemporary retail. In F. Brooksworth, E. Mogaji, & G. Bosah (Eds.), *Fashion marketing in emerging economies—Strategies, tools and insights for fashion brands*. Springer.

Bardey, A., & Nessim, Y. (2021). The rise of female empowerment in Egypt: The fashion psychology behind their attire and armour. In F. Brooksworth, E. Mogaji, & G. Bosah (Eds.), *Fashion marketing in emerging economies—Strategies, tools and insights for fashion brands*. Springer.

Bardey, A., Turner, R., & Mehdiratta, U. (2021). Fashioning the future generation: Generation Z Indian consumers' attitudes towards Western and Indian Fashion. In F. Brooksworth, E. Mogaji, & G. Bosah (Eds.), *Fashion marketing in emerging economies—Strategies, tools and insights for fashion brands*. Springer.

Bardey, A., Turner, R., Mehdiratta, U. (2022). Fashioning the future generation: Generation Z Indian consumers' attitudes towards Western and Indian Fashion. In F. Brooksworth, E. Mogaji, & G. Bosah (Eds.), Fashion Marketing in Emerging Economies (Volume 2) – South American, Asian and African Perspectives. Cham: Springer.

Brooksworth, F., Mogaji, E., & Bosah, G. (2022a). Fashion marketing in emerging economies: An introduction. In F. Brooksworth, E. Mogaji, & G. Bosah (Eds.), *Fashion marketing in emerging economies (volume 1)—Brand, consumer and sustainability perspectives*. Springer.

Brooksworth, F., Mogaji, E., & Bosah, G. (2022b). Fashion marketing in emerging economies: Conclusion and research agenda. In F. Brooksworth, E. Mogaji, & G. Bosah (Eds.), *Fashion marketing in emerging economies (volume 1)—Brand, consumer and sustainability perspectives*. Springer.

Camacho, G. (2021). Sustainable fashion: The case of a Mexican BCorp. In F. Brooksworth, E. Mogaji, & G. Bosah (Eds.), *Fashion marketing in emerging economies—Strategies, tools and insights for fashion brands*. Springer.

Gökerik, M., Gürbüz, A., Erkan, I., Mogaji, E., & Sap, S. (2018). Surprise me with your ads! The impacts of guerrilla marketing in social media on brand image. *Asia Pacific Journal of Marketing and Logistics, 30*(5), 1222–1238. https://doi.org/10.1108/APJML-10-2017-0257

Griffin, C. (2021). Fashion analytics in Africa & Middle East: Strategies, tools and, insights for fashion brands. In F. Brooksworth, E. Mogaji, & G. Bosah (Eds.), *Fashion marketing in emerging economies—Strategies, tools and insights for fashion brands*. Springer.

Huang, R., Lee, S. H., Kim, H., & Evans, L. (2015). The impact of brand experiences on brand resonance in multi-channel fashion retailing. *Journal of Research in Interactive Marketing, 9*(2), 129–147. https://doi.org/10.1108/JRIM-06-2014-0042

Jacob, R. (2021). Fashion weeks & customer experiences in emerging markets. In F. Brooksworth, E. Mogaji, & G. Bosah (Eds.), *Fashion marketing in emerging economies—Strategies, tools and insights for fashion brands*. Springer.

Joseph, D. (2021). Towards understanding how Nigerian fashion brands influences customer purchasing behaviour. A case study of Nigerian fashion brands. In F. Brooksworth, E. Mogaji, & G. Bosah (Eds.), *Fashion marketing in emerging economies—Strategies, tools and insights for fashion brands*. Springer.

Kaur, J., Mogaji, E., Wadera, D., & Gupta, S. (2022). Sustainable consumption practices in Indian households: A saga of environment management linked to Indian ethos and generational differences. *Society and Business Review,* ahead-of-print(ahead-of-print). https://doi.org/10.1108/SBR-08-2021-0132

Kay, P., & Young, C. (2021). Afloat in a changing COVID-19 world: The rise of artisanal fashion in India for brand story relevance in challenging times. In F. Brooksworth, E. Mogaji, & G. Bosah (Eds.), *Fashion marketing in emerging economies—Strategies, tools and insights for fashion brands*. Springer.

Kay, P., Young, C. (2022). Afloat in a changing COVID-19 world: The rise of artisanal fashion in India for brand story relevance in challenging times. In F. Brooksworth, E. Mogaji, & G. Bosah (Eds.), Fashion Marketing in Emerging Economies (Volume 2) – South American, Asian and African Perspectives. Cham: Springer.

Kharuhayothin, T., & Patarapongsant, Y. (2021). Will I follow my ideal self everywhere? Exploring consumers' perceptions towards fast fashion influencers on Instagram. In F. Brooksworth, E. Mogaji, & G. Bosah (Eds.), *Fashion marketing in emerging economies—Strategies, tools and insights for fashion brands*. Springer.

Lang, C., & Liu, C. (2019). The entrepreneurial motivations, cognitive factors, and barriers to become a fashion entrepreneur: A direction to curriculum development for fashion entrepreneurship education. *International Journal of Fashion Design, Technology and Education, 12*(2), 235–246.

Mackie, L., & Campbell, D. (2021). Sustainability in the supply chain. In F. Brooksworth, E. Mogaji, & G. Bosah (Eds.), *Fashion marketing in emerging economies—Strategies, tools and insights for fashion brands*. Springer.

Mogaji, E. (2020). Impact of COVID-19 on transportation in Lagos, Nigeria. *Transportation Research Interdisciplinary Perspectives, 6*, 100154.

Mogaji, E. (2021). *Brand management*. Springer.

Mogaji, E., Adeola, O., Adisa, I., Hinson, R. E., Mukonza, C., & Kirgiz, A. C. (2022). Green marketing in emerging economies: Communication and brand perspective: An introduction. In E. Mogaji, O. Adeola, I. Adisa, R. E. Hinson, C. Mukonza, & A. C. Kirgiz (Eds.), *Green marketing in emerging economies* (Palgrave Studies of Marketing in Emerging Economies) (pp. 1–16). Palgrave Macmillan. https://doi.org/10.1007/978-3-030-82572-0_1

Mukonza, C., Hinson, R. E., Adeola, O., Adisa, I., Mogaji, E., & Kirgiz, A. C. (2021). Green marketing: An introduction. In C. Mukonza, R. E. Hinson, O. Adeola, I. Adisa, E. Mogaji, & A. C. Kirgiz (Eds.), *Green marketing in emerging markets* (Palgrave Studies of Marketing in Emerging Economies) (pp. 3–14). Palgrave Macmillan. https://doi.org/10.1007/978-3-030-74065-8_1

Nayak, R., Akbari, M., & Far, S. (2019). Recent sustainable trends in Vietnam's fashion supply chain. *Journal of Cleaner Production, 225*, 291–303.

Nguyen, P. N., & Mogaji, E. (2021b). Emerging economies in fashion global value chain: Brand positioning and managerial implications. In F. Brooksworth, E. Mogaji, & G. Bosah (Eds.), *Fashion marketing in emerging economies—Strategies, tools and insights for fashion brands*. Springer.

Nguyen, P. N., & Mogaji, E. (2021c). A theoretical framework for the influence of green marketing communication on consumer behaviour in emerging economies. In E. Mogaji, O. Adeola, I. Adisa, R. Hinson, C. Mukonza, & A. Can (Eds.), *Green marketing in emerging economies*. Palgrave Macmillan.

Pstyled , Y, N & Bardey, A. (2022) The Rise of Female Empowerment in Egypt: The Fashion Psychology behind their Attire and Armour. In F. Brooksworth, E. Mogaji, & G. Bosah (Eds.), Fashion Marketing in Emerging Economies (Volume 2) – South American, Asian and African Perspectives. Cham: Springer.

Sandes, F.S. (2022). A Closer Look at the Menswear Market in Brazil. In F. Brooksworth, E. Mogaji, & G. Bosah (Eds.), Fashion Marketing in Emerging Economies (Volume 2) – South American, Asian and African Perspectives. Cham: Springer.

Sestino, A. (2021). Fashion brands and emerging markets opportunities: A literature review from a consumer behaviour perspective. In F. Brooksworth, E. Mogaji, & G. Bosah (Eds.), *Fashion marketing in emerging economies—Strategies, tools and insights for fashion brands*. Springer.

Index

F. Brooksworth et al. (eds.), *Fashion Marketing in Emerging Economies Volume II*,
Palgrave Studies of Marketing in Emerging Economies,
https://doi.org/10.1007/978-3-031-07078-5

R

S

T

W

GPSR Compliance
The European Union's (EU) General Product Safety Regulation (GPSR) is a set of rules that requires consumer products to be safe and our obligations to ensure this.

If you have any concerns about our products, you can contact us on

ProductSafety@springernature.com

In case Publisher is established outside the EU, the EU authorized representative is:

Springer Nature Customer Service Center GmbH
Europaplatz 3
69115 Heidelberg, Germany

www.ingramcontent.com/pod-product-compliance
Ingram Content Group UK Ltd.
Pitfield, Milton Keynes, MK11 3LW, UK
UKHW040225290926
15471UKWH00001B/6
* 9 7 8 3 0 3 1 0 7 0 7 9 2 *